A Life in the Shadowlands

John Stokes

Grosvenor House
Publishing Limited

All rights reserved
Copyright © John Stokes, 2025

The right of John Stokes to be identified as the author of this work has been asserted in accordance with Section 78 of the Copyright, Designs and Patents Act 1988

The book cover is copyright to John Stokes

This book is published by
Grosvenor House Publishing Ltd
Link House
140 The Broadway, Tolworth, Surrey, KT6 7HT.
www.grosvenorhousepublishing.co.uk

This book is sold subject to the conditions that it shall not, by way of trade or otherwise, be lent, resold, hired out or otherwise circulated without the author's or publisher's prior consent in any form of binding or cover other than that in which it is published and without a similar condition including this condition being imposed on the subsequent purchaser.

A CIP record for this book
is available from the British Library

Paperback ISBN 978-1-83615-419-8
eBook ISBN 978-1-83615-420-4

Preface

The Shadowlands is like a parallel universe that exists in our society, mostly ignored and largely unseen. Young people in the Care System, abused, neglected and disconnected, live out often broken lives that are rarely visible to most people. 'Out of sight and out of mind', each child seemingly with their own personal cloaking mechanism that hides them from the gaze of mainstream society, except in moments of extreme fear, anger and trauma. Young voices that are rarely heard and even more rarely listened to or understood. They live in the Shadowlands, sometimes for their entire lives, often being mistaken for demons rather than the victims that they mostly are.

They just need to be loved rather than feared or despised. Their only protection is their invisibility and the people who work with them and look after them. Youth Workers, Children's Home staff and Foster Carers. I have been all of the above as I've journeyed through the Shadowlands for almost 40 years, exploring a world totally alien to anything that I had experienced in my first 30 years.

This book is just a glimpse into this other world, A window into it or maybe even a portal. It's the story of my journey that has led me through the Shadowlands. The highs and the lows, the joy, the despair, the excitement and the intense trauma. The stories of a Foster Carer and his Foster Children surviving an underfunded and far from perfect system that can still all too often fail children and their carers despite the best intentions.

Many times, over the years, after regaling stories of my life as a Foster Carer, people have told me that I should write a book. Telling stories of the adventures of my various foster children, their deeds, their misdeeds, their sheer recklessness and bravado. Their ingenuity, their triumphs and even their glorious failures. Moments of magic, moments of horror with children that often embrace risk-taking and challenging behaviour on a daily basis. It has long been my aim to write this book. I have written many successful pieces on fostering issues for the media, but the magnitude of writing a whole book requires a discipline that is on another level, and one that escaped me for more than a few decades.

I had always considered that it would be a book about Foster Care, using actual events to highlight various aspects of fostering. Whilst I have maintained an element of that in this book, its concept has evolved since I first started writing. That was back in November 2018 whilst I was staying in a former Monastery (now a four-star hotel in Southwest Spain). It is a place that has, for the most part, retained its former tranquillity and calm. My visit was during the winter, so well into the off-season. The silence in the impressive hallways and cloisters would have pleased any lingering ghosts of a religious persuasion. Fortunately, the sparse wooden furniture had been replaced by a vast range of luxurious sofas that I suspect would have been frowned upon by those same ghosts of the past.

Leaving the noisy, narrow, bustling streets of cafes and bodegas outside and stepping into a place of such tranquillity was everything that I had yearned for in order to relax and recover after some hectic days of fostering. Well, admittedly, a steady supply of some excellent Rosé also helped enhance the experience. The absolutely overwhelming feeling of suddenly being in a place where I was meant to be was like an epiphany. Well, maybe that was the Rosé effect. As a person of no religion, an epiphany did seem somewhat unlikely, but something deep in my soul said that this was to be my time for reflection. My state pension had kicked in a few months earlier, so reflecting on my life at 65 seemed about right. I had waited a long time for this moment.

Over the following days, the writing bug overtook me, whilst I was rarely disturbed and I felt more creative than I had for a very long time. It was like a tap turned on at full force. Words flowed but without any plan or real direction. There were random thoughts about fostering and memories of various adventures in my career. What followed was a succession of mostly unconnected paragraphs on the broad theme of fostering, linked only by statements of acquired wisdom. Words that I felt able to impart, being myself a newly self-appointed Elder.

On returning to England, I was feeling really pleased with myself, having finally started the book. Sadly, it was to be quickly filed away to be replaced by Immigration battles for a foster child and the usual steady demands of fostering. Before I knew it, we were in a pandemic. Thereafter, I occasionally revisited my Spanish writings but had lost all momentum and lacked any clarity on how to proceed.

It was almost five years later, having reached my 70th year, that another trip abroad was to inspire me to return to my writing. I had made random notes over those years that I had added to my writing file, They were mostly pearls of fostering wisdom, but again without having any real idea on what my book was to be centred on other than the all-too-wide brief of Foster Care. Having a siesta on a very hot August afternoon in the northern Albanian city of Shkoder, I reread my earlier efforts and realised that the book must really be about me and my life. I had veered off previously because to do that seemed to me to be putting my own self-worth above that of some far more interesting subjects, people and issues. I somewhat reluctantly accepted that I was the thread that held this book together, the one thing that could bring all my writing together. Being a somewhat modest man, the thought of an actual autobiography seemed at first quite ridiculous. As I reached 70, I had started to list my achievements and realised that maybe they did amount to something and that as one of the first single men to foster in the UK I did have a rather unique and personal perspective that I could share.

Using parts of my original writings, I had about a third of my book finished by the time I said goodbye to the Hotel Blini and returning home I completed the first manuscript within a month. Whilst I am certainly not the typical Foster Carer. I hope the book gives a flavour of life as a Foster Carer and the challenges we face on a daily basis. I want it to show how much we Foster Carers learn from experiences that enrich both our lives and of those we care for. My life working with children was not initially as a Foster Carer but as a Residential Social Worker, a Youth Worker and mentor since the late 1970s. I am passionate about Foster Care, so I have in this book expressed a very personal opinion on where I think Foster Care and the wider Care System can be improved upon. I would also like to think that whilst it is a book that may well appeal to Foster Carers and our colleagues in the Care System, I really do hope it also appeals to the wider public that are largely oblivious to the crucial work that we do.

Chapter 1

July 14th, 1990, and I was in Paris. With me was Wayne, a young car thief who I had been working with in a Children's Home near Bristol. I was there to fulfil a promise that I had made to him a few months earlier. We had struck a deal that if he stopped stealing cars, then I would take him to the next concert by his favourite musician, Jean Michel Jarre. I had wrongly assumed that it would mean getting tickets for one of the shows on his next UK tour. How little I knew. Jarre only did large-scale events and not tours and the next one was to be in Paris. For me though, a promise is a promise, so here we were in Paris on Bastille Day for the concert at La Defense.

Wayne, for his part, had tried hard to keep his end of the deal by reducing his offending fairly drastically. That in itself was quite an achievement. Stealing cars was like an addiction and instant cures were beyond any reasonable expectations. Nobody who ever knew Wayne expected him to become an upstanding member of society and he was most certainly not going to disappoint them. Since making my promise to him, Wayne had spent the previous two months keeping out of police cells and courts. In my inexperienced naivety, I took that to mean that he had curtailed his criminal activities. Only much later was I to discover that it was more by luck than judgement that he had managed to evade the attention of the Avon and Somerset

Constabulary for an extended period. His offending had continued unabated and it was only the inefficiencies of the local police that ensured our Paris trip went ahead.

He was definitely not the only prolific car thief in the area at that time, but unlike most of the others, he wanted more than just notoriety, street credibility and the sort of adrenaline rush that is the lifeblood of teenagers. All of those things were naturally part of it, but it was more about his intense desire to be the absolute best at what he did. Wayne had no desire to be just another car thief because he needed to be the best car thief before he could move on to look for his next challenge. He would never be a follower because, by definition, that would mean that there was someone better than him. Car thieves were akin to graffiti taggers. They were all trying to get noticed whilst making use of a fairly limited skill set. Adding a screwdriver and some bravado to that adolescent-fuelled adrenaline was all that was needed to become a car thief. Then add to the mix a few disciples who could bear witness to one's exploits and voila! You have the perfect recipe for a new street legend.

Wayne though, was blessed with an above-average intelligence for a car thief. He was more of a Banksy than a Graffiti tagger amongst the young criminal fraternity, always wanting to develop his art and take it to another level. Car theft would never keep his interest for long, not whilst there was a whole world of opportunities waiting for a more intelligent and creative criminal. Outwitting the local police was hardly a challenge worthy of pursuing for any length of time. It kept his teenage followers happy, but all too soon it felt like he was standing still without new challenges.

He was like an ant, always moving and never still and his hands needed constant engagement. The description of being a 'live wire' was probably never more aptly applied to someone. His ever-busy hands were constantly trying to keep up with his brain that burned through life like a firestorm. From the first moment that I met him, it was like he was plugged into an electricity generator, sparking off people and situations around him and sending out shockwaves to anyone that got too close. He really should have come with a safety manual or at least an on-off switch because just trying to keep up with him could be totally exhausting. People either love Wayne or they hate him. He is Marmite! You could be entranced by him or enraged by him, but you could never ever be totally at ease with him. If Wayne appears to be chilled then it means that he has either taken some illegal substances or is about to strike either physically or vocally. Either way, it's best to keep at a safe distance.

My first ever meeting with Wayne was in Kidlington Young Offenders Institution in Oxfordshire. A county that always had many esteemed residents also back then had some notorious younger residents. Campsfield House was, in the late 1980s, home to all manner of young criminals who the courts had deemed in need of incarceration. They had been sent there as punishment in the hope that a custodial sentence would cure their criminal activities. In my experience, the effects of confinement tend to have precisely the reverse effect. As Wayne and many others have told me, the outcome really should not be surprising. If you take a bunch of car thieves and burglars and lock them up together, then when they come out, they will have shared their combined knowledge of crime and become better criminals with more refined skills. Wayne was to be a case in point.

After arriving at Campsfield House, I was escorted into a bleak room in the prison block and then waited for the appearance of the boy that I had been asked to key work. The room was devoid of furniture or decoration save for a table covered in initials carved into the surface. The table was flanked by two sturdy wooden chairs and was everything that I had expected it to be from TV shows and my now regular visits to police stations. I was fairly new to being a residential Social Worker, a term that was then used to describe both qualified and unqualified staff in Local Authority Children's Homes. I had been asked to take a look at this young man who was due for release shortly. He would then be placed at our Children's Home, where I would be his allocated key worker.

It was my first visit to any prison facility, so I went that day with a mixture of excitement and trepidation. First impressions confirmed my fears that the atmosphere would be oppressive. This was not a place where smiles would be forthcoming, nor many pleasantries exchanged unless delivered with sarcasm. Escorted from the main gate across a barren yard, then stopping briefly for another grim-faced officer with his huge canine companion. The dog I understood was there to alert his controller of any possible exposure to illegal substances that visitors like me may have had. Unlike plenty of other social workers, weed played no part in my social life. I had no fears of drug detection unless contact with my young charges at the home was sufficient to alert the hound. I was cleared through and we then proceeded on to another building. Once inside,

I was asked to empty my pockets into a metal tray, which would be held until my return. Icy cold stares were apparently the norm for staff and canines alike here. Instructions were curtly given and conversation was not encouraged, judging by the brief and direct responses from officers. I was then led through a series of empty corridors with the uncomfortable silence broken only by the echoing footsteps of my escort's boots and his jangling keys. At each door, he produced a mass of keys which he sifted through before then unlocking and re-locking each thick metal door in succession.

Eventually, we reached the interview room where I was asked to wait before being locked in alone. Solitary confinement only added to my discomfort. This sparse room, I mused, had no doubt seen its fair share of hostile and futile interrogations. Occasionally, on our march through the building, I had heard various disembodied shouts and cries. I listened to my escort's footsteps as his boots echoed far down the corridor until another heavy metal door slammed, bringing total silence. Ten minutes passed before I heard distant doors opening, then slamming shut and boot steps approaching. Those jangling keys preceded the door opening as an officer brought this slightly built young man into the sparse waiting room. Wayne bounced in with a walk that reminded me of George Cole's Flash Harry in the St. Trinian's films. Flash Harry was a Spiv. Is Spiv even a word these days? I'm not sure. Well, if not, then I guess younger readers will now be pausing to check on Google.

That first image of Wayne stuck with me, although later on, as I got to know him more, another famous

George Cole character came to be even more appropriate as a likeness. Wayne is the perennial wheeler-dealer and Arthur Daley is the closest character resemblance that I can think of to him. A lovable rogue. Well, lovable as he became to me, his friends and other associates. The first glance that I got from Wayne as he was led into the interview room was a piercing cold stare whilst slowly nodding his head in a knowing gesture, as though to say to me without words, "yes, I've got your measure". Despite being fidgety his gaze remained concentrated on me and went from cold to icy. I guessed that it was meant to intimidate and to some extent it worked. Intimidation was probably a little overused in this depressing place and I had already witnessed better attempts that day since entering the prison. Like many other young people in the system, it soon became apparent that Wayne held a particular disdain for Social Workers and Care Home staff. He sat down, but he couldn't sit still. His hands and eyes rarely settled in one place for long. He was flippant in his responses to my questions and occasionally got angry when his eyes would fix again into that penetrating stare. He was mostly dismissive of me, except when he would talk about his adventures. This was a performance on his part. For all the scrutiny that I was there to do, I sensed that his scrutiny was more direct and decisive. Everything about his performance was, in fact, a series of probes working out if I was going to be of any interest to him or of any use to him. That was certainly far from a given.

It was whilst describing his criminal exploits that he really came to life and the enthusiasm erupted in his voice and mannerisms. He would laugh aloud at his own banter, not unlike the Joker in the Batman movies. It was all very manic and quite unsettling. All the while it felt like the whole scene being played out was one of intentional distraction whilst he probed me for responses. He was assessing me, probably more out of boredom than genuine interest. Upon his upcoming release from custody, I doubted that he would have much interest in me or my attempts to befriend him. He would occasionally relax me with a joke or a story but then in a flash return to a cold disinterest and blank stare.

He only gave me snippets of information about his life before entering the care system, except when he talked about his stepfather, the 'fat bastard'. Those moments of anger however, caused the joker's mask to slip a little and gave me a glimpse of the pain he had probably endured that had undoubtedly hardened his attitude to life and adults in general. I had carefully digested his case file before my visit and reading between the lines, he appeared to be callous, with a complete absence of compassion, care or conscience. One of the first things that I learned working in Childcare was the necessity to read between the lines in Social Workers' reports as they have a tendency to tell you what they want you to hear rather than what you need to hear. Reports are often sanitised for consumption, arguably in order to stick to the facts rather than conveying personal feelings or impressions. This of course is correct and professional and Social Workers' reports are constantly scrutinised for errors so it is safer not to be too explicit or speculative. Over my many years as a Foster Carer I have however learned that all too often the initial reports on a child may indeed be factual but may also omit to mention some very relevant information. That is especially true when a Social Worker is trying to encourage a Foster Carer to take on a challenging placement. Not that I have ever come across a placement that is not in some way challenging

An example that comes to mind is a report I was given on a potential new arrival stating that the boy had some problems around hygiene. When taking on a teenage boy, that does not exactly leap off the page as something that is unusual or of great concern. Several weeks into that placement however and the aroma of urine in the house became somewhat overpowering. The cause of this was only found when the fuse blew in the electricity cupboard below the boy's room. His room had floorboards and he had been using one corner of the room as a toilet. Dripping urine and fuse boxes are not a good combination. I later discovered that this was in fact behaviour that had also happened in past placements, something that would have been useful to know when taking the placement on. It would, I think, have meant that the placement, from my perspective, would not have been taken on and from the boy's point of view it would have avoided another unsuccessful placement. It was something that we didn't get over, as it was one of the few behaviours that I was just not prepared to cope with. As carers we cope with all sorts of behaviours, but each of us has our Achilles heel, I think. Living in a house with such a disgusting smell was not in my skill set and as he by then had progressed to defecating in his room, the red line had totally been crossed. Had he been a much younger child, then I may have felt different, but I only looked after teenagers.

It took a complete refurbishing and redecoration of the room before the house became bearable again, but even then, I still seemed to smell urine around the house. It was a rented house and it never really felt like home again for me. We moved house a few months later.

Getting back to young Wayne and reading between the lines of the report, I realised it was written by someone who was trying not to be too negative but nonetheless had been left with a distinctly negative impression by both Wayne and his Stepfather. Despite all those negative traits, there was, even in that depressing prison room, some humour from Wayne. Yes, it was mostly manic, but just like with the Joker, there was, amongst the sneering, the mocking and the tales of shocking escapades, something distinctly fascinating and compelling. His blunt and direct descriptions of people in his life made me impulsively laugh on several occasions, much to his pleasure. Wayne does not waste words and says it as he sees it, without worrying about giving offence. He knew how to be polite, but to him it was unnecessary.

When I made reference to the aforementioned difficulties in his relationship with his stepfather, his response was: "Difficulties? There won't be any f***ing difficulties when I kill the fat bastard."

My rapid powers of deduction ascertained that Wayne appeared to have a bit of an edge and maybe just a few anger issues. It was very apparent that he didn't waste words or time with people who failed to come quickly to the point. I sensed bullshit would not be favourably received. His words and reactions were like firecrackers going off, quite unnerving in the confines of that prison room. He had no doubt realised that I was a little jumpy and was playing on it for his own amusement. Perverse I know, but I was beginning to like him. No danger of boredom with this one I mused. Boredom to me was the worst so I knew immediately that Wayne would never be boring. I had already realised from my days in Knowle West that I enjoyed working with people who were nothing like me, especially if they were humorous.

I had always been honest, well-behaved and relatively shy, even as a child. My humour was probably my saving grace when making friends as a child. I was not built for fighting, risky or daredevil behaviour. I was probably categorised as sensitive and about as far from an Alpha male as one could get. That has never changed. This young man with the icy glare, fidgeting in front of me, was the antithesis of me. We seemed to be from different worlds and yet he was not a kid from the estates, but rather, like me from a distinctly middle-class home and family. I wondered as to whether the broken family had been the crucial factor in the way his life had developed. Alternatively, maybe he had just become feral after running away and discarding his home and family.

Was the stepdad just a convenient excuse? Maybe he was, but the damage was done anyway and if Wayne were a car, he would have been written off long ago. As a young person in the care system, he was already written off by so many people anyway. There was, I have to say, a low level of expectation in Social Services as to what could be achieved with Wayne. Maybe bits of his life could be salvaged, but a complete restoration was not on the agenda. The child was long gone in this boy and the steely man he was to become was already being fashioned. Nobody was going to change this boy.

I knew that from that very first encounter, but I hoped that I could give him a few more options as to his destination in life. Right side of the tracks or wrong side, where would he end up? He was intelligent, responsive, inquisitive, arrogant and fearless. He would undoubtedly be very challenging, so he ticked all the boxes for me as a budding masochist. Whether he would see me as enough of a challenge to warrant his interest, I somewhat doubted. From what I had witnessed it would more be a case as to whether I could be of use to him. That would be possibly my best way to get behind this manic jokers mask. I had no idea how that would happen, but I sensed something behind that mask that I could work with. I felt that I had made some sort of connection with him that day, but other than humour, not something that I could as yet identify.

As I made my way back to Bristol, my thoughts were totally consumed by the meeting with Wayne. Not for the first time in my working life, I felt a compulsion to engage with someone who could potentially be my Nemesis. I didn't overthink or analyse my own motives at the time, nor really for many years afterwards. Looking back now I realise that although I lack the physicality or mental strength to be a daredevil, at least in the traditional sense, I do however, get my buzz from playing mind games with those that are most challenging and those that are actually the antithesis of myself. Rather than a physical confrontation, which I would surely lose, it's more of a mental jousting. It doesn't work so well with those young men who rely only on brawn over brains. Just like a chess game, I really need the mental challenge of getting inside my opponent's head, of gaining an understanding of that person that is denied to others. Bluntly speaking, then what's the point of getting inside someone else's head if not to gain knowledge? If you can read and understand someone by what they present to you, then there is little to gain by probing further into their psyche. In my experience, the purpose of delving deeper into a troubled mind is twofold.

1. it can lead to that person disclosing information that they have never before disclosed, although that can be a painful experience, especially for the young person. As a Foster Carer we want to build trust with our Foster Children, but if what we discover is of a serious nature, then we have to share it with Social Workers, thereby meaning we have to tread so carefully by letting the child know that we have to report any serious disclosures. Naturally, that can lead to a reluctance to trust, which is why these things tend to happen very slowly and take a long time.
2. Mental jousting is fine, but there is an element of win or lose and some of the young people that I have cared for are extremely intelligent. Usually, that is not in the accepted sense of educational qualifications. Anyone who works in the care system knows that the percentage of young people in care gaining educational qualifications is still extremely small. It's never a good idea to use educational qualifications as a guide whilst assessing a care-experienced young person. Trauma and damaging life experiences can inhibit the potential for educational development. At the same time, they can lead people like Wayne to use their intelligence in many other

ways, both good and bad. The challenge for people like me is to find a way to unlock their potential so that they can use it in a positive way rather than in a negative way. Trust is of primary importance and that, as I have said, can be a slow process where a mentor has to be patient. Push too hard when you get closer to a subject and all can be lost in that relationship. When I say about getting inside a subject's head, it is not in an invasive way but more by invitation from the subject. It's about understanding their pain, their motives, their behaviours and how their thought process works. Do it right and you can be fairly accurate in predicting their reactions to situations. That can then really help you to work with them in developing strategies for dealing with problems that they face. If they become more confident at avoiding difficult situations, then it follows that they will cope better with their lives and with increased self-confidence may be able to better release their potential. The downside is that to gain trust, one often needs to reveal more about oneself to the subject and that can be risky and not done without great thought.

Never, ever underestimate the child or their level of intelligence and never assume that they are not more perceptive than they appear or even more perceptive than yourself. Intelligence crafted by pain and trauma can outmanoeuvre some very clever people. Teenagers like Wayne survived on their intelligence, which is easy to miss if you assume stupid behaviour is the prerequisite of stupid people. Many of the young people that I have looked after have witnessed and survived traumas that most of us couldn't comprehend. We learn from life experiences, so it's fair to assume that someone who has survived many battles may have learned much already in their young life, things that some of us don't learn in a lifetime. I learned from my parent's generation that survivors of war can be incredibly resilient and for these children their lives have constantly been at war. The children I look after are survivors, albeit very damaged ones. If as carers we can help them heal then they can be very strong and very adaptable in dealing with their future lives.

Admittedly, most of the young car thieves that I have met since those early days were not blessed with great intelligence so it hardly took Sherlock Holmes to chase them down. Wayne on the other hand was increasingly irritated by the banality of stealing cars for police chases, enduring endless police interviews and getting his social worker to defend his case in court. Steal a car then race it, chase and get caught and then repeat, soon became for him a continuous and pointless exercise. He no longer needed the kudos that stealing cars brought him so instead started working for an international gang stealing high performance cars for a good wage. Being too young to work legally or drive was not an issue nor really any particular inconvenience for Wayne. Rather than as previously looking to race the car, this involved stealing a high performance car and trying not to draw attention to oneself. That was more of a challenge especially at fifteen years old. He only got paid if he got across the country to the port and money was always better than kudos.

Wayne evolved from being a thrill-seeking car thief to a car thief with customers. He provided a service for his customers that others just could not match. He was a 'fixer', a risk taker, an innovator and a problem solver for customers. He remains generally so to this day, albeit 'usually' within legal parameters these days. His life to that point had given him no expectation of justice or family values and no requirement for a conscience. Society's rules and conventions were for him merely inconvenient inhibitors to expression and creativity. He expected to be exploited for his talents, but rather than worry about that, he would use those exploiting him as stepping stones that could be walked over and left behind in his rear view mirror, much like the police cars had been previously.

My first real experience of Wayne's problem-solving ability came a few months after that meeting in Campsfield House at that Bastille Day event in Paris. Over one million people were said to be gathered in the streets of Paris that day to witness the concert by Jean Michel Jarre. A good percentage of them were much nearer to the stage than we were, so like many others, I was resigned to us having to watch on one of the many big screens in the surrounding area. Wayne, unsurprisingly, was not easily deterred and had other ideas.

The trip to that point had been pretty disastrous from my point of view. I was well used to foreign travel and usually took enough cash to cover everything. We had taken a dedicated coach from Bristol to Paris for the event, but in my haste, I had run out of time to get to the bank. Not a problem, I thought, as I knew that I could get cash on the cross-channel ferry. It wouldn't be at the best rate of exchange, but the convenience on this occasion was the overriding factor. Back in 1990, cash was not as easily accessible as it is now. I had my bank card and cheque book which was the norm in those days. Once on the ferry I went straight to the currency desk to write a cheque for my French Francs, which was the currency before Euros were introduced. That was the moment that everything went rapidly downhill. It was a French ship and they did not accept English cheques, or English bank cards, only cash, of which I had little. I had been given a small amount, about £30, by the boss at the Children's Home to cover Wayne's food costs. It was only a one night stay as the other night would be on board the coach so that amount seemed quite adequate at the time. I was to keep receipts for other expenditures to be reimbursed upon our return. In 1990 my bank card was no good in Europe and my bank card was no good in a French cash machine.

This trip was going to be on a tight budget, to put it mildly or, as Wayne more succinctly put it, "We're fucked"

Wayne was apparently less than impressed and loudly scornful of my lack of preparation. A liberal amount of salt was painfully rubbed into my wounded pride. He was, of course, keen to share news of our plight with our fellow coach passengers when we re-boarded the coach to continue the journey to Paris. He had quickly become the focal point of attention of three lads sitting adjacent to us. Wayne naturally was never one to ignore a captive audience. It slowly dawned on me that Wayne was now at home in this environment where normal order had broken down. Panic was more my domain. Thanks to Wayne, by the time we reached the hotel in Paris, the three lads and a couple of other passengers had thankfully chipped in with some offers of food and drink to see us through the evening.

The next day was Bastille Day and we set off to the concert. The centre of Paris, manically busy at the best of times, had an extra level of intensity. Large screens had been set up in the streets to enable the crowds to view the show. We were told that a million people would be attending, so chances of getting any direct view of the stage would be near impossible. In fact, we found out later that two and a half million people attended the historic event. After what seemed like an eternity of walking on a swelteringly hot day, we did manage to get close enough to actually see the stage in the far distance. Myself and the three lads from the coach agreed that there was little chance of getting closer. That, however, was just the spark of a challenge that Wayne thrived on. He got us in a huddle and told us that he was going to pretend to pass out and when he did so then we needed to make a fuss and each grab an arm or leg. We should then carry him in the direction of the stage as far as possible.

The three lads were somewhat more enthused with his cunning plan than I was myself, but with some trepidation, I agreed to play my part. Wayne duly collapsed to the ground and judging by the shock on the faces of those around us, he must have been convincing. I have to say that I was struggling to keep a straight face. The four of us picked up the poor, lifeless-looking boy as requested and with shouts of alarm, moved towards the distant stage. Miraculously the sea of people parted in a Moses-like moment as we ran through the crowd screaming and shouting. The whole drama was amplified by shouts and looks of concern as we hurried through the mass of humanity, moving aside to let us through. I really don't think that flashing lights and sirens would have been any more effective. Eventually, we came into a surprising empty space, possibly created to counter a surge forwards by the crowd. A few nods between us and we knew that we had probably got as far as we could. We gently laid the still lifeless Wayne onto the ground where shocked onlookers witnessed a Lazarus moment as Wayne, seemingly hit by an electric shock, suddenly burst into life and leapt to his feet. The shocked faces turned to confused looks as these five mad Englishmen erupted into howls of laughter. Looking towards the stage, we knew that the object of the exercise had been a complete success. The concert was brilliant visually and musically and thanks to Wayne, we had a brilliant vantage point.

Reflecting on that escapade now, I think it was probably right there, in that moment, in the shadow of La Defense in Paris, that I first recognised Wayne's ability to instantly problem solve in difficult situations. It was sheer bloody genius and something I mimicked ten years later to get to the front of the stage for David Bowie at Glastonbury. I had taken Wayne and two other foster lads, Dave and Rob, to Glastonbury. The plan was to release Wayne and Rob (both by then total ravers) and let them try and blag a way into the main arena, whereas me and young Dave had no expectation of entry. As it turned out Wayne did his usual improvisation, dragging Dave through a tunnel under the fence before I had chance to catch a breath to object. Rob, howling with laughter quickly followed. Wayne and Rob were going for the full drug-addled Glasto experience and I had no intention of leaving a poor young innocent like Dave to be introduced to all manner of craziness. I had little choice but to follow through the rabbit hole into the main arena. Wayne and Rob disappeared to the rave tents, so Dave and I managed to find our way through the massive crowd to be right up the front by the time Bowie emerged later. A slight crowd surge, a sudden fainting and Dave and I were lifted over the barriers by security. What a view, what a performance and by Bowie too. He was as charismatic and outstanding as ever, but to this day the act of gaining illegal entry still sits uncomfortably with me. Dave, who is still with me 23 years later, finds it hysterical to this day.

Chapter 2

I had started working with young people five years before that adventure in Paris. In 1985 I began working part-time as a youth worker at Eagle House Youth Centre. Eagle House was situated in Knowle West, a neglected council estate in South Bristol. It was an area that I had known of from my school days at nearby Hengrove School. I say known of rather than 'knew' because as a middle-class boy from the distant suburb of Stockwood (well, about four miles distant), it was definitely not the done thing to venture into Knowle West unless you had a local 'guide'. The estate of newly built houses in Stockwood, where my family moved to before my second year of senior school, was another world entirely in comparison to Knowle West.

Hengrove School had a large catchment area with a wide demographic financially, although at that time (late 1960s), very little ethnic diversity. Two decades on, that was changing, but the reputation of Knowle West as a no-go area for outsiders had continued. That part of South Bristol remained very tribal orientated. The post-war housing estates of Hartcliffe and Knowle West were known for their social problems. Young people in those areas always saw each other as rivals, if not sworn enemies. The vastly more middle-class neighbouring areas of Hengrove and Whitchurch were the favourite go to areas for budding housebreakers and car thieves. They provided much easier and more inviting pickings.

Hartcliffe kids and Knowle Westers knew that messing on your own doorstep was more likely to ignite family feuds and could get very messy. If you caused a ruckus in Whitchurch or Hengrove the repercussions or retaliation would rarely come home to Knowle West. The police might reluctantly pay a visit, but victims in those areas would generally know better than to come to Knowle West looking for trouble.

One only had to navigate a set of traffic lights to enter Knowle West, but for outsiders intending to linger, it might as well have been fortified walls and a drawbridge. The reputation of Knowle West meant that all popular routes circumnavigated it rather than passed through it. There was nothing inside Knowle West that outsiders would be likely to visit, other than Broadbury Road Police Station, so visitors tended to be social workers who had been asked to act as appropriate adults for their young clients.

When I started working at Eagle House, it was more akin to Beirut than Bristol. Well, at least it seemed so to a naive and inexperienced middle-class youth worker. Located in the heart of Knowle West, the single-storey youth centre, built in the style of a 1960s school prefab building, was half hidden behind wrought iron gates and an imposing high wall that made the front yard resemble a prison yard. On my first night working there, tempers flared, arguments ensued and the shutters on the coffee bar quickly came down. All the kids were ejected from the building and as I and my colleagues were leaving stones and rubble rained down around us into the yard.

After being under siege for a while, a grinning 12-year-old walked calmly up to me as the dust from the rubble cleared and said, "Welcome to Knowle West. I don't think you'll be coming back."

A menacing 12-year-old brought my first night at Eagle House to a fitting close. I'm really not sure if it was pride or stupidity, but I did go back and absolutely loved it in the same perverse way that I was later to enjoy looking after teenage car thieves and delinquents. Looking back, Eagle House was my apprenticeship and what an apprenticeship it was. It has stood me in good stead. Working in Knowle West was pure adrenaline for me, like being a space traveller arriving on an alien planet, eager to gather as much information and enlightenment as possible. It was edgy, potentially quite dangerous with daily dramas on the streets, arguments, fights and all manner of anti-social behaviour.

Inside the youth centre building, as mentioned, there was a coffee bar. The metal shutters were pulled down at the first sign of an argument as had been the case on my first night. A few raised voices was all that it ever took to incite a massive overreaction. The customary pool table was in the foyer. Every youth centre seemed to have one back then. It had a badly ripped cloth cushion and a selection of pool cues, few of which had tips on them. There was chalk though, plenty of chalk, so chalking of pool cues was possible, in fact almost compulsory, even if totally ineffective. There was a dart board with blunted darts and in the inner room, a table tennis table and a wide selection of names on the walls, tagged in graffiti style. In the 1980s, this type of youth centre was very much the norm, as darts, pool and table tennis were of course the only necessary requirements for containing 50 to 100 rowdy young people. Over the following decades music and art studios became more commonplace in youth centres, no doubt as a result of the developing hip-hop culture. Well, that was the case at least until the Tories of recent years decided the Youth Service was a waste of resources and closed centres faster than restaurants have closed since Brexit.

Back in the 1980s, youth centres rarely catered for girls and they were even excluded from some exclusively 'boys clubs'. Places were often run by ex-boxers and army types who were not averse to handing out a good clip around the ear, or indeed relishing a good eye-to-eye confrontation. At least Eagle House had a female as its assistant leader. She was my sister-in-law, Christina, a person who pioneered many girl-centred changes at Eagle House and understood that most girls just wanted equal opportunities with the boys. That in itself was at conflict with the traditional youth club setting. As has been the case in many patriarchal cultures men and boys are seen to hold all the power and yet it is the women who exert the real power and control and, more often than not, sort out the disputes among the men. Too many misogynistic men have asserted their claims as hunter-gatherers, never questioning the alternate view that women send their men to fight and forage and then control them by fulfilling their basic requirements of food and sex. It's a fairly simple way to maintain order, reinforced by making sure their offspring conform to the same basic principles. Knowle West has always had strong matriarchs and they still hold the real power. In Stockwood, we knew our next-door neighbours but few beyond that. In Knowle West, people knew virtually everyone in the street and several other streets too. In Stockwood we had an occasional conversation over the garden wall but in Knowle West conversations were often shared across the road and down the street without any concern for privacy.

When I joined Eagle House in the mid-1980s the traditional and largely dated youth centre equipment quickly became almost obsolete as the exploding love of Hip-Hop took the UK's youth by storm. At Eagle House, two brothers, the Thompson boys (Jeff and Kirk aka Flynn and Krust) were instrumental in helping me organise the first ever Hip-Hop event for Knowle West. That event is now ingrained in local folklore by middle-aged Graffiti Artists and Musicians. Another helper was Bunjy, an inspirational young man who was a catalyst at the centre of all things musical among the local youngsters. Music was empowering for Bunjy and was to become his life. He introduced me to a guy called Patrick Hart who became key to the success of that early event. The collaboration with Patrick was the beginning of a partnership that, over the decades, led to my biggest successes, both in music and in the Care sector. We went on to organise many music events and tours and many years later set up our own pioneering and very successful Children's Home and mentoring business, Elevation Childcare.

Bristol Freestyle was the name we chose for that first event in Knowle West. What was unique about it was that it was an event that drew top performers and young people from other areas into Knowle West. It was not really a very large event, attracting just a few hundred rather than the thousands that attended some of the events that Patrick and I organised over the next decade. Despite the smaller numbers, it was significant for the actual effect that it had on those present, both performers and audience members. That was to be its true legacy and it is still remembered fondly to this day by the young people who were there and who are now well into their 50s. The 'Stuff of Legends', as they say.

The event was in two parts. In the afternoon, an open-air event in the field opposite Eagle House and then in the evening, a concert at the local Community Centre. The Newquay Road field was bordered on three sides by council houses, with the open side facing Eagle House. Patrick had brought in a well-known local DJ, Tristan Bolitho (Tristan B) and he had used his contacts to pull in some big names for the evening show. For the daytime stage, we hired a drop-side van, whilst across the road in Eagle House, Christina had talked the club manager Dave into agreeing to let young graffiti artists do their stuff on the walls of one of the rooms. Patrick took charge of the stage management and equipment sourcing and the afternoon event featured young and very young local talent.

Inside Eagle House, there was a real buzz, as various teenage Graffiti Artists took over. The buzz was probably caused by the fumes of the spray paints. Most Graffiti then was of course done illegally and therefore on the exterior of buildings, so there were not a lot of guidelines nor experience on the effects of spraying indoors. There were risk assessments, even back then, but it was hard to assess risks when there were so few precedents. That was part of the excitement that the new Hip-Hop phenomenon was generating for young people. It was fresh, vibrant, colourful and was in the process of creating a new breed of outlaws, new urban heroes both in music and art. All rules could and should be broken; therefore nothing in music or art was sacrosanct. Even for someone like me, in my early 30s, it was slightly unnerving. Having grown up in the generation of Peace, Love and Revolution, this particular revolution was somewhat unexpected and surprising. Had I not been working with young people, then much of it would have possibly passed me by and it would certainly not have influenced me in the way that it was to do from that day on.

The Hip-Hop explosion was maybe the first time that my own generation was pretty much out of the loop and made to feel totally out of touch. I guess it happens to every generation and is equally unwelcome by them. We had seen many of our youthful dreams, ambitions and ideas come to nothing and ironically, it had made many of us reluctant to let a new revolution succeed where much of ours had failed. There had been a natural transition for my generation, certainly for the predominantly white, rock-based one that I was part of. In the 1960s, the Beatles had changed everything. Lennon was the voice that spoke for us before giving way to Led Zeppelin-led Heavy Rock, Bowie's gender challenging version and on to Elton, Rod Stewart, Pink Floyd and Queen. Soul initially passed me by, regretfully. Bob Marley and Reggae had broken into my erstwhile rock-led obsession, but Hip-Hop was the big challenge for me. It seemed to be dismissive and irreverent towards my favourite music genres, but at the same time, it was hard not to recognise the effect it had on young people. I had to put aside my personal discomfort with the idea that Hip-Hop Artists could steal my favourite guitar riffs and use them to blend into their own tunes. At first, it just seemed like cheating and unoriginal (just like AI does now for many). Accepting it would be a slow process, one that I long tried to mask in order to work with these incredible young people.

Bristol Freestyle had a second part to it that was basically for the more serious Hip-Hop kids. When I had first spoken about putting on an event, the kids had liked the idea but assumed it would just feature local performers. Thanks to Tristan and Patrick, we were able to book some famous DJ's including the then World Mixing Champion Chad Jackson and celebrated DJ Cutmaster Swift. For well-known artists to appear in Knowle West was a game-changer for the event. One of the performers did get his nice motor broken into, but hey, what would an event be without a traditional Knowle West welcome.

Patrick brought some music friends along from Bedminster, another area in South Bristol. Pat had started his own youth nights in Bedminster, which were attracting hordes of youngsters. Using the Crypt at the local church, the Cryptic Youth Club had a growing reputation as a place where budding rappers and DJ's could do their stuff each week. The Cryptic Crew featuring Patrick were to be one of the highlights of Bristol Freestyle. Patrick, a good decade or so younger than me, was clearly a very charismatic character. With Indian heritage, good looks and an engaging charm, he was a complete natural in working with young people. He was also a rapper and DJ, so he pretty much had it all as far as the kids were concerned. An abrasive attitude towards authority and tradition really sealed the deal in his popularity. Hip-Hop loving kids were looking for new role models and new leaders. Pat was just perfect for them. Coming from a Catholic family, he had gone to the rival school to mine in Hengrove,

St Bernadettes, admittedly a decade after me, but the rivalry remained.

Ironically, my schoolmates regarded Bernadettes kids with some sympathy, especially having Nuns as their teachers. However, what their school did have was more ethnic diversity, being Catholic. St Bernadettes attracted Greeks and Italians, amongst others. A largely unrecognised Ignorance, due to lack of contact with other cultures and ethnic backgrounds, was in hindsight a real downside of Hengrove School at that time. It was of course another great benefit of Hip-Hop Culture in that it was much more ethnically diverse. I can't speak for the likes of Bunjy, Krust or Flynn, but growing up in a predominantly white community could not have been easy. That these were to be the stars to later emerge from Knowle West possibly demonstrates that Hip-Hop gave them a natural and comfortable environment to achieve their potential and excel. Whilst Eagle House perhaps gave them that first taste of their music potential, it was also true that they virtually all quickly migrated away from Knowle West musically to more culturally diverse areas.

Hip-Hop really did change everything for the youth in the 1980s and also ironically for me. What I did very quickly realise was that if I was going to be able to work with this new generation of kids then I needed to quickly put aside my personal musical preferences. It was all about enthusing and motivating young people and to do that Hip-Hop was clearly the way forward, the way for me to enable communication. Luckily, I also realised that to capture the interest of young people it was not about me getting down with the kids and imposing my interests, my likes, or even my philosophy on them and certainly not trying to be cool with it or even trying to look cool with it. I could adapt to many things but becoming cool was never going to happen.

I knew that I was in effect an irrelevance for the most part. It was a most unwelcome revelation and after much thought I realised just what I needed to be. I should become a conduit channelling their enthusiasm, their hopes, their dreams, their anger and their frustrations into positivity and opportunity. Opportunities for young people on estates like Knowle West were few and far between and usually illegal. Just saying, "don't do drugs", "don't do crime", were pointless unless I and others could show them viable alternatives. Knowle West may have been their fortress, their sanctuary and indeed their family, but there comes a time in a young life where that fortress becomes a prison. That prison may be invisible, but reluctance to move away from one's safe place can lower one's expectations, one's ambitions and one's motivation. Now please don't get the impression that I see living in Knowle West as similar to living in a prison, because wherever you grow up can become like a prison. Even the leafy suburbs of Clifton can feel the same for young people who desire something more than they have and who want new adventures. The difference between growing up in Knowle West and Clifton though is really just one word.

Opportunity!

One can create opportunities for oneself, but generally for young people opportunity is gifted, and not many opportunities were handed out in Knowle West. With the benefit of hindsight, that is what Bristol Freestyle was all about, although I can't pretend that I possessed such foresight at the time. Yes, I saw it as an opportunity for the young people to indulge their love of Hip-Hop, but I was too inexperienced to recognise the effect of Inspiration in a longer term sense upon young people. Eagle House was the start of my journey of discovery, almost as much as it was for many of those young people that day. Inspiration is not a one-way channel. As a conduit, I didn't get to choose the direction or capacity of flow. Opening up channels of Inspiration and of communication involved a whole network of people. Myself, Christina, Patrick, Tristan, Bunjy and many others coming together, working together and creating new networks that would in turn lead to new networks, long after we had moved on. Bristol Freestyle was but a brief moment in time, but it was, I believe, a catalyst for so many things, for many young people and a few older ones too.

In the decades that have since passed, many bigger events and bigger names have been recognised for helping to put Bristol on the map, both musically and in Graffiti terms, but that day in Knowle West was a ground breaker without doubt. A little ripple that led to a much bigger wave following afterwards.

Those days at Eagle House were indeed massively inspiring and exciting times. Although I had run a couple of boys' football teams previously, it was Christina who convinced me to become a part-time youth worker at Eagle House. I had no idea from my first day at Eagle House that my life's work would begin there and then and go on to involve so many young people. Youth work led to me becoming a Residential Social Worker in a local Children's Home, then a Foster Carer, then a Children's Homeowner and Mentor, amongst other things.

Fortunately, from the outset at Eagle House, Christina supported me working with the kids there. Now, perhaps I should explain as to why it was the assistant leader (Christina) who was making the day-to-day decisions at Eagle House. Surely the Manager would make the decisions, not the assistant. You would think so, yes, but the manager, a guy called Dave, who was about as useful as a chocolate teapot, albeit certainly not as sturdy. As manager he would appear to make the decisions unless something went wrong. He was, in effect, just a figurehead and a pretty hopeless one at that.

Dave was a fairly frail looking middle-aged man who seemed far older than his years. Imagine taking someone who looked like a rabbit in the headlights and putting him into one of the most challenging youth centres in Bristol. He was probably one of the most unfit-for-purpose appointments that has ever blighted the youth service and that is in a strong field of candidates. With Dave at the helm, the good ship Eagle House would have run aground long before had it not been for his more than able assistant.

How 'Dopey Dave' had ever got into youth work at all amazed me. A man devoid of any personality who would avoid making any sort of positive decision without first considering endless excuses for not doing so. He must really have seriously upset someone in the Youth Service to have been placed as manager in this long-forgotten outpost of youth work. It was like putting a librarian in charge of a street gang. The other possibility was of course that the decision makers thought that by appointing Dave they could invoke a convenient Titanic scenario. Dave would rearrange the deck chairs very neatly as the good ship 'Eagle House' plunged towards inevitable disaster. I doubt that there would have been too much disappointment in the youth work hierarchy if the place had sunk without trace.

Dave was not a problem for his superiors, as he would generally say no to anything that would involve any expense or risk. Costs would be kept to a minimum and users driven away by boredom, until such time as the whole place could be quietly shut down. At the very first sign of trouble, Dave would find an excuse to lock himself away in his office with his paperwork and leave his staff to deal with the inconvenience of local bored youths.

Initially he probably saw Christina as a blessing, as he could abdicate responsibility for absolutely anything when necessary and leave her to carry the workload. By the time he realised her capabilities it was too late and he had literally lost all authority to her and could do no more than spend his time frantically trying to take credit for her successes. It's possible, although unlikely, that his bosses were ignorant of his limitations but not a kid in the place had any respect for him whatsoever. Christina had undoubtedly realised that the real power in Knowle West lay in the hands of the women, even if the men believed otherwise. The staff were mainly local women who were related to many of the kids. With Christina running things the girls who attended really asserted themselves. Dave knew better than to take on the Knowle West sisterhood. Bravery was not a weapon in Dave's armoury. Well, actually Dave's armoury had long since become an empty warehouse, such was his ineffectiveness.

I was lucky in that there was a nucleus of musically talented youngsters at Eagle House who were supportive and instrumental in inspiring many other young people at the time. First and foremost was Bunjy who was integral to that first event. One of the other prime movers in that emerging scene was Knowle West boy, Tricky, who was to become famous as a member of Massive Attack and later as a solo artist. When I first encountered him, he was just a local lad trying to introduce another young man's head to a reinforced glass window. The Thompson's soon to become DJ's Flynn and Krust (as part of Fresh Four) Tricky and DJ Bunjy (Un, Deux Trois and now Laid Blak) were all teenagers that attended the club. For some years after the emergence of the Bristol Sound, other more socially cool areas of Bristol were acknowledged for their contributions, but sadly all too rarely Knowle West got a mention. Tricky did later pay homage to his roots with the release of his *'Knowle West Boy'* album in 2008. In one of his interviews for that album he described me as a mentor, massively exaggerating the truth without a doubt, but nice that he remembered me. He did reinforce the opinion when we met up again in 2008. Fame had not taken away his charm, but in truth he had never needed a mentor, as just like Bunjy and the Thompson boys he was always totally focused and uniquely talented.

Tricky actually referenced me in an interview he did around that time. He said this: "There was quite a few people who had a positive impact on me. A guy called John Stokes ran a youth club round the corner from where I lived. Everyone would hang out there, and they sorted us out with turntables and got us into making music."

I smiled when I read that quote which was published in a New York magazine. When you get to be a big star like Tricky the memory can play tricks on you. I never ran the place, nor wanted to, but the bit about the decks was true. In my naivety I signed an HP agreement on behalf of the boys to get them a set of decks. The plan was for them to pay me back in instalments. I think it slipped their mind after the first instalment, but it was worth every single penny to know that it was appreciated and fondly remembered. It was for them the start of their successful careers in music.

The music at Eagle House, the excitement it generated and the social engagement and communication that came from it was electric, despite my music preferences being so very different. It was one of the first ways that I found to engage with the kids. Eagle House was not just about Hip-Hop though. It was an important focal point for the local kids. Knowle West had a multitude of social problems, but once you were accepted there as an outsider, it was such a fascinating place for someone like me. These were not quiet streets. There was always something happening. Many of the kids were quite disconnected from the society that I had grown up in. Working with these kids was challenging but nonetheless rewarding emotionally. They mostly had little but wanted everything. There were other parts of Bristol, less socially deprived, where kids had more opportunities and more distractions, so could often be much less engaged with the area's youth services. Whilst through their lived experiences there was a great distrust of the provision for young people and of outsiders coming into Knowle West, there was undoubtedly a powerful energy amongst the young people. Admittedly that energy was often very negative, but for me that was the challenge, to turn negative energy into positive energy.

I didn't know then, but those two ingredients, Music and disconnected young people, were to be the foundations of my life's work. Two things that went hand in hand throughout my career. Everything I learned growing up was in the comfort of middle-class security. Honesty was a given because I didn't need to be dishonest. Holidays, possessions. were all taken for granted. If I needed new clothes they were bought. Suddenly, I was surrounded by kids, many of whom were given nothing of what I had taken for granted. If it wasn't given, then why not take it? That was an understandable philosophy.

Their parents had grown up the same way. Some of them had parents who robbed houses and got arrested on a regular basis. Parents who physically fought other parents, parents who beat people, parents who beat their kids and let them run feral. It was not all parents and not all families, a minority no doubt, but a very vocal and visible minority. Growing up we never saw police knocking in doors or people being handcuffed in our streets. I had nothing in common with these kids so how could I communicate with them?

Unlike Patrick I wasn't talented musically, or in any noticeable way. I clearly wasn't a strong person physically. Dopey Dave stood out as weak and ineffective in a community full of alpha males. Unfortunately, in their eyes I initially probably came across as a younger version of him, totally out of my comfort zone. It was at that time, right there, when I first learned to mentor, albeit operating in an instinctive survival mode and generally without any forethought or planning. I was totally out of my comfort zone, 30-plus years of life experience seemed absolutely useless. Instinctive reaction was how these kids survived from day-to-day. I had never been so out of my depth, it was sink or swim and I didn't know how to swim in these murky depths, but there was a surprising clarity as I was drowning. Grab a lifebelt, and for me Bristol Freestyle was that lifebelt which led to me understanding them better. I studied how they reacted to threats and to danger, how they didn't stop to think about right or wrong, as to whether something was legal or not, or what the consequences could be. No, they just reacted because instinct and reaction was how they had always survived. Risk taking behaviour (at least compared to my childhood) was right off the scale.

The one thing that was clear was that whatever the danger, whatever the risks, it was fun. Not just laughing at their own risky behaviour, but absolute whoops of delight from them when they did crazy stunts. I laughed so much at some of their antics that I forgot my fears. Strangely I was suddenly totally at ease in this alien landscape and enthralled by the whole experience. The energy, exuberance and joy of life in these kids was like a lightning bolt going through me and it was contagious. For someone like me who was averse to risk-taking it was exciting. I was fascinated by the untapped potential in these kids and the psychological aspect of how they had no need of normal societal behaviours, rules or conventions. They were mavericks that had torn up the rules. It's not a case of me voicing approval of their challenging behaviours so much as accepting that it would be a pretty dull world without mavericks, risk takers and opportunists.

Chapter 3

It wasn't just the music and graffiti at Eagle House that caught my attention. Having previously managed a boys football team in North Bristol. I was asked to take over the club's failing football team. Well it wasn't so much failing, as banned from the boys' club league. The team had been doing okay the previous season until an incident in a cup tie against the local rivals. The opposing centre-forward had been giving it out a bit physically and verbally. Tempers flared and there followed a bit of an altercation. The Eagle House goalkeeper, not wanting to miss out on all the fun, went and collected the wooden corner flag, ran up the field and promptly hit the aforementioned centre-forward across the head. The rest of the team piled on, the game was abandoned and the team was subsequently expelled from the league.

After considerable thought on the matter, I decided to start a team in a younger age group (under 14s), so as to avoid the possibility of previously banned players being involved. The league agreed to admit the new team and I went about recruiting new players, carefully avoiding selecting a few potentially violent players. Most of the lads, myself included, were Bristol City fans, so I thought it would be a good idea to ask the City for a player to come and coach us. Bristol City had almost gone bust financially and dropped through the divisions. Their new manager, former Leeds and

England legend Terry Cooper, had been on TV saying that the club, still on its knees financially, wanted to encourage more community involvement. He said his door was open to the community.

Well! Talk about a golden opportunity. I wasn't going to turn that down. The very next morning, I phoned into the club and asked to speak to the manager. To my complete surprise, I was put straight through to him.

"How can I help you lad?" was his warm response.

"Well," I said, "firstly, I would like to bring some of my lads down to Ashton Gate for a tour of the ground."

"No problem," he said, "just give me a minute and I will find out who it is that organises the tours."

After what seemed like an eternity, I could hear him come back into the room and pick up the phone.

"Are you still there lad?"

"Yes," I replied.

"Well. apparently, I do the tours," he said laughing.

Clearly, there hadn't been any tours since the club financially imploded. A skeleton staff ran everything on a shoestring budget.

"Anything else lad?" he asked.

"Well, I would like to have a player come to the club and do some coaching," I replied.

"No problem," he said, "what about tomorrow evening? You can come down about 5 pm sort out a date for the stadium tour and pick up a player."

I said my thanks to him and was absolutely buzzing that things were sorted so easily. Terry was a rare gem as managers go. The next evening, I drove down to Ashton Gate, where a very tall track-suited figure appeared to be waiting.

"Are you John?" he asked in a broad Glaswegian accent as I got out of the car.

"Yes, I am indeed," I replied.

"Well, the gaffer has asked me to come and meet your boys. My name's David, David Moyes and I've just signed for the club today." That explained why I didn't recognise him, but I was sure the boys would be suitably impressed. On the way back to Knowle, I warned him that the kids were not necessarily the politest of children. He quickly explained that he was from Glasgow, so nothing would phase him.

Well, the initial reaction was rather cool when we arrived. Just like me, they didn't recognise him. He introduced himself.

"I'm David Moyes and have signed for Bristol City today for thirteen thousand pounds."

"F*** off," said one little lad. "It was ten thousand".

Moysie looked at me and smiled. He wasn't fazed at all. A series of coaching sessions soon had the rabble organised and responsive. To think that my boys in Knowle West back then were coached by a man who went on to coach Everton, Manchester United and West Ham, amongst others. Who would have thought it? The man was a joy to work with. I bumped into him again at Ashton Gate many years later when, he was manager at Preston and he came straight over to say hello. He had not changed and I suspect that if I met him again, he would be just the same pleasant, affable guy he was then. He had that presence and manner that commanded respect with a generally quiet but firm assurance. I always felt that he would become a very good coach and it's been so pleasing to see the success he has had.

As for the football team? Well, two years later we got to our cup final. I hired a 52-seater coach to transport the team as a reward for reaching the final. That way, we had room for a few supporters too. The boys stepped off the coach like kings, bouncing past the opposition who were clear favourites. They cast envious glances at our arrival. The boys were walking on air and won the day, bringing the first trophy back to Eagle House for many years. The right motivation can make a massive difference and that day we beat the odds, the history and the local rivals.

It wasn't always so easy taking Eagle House kids anywhere. Driving the county minibus with kids opening the back doors as I drove and pelting people with rubbish as we passed by. We even took them to a country club on one occasion for a summer fun day for Bristol youth clubs. To say that they caused havoc would be somewhat understating the case. Not many of the other participants or guests warmed to them, except maybe the old couple in the sauna. They certainly warmed after two of the boys had loaded up the coals for the sauna. The highlight of the day was a chance to play American football against a top UK team. We had a bunch of 12 to13-year-olds and the odds and history suggested something would go awry. True to form, the captain of the football team got our lads to line up against these massive American footballers. He explained that the object of the exercise was to try and take out the wide receiver when he got the ball. I squirmed a little when he said, 'Take out the wide receiver'.

That sounded too much like an invitation for trouble. The kids from other clubs had gingerly tried to stop the giant of a man who was the wide receiver. Not so Eagle

House kids. They attacked en masse like a swarm of bees flying head-on, side-on and every which way. Boys were hanging on to each leg and arm, with others just launching themselves at him. Having felled the giant, they proceeded to pile on the poor guy, punching and kicking. It was a sight to behold and eventually the giant emerged from under a pile of bodies. He was probably never more grateful for his protective clothing. I have so many crazy memories of those mad Knowle Westers.

The couple of years that I spent at Eagle House were the most surprising and amazing learning experiences of my life. It was there that I learned my survival skills for working with troubled teenagers. I became a mentor without even realising it. Little did I know then, but it was there on the streets of Knowle West that my destiny was decided. Understanding and communicating with the minds of teenagers was to be my life's work.

As a teenager, it's pretty much impossible to understand your own mind, the raging hormones prevent that and yet those teenage formative years can define you for the rest of your life. Direction is often random; opportunities are missed. I guess it's why we need good parents or failing that then good mentors. Not realising your potential, not being able to realise it, or not having somebody recognise it is such a sad waste. To truly realise it, you have to really know yourself, understand yourself, your strengths, your weaknesses, your talents and your skills. There really is no magic age where you can do that.

Look at me. I am 70 years old and writing my first book. I am reflecting on my life, some of the many things I have learned and why at 70 I am still working.

Yes, one reason is that I neglected to sort myself a decent pension and the fact that there is no work pension for Foster Carers. When you're done, it's thank you and goodbye and if you're lucky maybe a certificate. Not so much a golden handshake as a golden shower. There should be a pension or something after such a long life of duty and maybe one day there will be, but not now and not in my time. We are all slaves to finance and the thought of no longer having an income and vastly inadequate savings is pretty scary. Foster Carers are always reluctant to say that money is a factor, but the bills don't pay themselves. Money is not my main motivation though, for remaining as a Foster Carer into my 70s. I still love doing the work, but more than that, it's about the thirst for knowledge that I have always had, especially in respect of young people. Helping them overcome the many things that can prevent them reaching their potential is my reward.

I had never realised that I possessed a thirst for knowledge until I was transported into another world in Knowle West. In fact, my reluctance to go into further education or my lack of interest in obtaining any qualifications would suggest the opposite. The only qualifications I ever got were a handful of GCE's at O-level and an A-level in English. The certificates for those exam passes arrived and were promptly put in a drawer somewhere, never to see the light of day again. They meant nothing to me, except wasted time in school. All that pressure of trying to pass exams just to prove that I could remember largely uninteresting information has left its scars on me. Why not instead find out what a child is interested in and then help the child learn more through studying that subject, or else maybe use that subject to gain their interest. We learned Shakespeare, Wordsworth, Keats, Algebra, Physics, Chemistry, etc, etc, on and on and almost all of it was mind-numbingly boring to me and useless for my entire life since. It put me off traditional learning and education for the rest of my life. A couple of years working with young people in Knowle West taught me far more about life than I had learned to that point.

My first job had been working in an office, because with my qualifications and experience, that was my destiny. I could dream one day of being an office manager. I didn't of course because I really didn't have a clue what I wanted to do and nothing in the education system had identified anything for me. I just walked out after a few weeks in that first job, totally unsure of what to do with my life. Hengrove School had given me no direction whatsoever and had not sparked any sense of creativity within me.

When I left that first job, my dad set me up in a confectionery shop in Bath and later in another in Hampshire, working with my mother whilst he was working as a director of a Building Federation in London. When I grew tired of it, he bought one for me and my elder brother Mike back in Bristol. It was okay for a couple of years and I started a football team for the paper boys, which was fun. That was my first real interaction in working with young people. I worked for my dad in his office in London after that. He must have despaired that I would ever really settle into anything, although he never once said so. Unequivocal support for me, he never once let me down. Homesick again, he found me a job back in Bristol, which could have led to a good position but it was office-based and my idea of hell. It was then that I started working a few evenings at Eagle House and nothing was really ever the same again for me.

My sister-in-law, Christina, was already a qualified youth worker and destined to become a senior figure in youth work. I was a part-time unqualified youth worker with absolutely no intention of training to become a man like Dopey Dave. Even worse, I could become a senior management person who could sit in an office and qualify for a pension after a lifetime of meetings and training modules. Much as I loved my time at Eagle House, I knew that the Youth Work structure was not for me. In a voluntary capacity, then yes, something like Patrick had done in setting up his own youth group, but I couldn't see that leading to a full-time paid position. I had already been enthused enough by Patrick to see possibilities of continuing to work with him, organising further events and youth groups. Unfortunately, it would probably never be anything that I could earn a living from, so any youth work would have to be a secondary interest.

Once again though, after a couple of wonderful years at Eagle House I really still lacked any inclination of a way forward career-wise until my cousin Terry suggested that I consider working in a local Children's Home. The idea certainly ticked a few boxes and it was a full-time position working with teenagers so it made a lot of sense. I had continued to develop music-based ideas with Patrick and had helped him organise a few very successful events in Bedminster. The Children's Home position would not affect my staying involved with Pat or being involved in his new music project 'Freshblood'.

The Bedminster Fun Days, as they were called, were similar to Bristol Freestyle, only bigger and with much larger attendances. They were held at Bedminster Skateboard Park, where there was plenty of wall space for the young Graffiti artists who were by then beginning to get far more organised, thanks to another Youth Worker, John Nation. He was working at a youth centre in the Barton Hill district of Bristol, another working-class area, more known for its high-rise flats than sprawling council estates.

John Nation was busy creating a hub for Graffiti artists at another bland-looking youth centre in Barton Hill (aka the Dug-Out). Those young Artists from Bristol Freestyle, along with many others migrated to the Dug-out. It attracted budding Graffiti artists from across Bristol and beyond. Whilst Banksy might have later put Bristol on the worldwide Graffiti map, John Nation was the pioneer who created the environment that caused the explosion of Bristol Street Art. That explosion would later lead to the emergence of artists like Banksy and Inkie and a plethora of extremely talented street artists that still today keep Bristol at the centre of UK Street Art. John is rightly recognised as the Godfather of Bristol Graffiti and these days gives guided tours of Bristol Street Art for hordes of tourists on behalf of the City of Bristol. It is impossible to underestimate the influence of this one modest man on the Street Art culture of 21st-century Bristol and yet to the majority of Bristol citizens, he remains largely unknown. Sadly, even now, the measure of success in Bristol is all too often attributed to people who have made wealth for themselves rather than people who have added to the richness of our city and its culture.

Much the same could be said about Patrick, who has contributed so much to the fabric of our city with little recognition. The Bedminster Fun Days attracted hordes of young people, along with the elite of Bristol's emerging talent. That talent, over the next few years, was to finally put Bristol on the music map. Pat's Cryptic Crew evolved into another music collective, Freshblood, featuring well-known local Reggae artist Dan Ratchet. They quickly became stalwarts of the Bristol scene and were known for attracting a large teenage following. Pat was known for his English rap style, at odds with many UK rappers who simply sought to mimic American rappers.

By that time, both Pat and I were looking to start a new project encouraging talent. Using the same name, the Freshblood Organisation was created. We set up a recording studio both for Freshblood and also other young artists looking to get into the business. Pat as a DJ and a rapper became a mentor for many young performers.

The events that Pat and I were to organise over the years following the Bedminster Fundays created ripples of their own, but even back then there was a clique in the Bristol Music Scene that you either had to follow or else be largely ignored by Bristol's largely middle-class arty crowd. Pat was never a follower, or someone who would give the time of day to people who were so up on their own egos or self-promotion. Back in the late 1980's, well before the Bristol Sound had emerged, Bristol was a music wasteland. Being a city with a large student population, the feeling generally was that the city had no edge. Life for the majority was comfortable and the only place beginning to show much creativity was the inner city St Pauls area, home to the city's largest concentration of migrant population, especially from the Windrush generation. St Pauls at that time was certainly at odds with Bristol's sleepy middle-class image.

The arty London set that were to flood into the city following the music successes in the early 1990s had fortunately not then set up camp, or gentrified Bristol's inner city. The student-led *Venue* magazine held the influence until their arrival, an influence that comfortably merged with the London exiles when they arrived to put their own spin on our musical history. Only two areas of Bristol mattered in many people's eyes. The student hub of Clifton and St Pauls. In that respect, not much has changed, but it explains why Freshblood and many others had to either fit in or sit on the outside of the music scene. The bulk of the Bristol Music and Art Scene that got the media attention at that time was mostly very elitist and exclusive. Patrick's work in Bedminster and Hartcliffe, my experience in Knowle West and John Nations Graffiti tribe in Barton Hill were never really part of that. Pat was not into bootlicking middle-class journos, so Freshblood, to this day, remain largely excluded from any recognition of their input into the fabric of those times. The Graffiti scene gained notoriety when Operation Anderson saw many of the artists arrested. John Nation had firmly planted the Graffiti flag at the forefront of Bristol Art and Culture where it has remained ever since and is now known around the world.

In the 1990s myself and Patrick, by means of the Freshblood organisation, created some amazing events that built on the reputation of Bristol Freestyle and the Bedminster Fun Days. Bristol Safe Music was one of the first events that addressed youth crime and drug-related problems. Held in Eastville Park, which has since become synonymous with large music events, it featured chart-topping US group PM Dawn in their first ever UK appearance. Members of Bristol Legends, Massive Attack, although not appearing, were there filming the event from a truck at the back of the crowd.

Following that success Freshblood were recruited by the local council to organise youth events in Kingswood Park two years in succession. The last event proved so popular (apparently the largest ever gathering in Kingswood Park) that the following year we were asked to produce a scaled-down event, which we politely refused. By that time, Patrick and I had opened a very successful record store in the area that included a new recording studio home for Freshblood. Although large-scale commercial success eluded Freshblood, their appearances always generated excitement with audiences from Amsterdam to North America. Along the way, we introduced many young performers to their first big audiences and Freshblood produced their first records. We never saw ourselves as mentors in those days, but that was exactly what we were.

There are many experienced and successful Bristol artists since the 1990s who were either inspired by our events or got their first studio session with us. That for me, is more important and more rewarding than any brief commercial success. The music business is notorious for destroying the lives of young people and to have supported young people at the start of their music careers and helped them avoid the all too common exploitation that comes with it stands among our finest achievements.

One young man who came looking for help was a local lad, Mikee Freedom. He had personal experience of that exploitation. He was asked one day to provide a rap for a tune that had failed to chart despite several releases. The song was a track called Devotion, or to give it its full title, '(I wanna give you) Devotion'. It became a worldwide hit and reached number one in many countries. Yet a few short months later Mikee was virtually destitute having received hardly anything in royalty payments despite the song's success. His health suffered and whilst the song producers went on to further successes, young Mikee, only 21, was jettisoned. Their success had been achieved and Mikee had become surplus to requirements. Duty of Care to young people in the music business is rarely a consideration.

Mikee was a success and yet his life was failing. Such is the nature of the music business. In my younger days, there was a saying when Fish and Chips used to be wrapped in newspapers:

TODAY'S NEWS IS TOMORROW'S CHIP PAPERS

It summed up how news stories quickly lost their value.

FAME IS FLEETING

Might be a more suitable equivalent for many young people in the music industry.

Pat took Mikee under his wing and at least managed to get him some overdue royalties. Mikee was added as a guest performer to the Freshblood stage set. In the eyes of the audiences, the young man was a star, although he had never been able to perform Devotion to a live audience. His former producers may have given him a moment of fame, but it was Pat and Freshblood that gave him an opportunity to enjoy it. When we took him to Amsterdam, it was apparently his first trip outside the UK. I will never forget walking past the houseboats with him in Amsterdam and hearing Devotion blasting out. The pure joy on his face was there again when he stepped onstage at the venue that night in front of a heaving mass of people. His previous producers attempted to prevent him from performing the track, but gladly, to no avail. His all too brief success with Devotion was to lead to many years of legal battles to establish his rights to the track. At least with us, he got to enjoy it. In music alone, countless young people benefitted from Pats guidance and mentoring. I learned so much from him in those early days that was to help me mentor children in the following decades. Pat is one of those Bristol legends that even now does not get the acclaim he richly deserves for his contribution to music, mentoring and Radio broadcasting. To this day he is always encouraging young and emerging talent. Many times, in recent years I have been asked by people as to why his contributions, (and mine for that matter, after 30 plus years of Fostering) have failed to get recognised by the powers that be. We clearly don't know the right people or say the right things. That'll probably be it.

John Nation is another classic example of a lack of formal recognition. As someone who has appeared in Graffiti documentaries around the world and is appreciated by so many great artists he should be more prominent in his own city. His work today, showing thousands of tourists around the Graffiti sights of Bristol, is brilliant and of great benefit to our city.

I have long believed that rather than braving all weathers to convey our Graffiti landscape and history to tourists, he would be better served curating a Graffiti museum that would attract tourists in their hordes. Bristol is the uncrowned capital of UK Street Art and the city has missed a massive opportunity in not developing a permanent museum/showpiece to it. A place where our artists could be justly celebrated and where young artists could come to learn and practice. In John, they already employ the ideal curator. Sadly, Councils rarely have the necessary vision to develop such ideas.

The amazing Upfest festival attracts Graffiti lovers from all over the UK and artists from around the world. Sadly, like most music and art events, it is affected by a lack of funding. As a result, it has become a bi-annual rather than an annual event. I despair at how the leaders of our great city fail to acknowledge or capitalise on the talent within its populace. For decades, they refused to remove an abhorrent statue to the slave trader John Colston, lauded for centuries as a great benefactor of our city. Bristol's main Concert venue, until very recently, carried his name. The statue was finally toppled by our own citizens in an event that made headlines around the world, an event that led to similar events in the USA. That's what happens when Bristol leads the way. With all the wealth now generated by businesses within our city it really is time that new benefactors stepped forward and contributed more to art, music and culture here. I live in hope but will not hold my breath. If the museum of Street Art was ever to be created here, then I suspect the powers that be would engage some arty type from London to curate it rather than a real legend like John Nation.

Getting back to my story, as the 1980s were drawing to a close then so was my time at Eagle House, I was prepared for my next challenge, that of working in a Local Authority Children's Home. I had lost my fear of being out of my depth or of not being able to cope with difficult situations. Eagle House was my research lab where I was able to study all sorts of teenage behaviours. There were many volatile situations, some resolved well and others not so well by staff members. In a way, the latter were more beneficial to me because I could learn from others' mistakes. Just studying Dopey Dave at work was a lesson in what not to do.

Eagle House was the spark that lit the flame for me. Working with kids in groups and also individually, gained me so much experience. It really was the perfect training ground for anyone who had aspirations of working with young people. The kids would constantly challenge me and test my patience and resilience. They exhibited all manner of challenging behaviours, which were to help me so much in adjusting to full-time work in a children's home and later as a Foster Carer. I was really looking forward to starting my new job as a Residential Social Worker after failing so many times to find any sort of career that I wanted. I hoped that at last, I could do something where my father wouldn't have to sort it for me.

My dad had stuck by me in every difficult time that I had faced. He never once turned away or failed to support me, even when I neglected to take his advice on occasion. His love was unconditional, as it was to all his children and grandchildren. He was not one to say. "I told you so," if I messed up after ignoring advice. I think he was pleased that I had found something that

I so wanted to do and even a few years later, despite his reservations when I first became a Foster Carer. Right up until his last day on Friday 13 April 2007, he was protecting me and his loved ones. It was literally the habit of a lifetime and yes Friday the 13th. I wasn't superstitious but perhaps he was having a last laugh with me.

I will never forget standing in a phone box in the town square in Boussac in central France when he called me to tell me that his body could no longer take the dialysis that he had been receiving for years. He only had a couple of weeks at best. We were on holiday with friends for the week and he said not to spoil the holiday as he would wait for me and my most cherished boy Dave to return . A week later, we were on our way back and stopping overnight in Paris. Dave wanted to go to the top of the Eiffel Tower the next day. I called Mum, who told me that the end was very near, so me and Dave left for home immediately. I drove in tears throughout the night to Calais for the ferry and then back to Bristol, fearing that I would not get a chance to say goodbye. As ever, Dad was not going to let me down. Wednesday and Thursday were mostly spent with family visiting Dad. He was frail, but nothing looked imminent. As we went to leave that afternoon he sat up, called me over, shook my hand and said thanks and told me to look after Mum. At that moment, the baton was passed on.

That evening, I took Mum to see family, but she was violently sick on the way home. I got her to bed and stayed with her. In the early hours, the hospital called to say the end was near and that he was calling for Mum. I had to tell them that she was too ill to attend. His last words to me the previous day had told me my priority and I knew he would know. My brother Tony went to the Hospital until me and Dave turned up in the morning. Dad was sleeping, but we were told that he wasn't likely to wake up. Me and Dave sat with him. It was peaceful and the hospital said it could take hours. I decided to take Dave out for a walk to get some air and minutes later, the hospital called to say that he had passed. I felt, and still do, that despite his condition he was aware of our presence and didn't want us to witness his final moments. Thinking of others as ever.

We, as a family, were not given to outward displays of affection or emotion towards each other, yet every one of his children knew they were loved and had always been loved. After he had passed, I wished that I could have broken a lifetime's reticence of saying, "I love you". It just wasn't me to say that. Yet now, as I am an elder myself, I realise that he always knew that. I know those who love me and those who don't, just as I am sure he did too. It's people's actions that can tell you what their words might not. I know that plenty of the children that I have looked after have had a love for me that has been difficult to express in an all-male household.

There were little, if any, experiences in my childhood that prepared me for a life working with extremely challenging children. The one thing that did was that feeling of safety, security and unconditional love that my parents had infused in me. That, more than anything, has got me through so many difficult situations with children. Even as a parent, if you don't have the right answers for them or even really know what they want, then however bad their behaviour or situation is, just stand by them with your support and unconditional commitment. Don't ever waver because not being there even once for them is one time too many. I like to think that I have been there without hesitation for many young people. Unconditional love doesn't need to be said. Expressing love was never my thing anyway. Feeling it, yes, expressing it, no. Just like those little words that I couldn't say when he said, "Look after Mum"

"I love you Dad."

Chapter 4

Bathurst House was a Local Authority children's home in Thornbury, a satellite town of Bristol. The home was a two-storey building typical of care home facilities of the period. It housed up to 16 young people, including two who resided in a single-story extension at one end of the building, to the left of the entrance. That was the independence bungalow where young people would get a feel of independent living before leaving the care system but could still enjoy the benefit of staff support if necessary.

The home was run on a shift system, so at any given time at least two staff would be on duty working 24-hour shifts. The shifts would start and end at 3 pm and the two working overnight would each have a room where they could sleep, assuming all was quiet. When I walked into Bathurst on my first day, I had no idea that waiting for me would be the best local authority staff team that I would ever be part of. There was a lot of experience in the team that was to make it easy for me to settle in, and as a new member of staff without any relevant experience I was carefully looked after from that first day.

I am not sure if Bathurst House was designed to be a children's home when it was originally built. If it was, I can only assume that the design was approved by children rather than Residential Staff. The main building was really quite long from one end to the other. Downstairs there was the fairly small office, a staff sleeping-in room, the

TV room and leisure area, a good-sized dining room and a large kitchen that resembled an industrial kitchen with all the metal surfaces. With the various doors leading through the place, it was virtually impossible to hear any noise from one end of the building to the other. All sorts of mayhem could kick off in the kitchen without anyone in the office knowing anything was happening. The kitchen tends to be a dangerous place in childcare. Children naturally hang around the kitchen looking for food or making food and it's often where arguments kick off and quickly escalate. Most of the equipment in the kitchen at Bathurst was locked away to reduce risk, but no system is perfect.

At each end of the building were staircases which led upstairs to a long corridor of bedrooms, with a staff sleeping-in room at one end. The design was really not fit for purpose because as soon as there were any problems, there were several options for escape routes downstairs and out of the building. This was of particular benefit for residents sneaking friends in and out of the building, especially at night. It felt like a rabbit warren where anyone could hide or disappear quite easily. As a good percentage of the young residents had nocturnal criminal habits, this did not make our job as residential staff any easier. Bearing in mind that overnight there would generally be only two staff on duty, then it was fairly easy for either or both to get fairly isolated. It was almost impossible to monitor movement in and out of the building as there was no CCTV. Doors were not the only means of entry or exit as there were plenty of accessible windows.

The residents at Bathurst were all teenagers, boys and girls, mostly aged 14–17. With a fairly large group living there at any time, the possibility of arguments breaking out was high. Any noise or altercation tended to bring everyone else out of their rooms, whether just to observe or to join in. Simple arguments quickly escalated to involve multiple residents in multiple locations around the building, so it could feel like firefighting, where the two overstretched staff members had to quickly determine which situations to tackle first. Naturally, with only two staff at night, there was also the consideration of each being able to watch the back of the other if possible. Incidents could happen simultaneously at opposite ends of the building and on different floors, so containment was not always easy. These days, Local Authorities tend to run much smaller facilities for easier operation. Even then, larger group homes were being reduced. In Bathurst, many young people slept in shared rooms, but that was on the wane even then.

I learned very quickly about the importance of working together as staff members whilst on the night shift. One of the two staff members would be the shift leader, so I would take my lead from them as my senior and even in the first few weeks there were several shifts that I needed to be talked through. I quickly built up some good relationships with other staff and with some of the young people. In most institutions, there tends to be a hierarchy amongst the residents and Bathurst was no exception. Most of the residents would defer to the top dog, although there were a couple of outliers, both of whom were socially awkward and never really part of the main group.

Shaun was a tall, gangly youth with autism and very likeable. He was rarely a problem and eager to please the staff. Andrew was more distant, with unkempt ginger hair and generally a rather unpleasant and lingering aroma. His personal hygiene was of no concern to him, just to everyone else. He had eyes that were always wide open with an unnerving stare. When speaking to him, it often felt that he was looking elsewhere and was somewhat vacant save for the occasional inane grin. His hygiene alone made people want to keep their distance. Certainly not a lad that I could feel at ease with. He was like a dormant volcano that could suddenly erupt with fury and he had done so several times in my first few months of working there.

An incident with Andrew emphasised the need for two staff members to work together in a crisis. I was on duty with a colleague, Mary, who was brilliant at dealing with challenging situations. Mary was the senior staff member on our shift. However, a confrontation arose outside the front of the building with Andrew, who was threatening her with a sharp knife from the kitchen. Mary was trying to calm him down without making any obvious progress. She had several disagreements with Andrew over the preceding days and he had been verbally aggressive towards her. As I had built a fairly good relationship with Andrew, I put myself between the two of them and deflected his attention. He was very aggressive and did not really respond, although he was talking to me whilst glaring at Mary. I suggested that Mary leave us to talk, knowing that she would not be far off but at least out of Andrew's field of vision.

Andrew was still extremely angry, but he had at least lowered the knife, which he still gripped tightly. Whilst talking to him, I slowly edged closer, getting close enough to put my arm around him. That's not something I would normally do in any situation, but it worked. Suddenly, from being completely tense I felt the power drain out of him. To this day, I have never since experienced anything like it. It was like I had taken his batteries out and it sent a shock wave through me as I felt his energy dissipate instantly. At the same time, I had my own adrenaline rush. His body totally relaxed and his usually very blushed complexion looked drained. It was an extraordinary moment. It really felt like my touch took every last drop of energy from him and transferred it to me. It was an incredibly powerful and unique experience. Feeling confidently in control of the situation, I gently took the knife from his grasp.

Having visibly drained him, he looked ready to drop to the floor. I had, at that point, no idea at all where Mary was, but knowing everything she had told me about working together, I sensed that she was close by. With my arm around him I led him towards the building, which was seemingly deserted, the other residents having fortunately missed the altercation. Had there been an audience, then things may well have escalated and turned out very differently. On reaching the building, I led him through the side entrance into the kitchen, depositing the knife as we passed through. We went through the dining room, down the corridor into a small room on the ground floor in the centre of the building. It was a room that we often used for private one-to-one conversations. Once inside, I closed the door and we both sat down. Not once did I catch sight of Mary, or anybody else, yet I sensed that the second that the door closed, she would be close enough to come to my aid if necessary. My senses did not betray me as Mary was later able to tell me what she heard of our conversation.

From that day, I never had another altercation with Andrew. When writing up the episode in the diary I noticed that it was the night of the full moon which made me laugh and jokingly mused that Andrew must be a Werewolf. Sometimes we had dark humour amongst the staff, as a way of lightening the mood. Certainly the extraordinary power of the moment felt like it belonged in a supernatural film. A couple of days later, my curiosity got the better of me and I checked back against previous incidents with Andrew and found that the two most dramatic ones had fallen on full moons. From then on, I nicknamed him Moon Boy amongst the staff and always drew a few laughs when I occasionally warned staff to be vigilant when the moon was full.

It was probably a year later, when Andrew had moved on to independent living, when I got a call that he urgently needed to see me. I went to his flat in Bristol, which was every bit as filthy and disgusting as I had feared. His kitchen was full of overflowing rubbish bags, a half-empty can of beans, mouldy bread and discarded pizza boxes. It had become a haven for masses of tiny little flies. His fridge had little else but long-soured milk and pans that had been burned black and still contained charcoaled remnants of food. The smell was absolutely overpowering and felt like it was suffocating me. I decided not to venture into the bathroom as that may have been literally a step too far for my senses and my stomach. Over the years, looking after teenage boys, I seemed to develop an ability to avoid smells by not sniffing in confined spaces. Boys would be complimenting themselves on powerful smells that they released in the car and I would be oblivious to them.

Andrew, that day, was one of many care-experienced children who I have witnessed over the years, who looked totally lost, having been virtually abandoned to their fate upon leaving the care system. That day, as I adjusted to the surroundings as best as I could, I really needed to sit down to put him at ease. The sofa had assorted stains of dubious origin and some not so dubious that I unsuccessfully tried to banish from my thoughts. My imagination was sending me messages that I really needed to delete. I suspected that there was somewhere an empty skip from which his furniture had been removed.

The timid-looking Andrew, who then sat down next to me, was akin to the boy that I had put my arm around on that day at Bathurst. I sensed that the fact that he was sitting so close to me meant that he was going to be in need of my arm again before we were through. The difference I suspected this time was that it would not be so much to drain his energy, but maybe to return some to him. His eyes were watery, the pupils like islands in a reddish sea of tears. His whole demeanour was almost lifeless and once again his face was drained of colour, contrasting with his red eyes. Once we had got through the seemingly pointless 'how are you' type exchanges, we came to the reason he had called. He told me that he had recently 'entertained' (my word, not his) a number of men from the neighbouring park in exchange for varying amounts of cash. It was, for him, a way of surviving from one day to the next, a skill he had developed at Bathurst. He then told me that the previous evening he had gone to the park and brought a man back with the same intention of quick cash. Once inside Andrew's flat, the man swiftly dismissed any attempts at negotiating a price and promptly forcibly and violently raped him. The tears flowed unabated as he described how he was powerless to stop this strong and aggressive man from overpowering him. He was unsure how long it lasted, only that it seemed to go on and on and was coupled with numerous punches, resulting in a severe beating. There was no anger in his voice; the poor boy was broken and he had absolutely no energy left for anger, only guilt. In contrast, listening to the horrendous details filled me with pity and a simmering rage.

The tears continued and I had moved well past any personal concerns of hygiene with my arm wrapped around him as he sobbed uncontrollably. This time there was no transference of an energy force, both of us were totally drained, but in a few minutes I would be returning to my normal life, leaving him with his demons. Instead, there was an emotional transference of shame, guilt, hopelessness and despair. All I could do was offer words of comfort and reassurance, but it all felt so overwhelmingly inadequate. Despite feeling helpless myself, I could see my words were very much needed. My own anger needed to be put aside in those most desperate of moments. Only much later, when I got home, did I acknowledge the anger and the rage that I had withheld. Then with no one else around it was my turn to release the tears for a boy whose life was forever changed. I had looked into his soul and seen the gentle boy that few could ever see, drowning, gasping for breath with nobody else in the world to turn to.

That anger came later when I was alone, but first I had to try and let him feel safe again, even if it was just for a few brief minutes. The police had been and apparently not stayed a moment longer than they needed to. They had taken details, shown some token concern, but very little real sympathy. He doubted that anything would come of their investigations and he was sadly proved correct. They had given him the impression that this was not an unusual situation for a rent boy and that given that, then it would be hard to prove as being non-consensual sex. In my time in both Residential work and Fostering since that time I have all too rarely received a satisfactory response when dealing with Police Officers when sensitivity was required. In my wide experience, there is, in my opinion, a totally different attitude from many police officers towards children in the care system. Sympathy for them that is sincere seems all too rare. Many, many times, I have been given the impression that the police have rather more important and less time-consuming things to do than follow up issues affecting children in care. The often overused phrase of, "We are not social workers," that, I have heard all too often over the years.

At that time, being still quite new to Residential work and the Care system, I had little experience of what happened to young people when they left care. I had hoped that Andrew was an exception in being cut hopelessly adrift, but sadly as time went past, I realised that he wasn't. There were some who made successful transitions to independent living, but all too few in comparison to so many others who did not and still do not. For some children, their time spent in care ,especially in foster care, is the only period of stability they experience in their entire lives, the only time when they are truly cared for. Life is a challenge for any young person leaving home, but for those in the Care system it is so much more difficult and it is riddled with obstacles that our own children fortunately do not have to face.

In the Care system today, there have been improvements in support and consequently in outcomes. There is, however, still a huge amount of improvement that needs to be made before it can be said that those leaving care have what they need and what they deserve, for their future wellbeing. I am currently working with a Care-experienced young man, now 25 years old, who over 30 years on from Andrew's time, still demonstrates the shocking levels of support that I saw with Andrew. Marcus, another young man, all but abandoned after leaving Foster Care and, as a consequence, unable to ever reach his potential or even adequately manage his day-to-day needs. Walking into his flat and I could be walking into Andrew's flat in the early 1990s. Every bit of my description of Andrew's flat now applies to his. Here we are now and it's like being stuck in a time warp. and some things have not changed for the better at all. It's horrendous, it's appalling and it should, in every case, be unacceptable to abandon these young people to a lifetime of pain, hurt and misery.

Vulnerable young people are being abandoned, neglected, ignored and left open to all manner of exploitation and abuse. People just saying that it's the best we can do with the available resources do not get it. We all know Local Authority budgets are inadequate, yet plenty of money is needlessly spent with the private sector in Childcare. We see the Government handing out billions to profiteering companies, whether it be for PPE, inadequate and cruel immigration policies, or Hedge-fund backed Childcare operations. Unfortunately, adequately supporting Care experienced young people (or migrants for that matter) neither wins votes nor lines the pockets of their rich friends. Until that changes, these vulnerable young people will be forced to endure their often miserable existence.

I feel almost guilty having happy memories of my time at Bathurst House but I do often think back to those early days in Residential, especially my amazing colleagues who taught me so much and inadvertently prepared me for my fostering career. My favourite colleague was Sue, a little firebrand, a pocket dynamo, who never seemed fazed by any situation or intimidated by anyone, neither by any child nor any manager at any level. I knew then that she was destined to make an impact on Social Services and indeed she did. On quieter nights at Bathurst, Sue and I would go down to the kitchen, make some hot chocolate and talk into the early hours of putting the world to rights. We shared a mutual passion for our work and an intolerance of poor standards, attitudes and performance. We both wanted better outcomes for the young people, especially with the after-care service and its insufficient support. Sue didn't waste words, especially when two in particular would usually suffice in certain situations. She got directly to the point and had no time for excuses, especially from superiors. Above all though Sue was fun and especially in the difficult work that we did, then fun, when appropriate, was absolutely a way of finding balance in our work.

Fun may not seem to be a necessary requirement when dealing with the aspects of society that we have witnessed. The abuse, the abusers, the overdoses, hospital visits, prison visits, the appalling families that many of our young residents had endured and all too often returned to. A sense of fun can be vitally important when one has to deal with the darker aspects of society, that fortunately, few ever bear witness to. The only way you can survive some of the horrors we saw and that I still see as a Foster Carer is to be able to enjoy the little moments of fun with colleagues and fellow carers who truly understand. Those things that we wouldn't or couldn't share with our own families, friends and loved ones. The world we have witnessed can be dark, sometimes very dark and unforgiving and is mostly not for sharing. It is however necessary for our own mental health and wellbeing that we can find some light amongst the darkness, some hope, some joy and some fun or else it's all too easy to get lost in the pain and misery of those that we look after.

When I first started at Bathurst, the manager was a guy called Keith, a man who knew how to lead and how to demonstrate leadership, but at the same time he was one of the best people I have ever known for knowing when a staff member was struggling or in need of support. One of the first things he said to me was that in order to do the job well, when you walked through the door at 3 pm you needed to leave any problems from your personal life at the door. Coming to work with your mind elsewhere would lead to problems and he was right. Taking that a step further it also meant that the reverse was true. Taking your problems home with you could be just as damaging. Keith also had a great sense of humour and realised that doing the job we did that we would need those moments of levity now and again, especially between staff. He always knew exactly where and when to draw the line though when the job demanded. A natural leader who led by example!

We certainly did have our laughs though and it bonded us as colleagues and helped make us into a strong team, a strong and caring team. In that long hallway upstairs in Bathurst, I'm sure our laughter sometimes reached the ears and the curiosity of our young people. Especially those shifts with Sue, who has such a mischievous laugh. There was a particular night that I recall. It was one of those nights that our shift went far into the early hours. Hyped up young people going in and out of the building, police visits and all sorts of other noisy interruptions had occurred that night. The new day's dawning was not far away when the place was finally settled and at peace. The customary mug of hot chocolate was needed more than ever. Ah, but if only life in a children's home were that simple.

I went quietly through the silent building to the kitchen to make our drinks. Having put the milk in the saucepan, I went to light the gas hob. The hob lighter was broken and the only box of matches was empty. I hunted around the kitchen to no avail. Two non-smokers on duty, so no lighter. Most of the kids were smokers, but after the night that we had just experienced they were finally settled, so no chance there. On almost any other night, there would probably have been one of them sneaking around the unit, but after all the excitement they too were completely exhausted. It was then that I thought of all the times I had picked up both spent and unused matches on floors around the unit. So, there I was at 3.30 am on my hands and knees crawling around the floor in the faint hope of finding an unused match. Checking the floor in three rooms and the corridor I found plenty of dead ones but not one unused. Then almost despairing, after checking down the back of the sofas and armchairs EUREKA! I had finally found a live one. Like a gold prospector finding a gold nugget I kissed it and hurried back to the kitchen gently holding my precious discovery.

Once back in the kitchen, a feeling of dread came over me. I had the empty match box, but what if the match was a dud or went out before igniting the gas. decided that I had better turn on the gas first to reduce the risk of failure. There followed a couple of very worrying failed strikes but then BOOM! In the silence of the night, it felt like an explosion echoing down the empty corridor. Luckily, apart from a singed finger, no damage was done. It just remained to get the jar of chocolate and two mugs. I went over and opened the cupboard but NO! The cupboard was bare. Not a single cup or mug. I waited for the milk to come to the boil, moved the pan over and diligently left the hob alight just in case it took a few minutes to locate some mugs and the one live match was now spent. There I was, once again back searching the various rooms looking for discarded mugs. How could there be none? Finally going into the office, I found one. I scuttled back to the kitchen, searched every cupboard again and located a gravy boat. Beggars can't be choosers I thought !

Life had come down to crawling around the floors of a children's home in the middle of the night and drinking hot chocolate out of a gravy boat. What times they were and Cadbury's Drinking chocolate never ever tasted as good, or was as satisfying, as it was that night. A memorable night was thus brought to a fitting close. A night that led to Keith howling with laughter the next morning when reading my account of the Hot Chocolate Saga in the night's log. Keith, of course, had appeared early to check on our well-being after hearing of our busy night. I think it was when we had our next staff meeting that he suggested everyone read my account. That I think was the moment that Sue said, "John, you have a way with words, you should write a book."

"It only took me a little over 30 years Sue, but I have finally taken your advice."

I like to think that the tale would resonate with any residential workers, past or present, in Children's Homes. It's an incredibly demanding job, physically, mentally, emotionally and burnout is all too common. The upside of it is that you can get to work with some amazing people and get a perspective of life that few others can ever have. You also get to meet some amazing young people, many of whom show incredible resilience, despite their immensely troubled lives.

I learned so much from the other staff members at Bathurst House. Apart from Keith, Sue and Mary the standouts were another Keith, (Keith B) a deputy manager ,along with Penny, Lucy and Roy. Each of them had different qualities, different styles, but what a team. Others came and went, but that was for me the super team that was never equalled.

Roy Hackett was an inspirational character and a reference point for me so many times in my career. Roy was a typically bubbly Jamaican. He was one of the Windrush generation that has added so much to our culture in Bristol and in the UK. He was the elder statesman at Bathurst, a man then in his early 60s, which, given his energy, didn't seem possible. With all due respect I wondered why he was still doing such demanding work at his age and in a relatively lowly position equivalent to mine. He told me that he had never wanted to be a leader and was happy being a soldier and not a General. The irony of that statement didn't become apparent to me until many years later when I read about this man Roy Hackett, who had helped to organise the Bristol Bus Boycott in the 1960s. The boycott challenged the racist employment policies of the Bristol Omnibus Company, who were refusing to employ Black or Asian crews. The successful campaign was a major milestone in British race relations and had a national impact. It has been considered by some as a factor in the passing of Race Relations Acts in 1965 and 1968. Roy went on to become a leading Civil Rights Activist and was many years later to be awarded the OBE for his contributions. In all the time that I worked with him he never once mentioned anything about his achievements, just demonstrating what a modest and humble man he was. He would always praise me for my work with young people, work that absolutely paled in comparison to his amazing achievements.

I only knew Roy back then as a colleague who had an aura of calm surrounding him. He had a way of defusing difficult situations without ever having to assert himself, except in the most laid-back of tones. He really was the Obi-Wan Kenobi of our team, a man who used wisdom and gentle persuasion in every situation and a man who was never shown anything but the greatest respect by every child and adult he encountered at Bathurst. Perhaps when compared with his struggles when he first came to the UK as a young man, the hostility and discrimination that he faced, then a rowdy child was nothing to get too excited about or upset by. I so envied his ability to quell a disturbance and remain calm in difficult situations. I tried to capture that essence of calm so many times then and throughout my fostering career. He, more than anyone I have ever worked with, was the role model that I tried to emulate.

The other aspect of Roy was his humour which added so much to my time at Bathurst. His loud bellowing laugh, his cheeky grin, his wink and his chuckle. He seemed to charm every man, woman or child that he came across. The ability to stay apparently relaxed, to avoid hasty and poorly executed responses, to keep smiling in a crisis. That was Roy, a diamond of a man if ever there was one. He mentored me and I really didn't realise it. I had become a mentor before Bathurst, but after learning from Roy I became so much a better one. He was young for his age, but in terms of wisdom an elder ahead of his time. I was lucky enough to meet him again in recent years and be able to thank him for his guidance and his influence. He modestly dismissed the plaudits as he always had done, but of all the legends that I have met in my life he stands above them all. Now an elder myself, I appreciate that I was blessed to know the man and learn from the man. His legacy his huge and his influence remains with me and so many others.

Chapter 5

It was at Bathurst that I was first introduced to the inside of police cars, police stations, prison and Court proceedings. When you get to be responsible for looking after young car thieves, there really is no choice. The late 1980s and early 1990s were to see car thefts hit a peak in Bristol not matched again until very recent times. It is generally very much more sophisticated these days. Whereas back then a screwdriver was probably the tool of choice, these days it is all about computer technology. The more brutal and physical way of breaking into a car has evolved, nowadays, a thief only needs a special type of computerised gadget. One that can unlock any of the keyless entry vehicles simply by activating the owner's remote lock from a distance away from the house. Many people tend to leave their keys just inside their front door, where they can easily be remotely activated by thieves. People would previously break into a house, pick up the keys, unlock the car and drive off, or just simply smash the window to get into a car. Nowadays, actually breaking into the car or the house is virtually obsolete. The car is unlocked and often starts before the thief appears. It's just a case of jumping in and driving away. Much less risky and easier for gangs to do multiple thefts in one night.

The boys at Bathurst were much less sophisticated back then. It was all about the simple act of joyriding.

Damage to the stolen car was of no consequence or concern to them whatsoever. Wayne, who could see the financial benefits of working for gangs, was the exception rather than the rule back in the 1990s. The first car thief that I worked with was more typical of the type of youngster doing the TDA's (Taking and Driving Away). Jason was an engaging young man, not overburdened with intelligence, who just loved to show off. Taking young girls joyriding was his way of impressing girls and his peers. Getting caught and arrested just added to his image. Beneath the charming exterior, he was quite a cold and callous operator. He knew how to get what he wanted with no real concern for anyone else. A large ego but little compassion or concern for anyone.

I soon got used to attending police stations with one or other of the boys from the home, often being required as an appropriate adult (someone who can accompany a child during a police interview). They were time-consuming affairs that involved an interview, fingerprinting, 'mugshots' as they now say and most often waiting hours for a solicitor to arrive. The outcome would usually then be a 'no comment' interview unless the accused had refused legal advice. They would be charged, bailed and given a court date a few weeks later. By the time of the court date, they would usually have re-offended, often necessitating the court date to be deferred pending further charges. This cycle could go on for months and when it eventually came to court, there might be many offences that had to be taken into consideration. From the point of view of the accused, further offences rarely worried them.

The sentence wouldn't differ much whether it was one or two offences or ten, twenty or more.

On the one hand, it was argued that the young criminals were abusing the system. On the other hand, one could say that the system was unfit for purpose and their actions were just proving it. What was clear was that it involved a massive waste of resources for the police, the courts and for Social Services. The court cases were often, in effect, just another waste of time and resources. Custodial sentences were rarely given and all too often the magistrates would be guided by Social Work reports, heavily laden with excuses based on difficult childhoods and the influence of others. Social Work reports would by nature highlight any positives without focusing on the negative behaviour. The young person would be told that it was their last chance before a custodial sentence, only to be returning again with another batch of offences a few months later with the same outcome. The seemingly endless cycle would continue until eventually, custody would at last be given. It was, however, understood by many of us that custody usually came much sooner and more severely for any black or Asian youngsters. There was at that time, little equality in the youth justice system and little diversity in the selection of Magistrates.

I stood in court many times listening to Social Work reports that were mostly works of pure fiction. I never once felt that massaging the truth for the Magistrates was serving any useful purpose. Actions have consequences and young people need to learn that particular lesson and not that they can use their Social Worker to mitigate their actions. I don't believe that prison is often the answer, but I do believe that society has a right to protection from young people with no boundaries. Many of those young criminals had grown up in families without firm behavioural boundaries and did not understand the concept of respect or responsibility. Coming into the care system, it was only natural for them to push against boundaries, which is why those boundaries needed to be more rigidly enforced. Enforcing firm boundaries can feel restricting but it can also give a sense of security, a feeling of being cared for, which many young people in the Care system had never experienced in their entire lives.

In those days, as a residential worker, I wasn't often asked to speak in court. The role was more of an escort and we deferred to the Social Worker for statements on the accused. That was to change when I became a Foster Carer, which for me was a far better situation. The police contact and the Court appearances were actually good learning for me. Even sitting outside courtrooms for many hours was useful in understanding the young criminal mind. Various residential workers, social workers and Foster Carers would bring their young charges to court. The kids would revel in being seen in court, sharing conversations about their misdemeanours with each other and even planning to offend as soon as their appearance was over. A young man with 30 offences would lord it over someone with only a couple. If only the magistrates could have heard those conversations, then they would probably have often been less lenient in sentencing. Having said that, there was a procedure which involved providing an alternative to custody. Sadly, all too often these were an ineffective deterrent and just a way of delaying the inevitable.

Among the young residents at the home, there was inevitably a hierarchy. The old expression of 'Top Dog' rang true. With a mixture of boys and girls in the home, each had their own leader. The inadequate design of the building with its multiple exits gave any 'top dog' plenty of scope for mischief and caused multiple problems for staff. A large home like Bathurst contained too many children from a child protection point of view. With so many potential quiet spots, bullying was easy and often went unnoticed. It was not difficult for children to arrange distractions from such events. Whether daytime or nighttime, as staff we knew that there were always many things that went unseen.

On the surface, it would appear that top dogs maintained order mostly by physical strength and a couple of able lieutenants. Unfortunately, there was often a darker side where drugs and sex were weapons of control. Occasionally, kids would be caught in compromising situations, but that was fairly rare. It was all too easy to manipulate fellow residents, well out of sight and hearing from the staff. Whilst some relationships were fairly obvious, other relationships and abuse were well hidden. As staff I felt we did an amazing job in the circumstances, but how much did we miss? Years later I found out much more about the hidden abuse that we never really saw.

One young lad was only 14 when he came into the home, easily the youngest and most vulnerable resident among some very streetwise and care experienced 15, 16 and 17-year-olds. He had been in Foster Care but exposed himself to the carer's daughter and his foster placement was quickly ended. Fostering teenagers is always a difficult balancing act, in meeting the needs of these children whilst protecting your own birth children. There is often no particular right or wrong way of tackling such incidents. There are so many variables. The sex and age of the foster child and the birth child for instance, maybe if the birth child is much younger and potentially at increased and unacceptable risk. The lad was unfortunate and looked especially nervous and vulnerable when he arrived. He was put into a shared room when he arrived, which wasn't unusual back then in the larger homes.

That other lad in his room was the nearest in age to him, but was a towering figure in comparison, well over six feet tall. That night the younger lad was allegedly raped, but aside from the young residents, nobody knew until I was given the details in confidence years later. By that time, the younger lad had long moved on and become a rent boy. He wasn't going to discuss or even admit that the incident happened. The older lad, had not shown any homosexual leanings, having a steady girlfriend at the time and for the staff there was never any indication of his intent or capability. I was never told if he was the person responsible, but at the very least he was complicit in the assault.

With a few older boys moving on in the following months, the older lad quickly rose through the hierarchy and became Top Dog, hooking up with the dominant female in the group in the process. Their relationship was clear and it was easy enough to make the wrong assumption that he maintained his position by just being the strongest male in the group. I was again told many years later that sex was apparently his preferred method of control. Having become a sexual partner of the dominant female, he helped her maintain her position. His trade-off apparently was having sex with most of the other girls and for that matter, most of the boys in the building. The exceptions were the boys who could have challenged his position but showed no inclination to do so.

It was quite a shock initially to find out about how this lad rose to dominance, but my feeling was that it was learned behaviour, and that he too had probably been a victim himself at one time. One of the things I learned working there was that things are not always what they appear to be. It was not uncommon back then for female staff to enter a girls' room in the morning to find a couple of girls in bed together. This was always dismissed as a normal girls thing, but had it been two boys our reaction would have been totally different. Young people in the Care system have usually had very much more trauma in their lives than our own children and have had to survive many things that most of us would find hard to comprehend. Try not to judge what these children have had to do and endure to survive; just be glad that our own children have not been exposed to such horrors. It doesn't always excuse the bad things that some may later do themselves, but it does help explain it. Abuse is a cycle that is not always easy to stop and victims often become abusers. People tend to find it easier to judge than to understand.

A few months later, some more children had moved on and the hierarchy changed once again, as more damaged children had to face the new challenges of living outside of the care system. Among the new faces was the young man who was to change my life after his release from Kidlington Young Offenders institution. The trip to the Paris concert had created a bond between Wayne and I that couldn't be broken, unlike my ribs unfortunately, that fell victim to his Karate kick one afternoon. Walking back from Thornbury High Street to Bathurst House. I happened across Wayne who unsurprisingly had a new willing audience of local kids. My presence was not what he wanted at all. We were no longer in Paris. This was the bad boy in full peacock display mode for his new audience and my presence was most unwelcome. My being there was a potential embarrassment. This was his territory now, his audience and I was neither invited nor wanted.

Wayne's way of avoiding embarrassment was a show of defiance, to warn me off. My mistake was to think that I could use humour to reduce the tension when in fact, it only heightened it. My presence was a threat to his image. In making his friends laugh, I only made things worse. He jumped up on the bench where moments earlier they had all been sitting. He then went into full martial arts combat stance, lashing out with his feet like a kickboxer, reminiscent of Jean-Claude Van Damme's style. My next mistake was not to be intimidated by his stance and to move towards him. I think it was more misjudgement than intent on his part. but I walked straight into one of his kicks that caught me right in the ribs. It was certainly a misjudgement on my part. I doubled up momentarily in shock then stood up, by which time he was apologising whilst suggesting it only happened because I moved forward. He was probably right but being in some degree of pain that I didn't want to admit to I brushed it off and went back to work.

Returning to Bathurst I reported the event but worrying about potential assault charges for Wayne, played down the incident. Keith B sent me home early as I was approaching the end of my shift. By the time I got home I was in agony and decided to try and sleep it off. Being in so much pain that it was quite impossible and after an excruciating night, with virtually no sleep I went to the doctors the following morning. He immediately sent me to the hospital for an X-ray. Two ribs were broken and I was given strong medication that virtually wiped me out. Even with the painkillers the pain was excruciating, until the sedation kicked in. I hardly slept for days and it was several weeks before I could return to work. Wayne was still full of apologies and thankful that it had not led to his being charged, which could have meant another custodial sentence.

On my part, there was no animosity because I knew that the whole situation that led to the injury could have been avoided with more forethought and sensitivity on my part. If anything, it only served to strengthen the growing bond between us in the following months. It was a few months later when we were talking Wayne suddenly suggested that I should Foster him. It came out of the blue really. We had been discussing his future and the likelihood that he would soon move on from Bathurst House. He was still only 16 and there were not too many options.

"Why don't you Foster me?"

I just responded with a laugh. "I am single and I am not a Foster Carer.

"You could be one though," he said. "Like Rob."

Rob was a single man who fostered, a bit of an odd character I remember thinking. Rob was a devout

Christian who had an unusual house where he had several foster kids. I say unusual, having visited it with a potential Foster Child for him. Each of his own Foster Children had their own TV, video and various expensive gadgets. Wayne had suggested once that it was probably done to buy their affection with gifts.

"He's definitely a bit dodgy," was Wayne's summation of Rob.

Rob also had a swimming pool, well at least one of those temporary ones that were to become the fashion for a while. In his house he had also built a loft room so as to be able to take an extra foster placement. I'm not sure that it would have met any building regs, as in order to create an extra floor he had squeezed in an extra staircase. There was insufficient headroom on the top stairs, so it necessitated having to crouch down virtually on your knees to enter the room. I was never quite sure how either the local council or Social Services had approved that, even with the shortage of available beds for placements.

Getting back to Wayne's suggestion about me fostering him, it was a thought that lingered over the following days. Was it such a crazy thought I wondered. I mentioned it to Keith B, who had by then taken over from the other Keith as manager following Keith S being promoted. He didn't dismiss the idea and asked for my thoughts. I explained to him that there was something about the idea that appealed to me, but I wasn't even sure if it could happen. If it could then what about the financial package? Would it be sufficient to compensate for giving up my job? I left it for him to make the necessary enquiries.

A few days later after a conversation with Keith S a suggestion was made to me. We could trial it whilst still keeping my job and if it worked then we could consider an application to become a Foster Carer. I would work day shifts at Bathurst and his placement would temporarily move to my house. It didn't take long to set up, unlike the Fostering application process, so we proceeded with a view of me becoming a Foster Carer once approved, but that I would continue to work at Bathurst on a job share basis initially. It was an unusual way to become a Foster Carer and I would still have to go through a lengthy vetting process, but it was the start of a new career. I officially became a Foster Carer a few months later.

Looking back now, I can't recall the specifics about how I managed to be a Foster Carer and a Residential Worker at the same time, but whatever we did, it worked. Had it not been for Wayne, then the idea of me becoming a Foster Carer may never have arisen. When I became a Foster Carer, I continued to manage to do the two roles for a while before leaving to concentrate on Fostering. However, with just Wayne to Foster it left me with plenty of time on my hands and I was soon offered another residential job at a different Children's Home. Keith S was the area manager, so I did not take too much convincing.

Mercas was a much smaller children's home, with just a handful of children at any given time. The manager was a lady called Jackie Johnson, who spent more time in the kitchen than in the office. It was a system that she made work. The kitchen, traditionally a very risky area to linger in with children, was Jackie's domain. She was referred to as being like a mother hen with the children. She would often be found sitting at the kitchen table with the children all sat around and not just at mealtimes. She had a very relaxed manner that put many of the children at ease, and it had a much more laid-back feel than I had been used to previously.

Whilst the place was more easy going, some of my most difficult days were at Mercas. I had to supervise family contact with one family. That was because the two boys who were placed with us had been badly abused and they could only have parental visits under strict supervision. It all made for a very difficult situation, not least for the boys. They had three other siblings who had all been taken into care at the same time. The abuse by their father had been one of the worst cases that I had heard of and by that time I had experienced some terrible cases. The boys were allowed supervised access with other family members, but none with their father.

Months of very difficult access visits passed before their father appealed his case. The details were so horrific that there was seemingly little likelihood of any change. However, the judge was to find that there had been a technical error made by the police officer who initially arrested the father. The evidence was clear, but the officer concerned did not follow the correct procedure. As a result, the judge overturned the original verdict and ordered that the father should be given back custody of the abused children. Like everyone else, I was in disbelief at the decision and appalled by it. Some days later, I had to bear witness to the boys and their siblings being handed back to this monster. The children were inconsolable and I have never forgotten that feeling of absolute rage that I experienced that day, towards both the father and the judge. Having got his children back this sick individual promptly moved away from England, condemning the children to further untold horrors.

I was never to hear of the children again and quickly decided that I no longer wanted to continue residential work. In hindsight, that really made no sense, as I was still a Foster Carer to Wayne. Assuming that I was to remain a Foster Carer, then I would have to find a way of dealing with monsters who abused children or just give it all up. At that moment all I knew was that I never wanted to be in that situation again, where I was literally given abused children back to their abuser. Rather than quitting immediately, I was advised to go on sick leave to give me time to consider. I had to see the doctor and was signed off for a few weeks from the job but not from Fostering. I did not know then that for decades thereafter every time I had a review where there was even the slightest question mark about my performance that stress related break would be used to justify criticism. Had I just quit it would have been so much simpler, which in fact was exactly what I did anyway, just a few weeks later.

Well over thirty years later and I have never again used the stress excuse for either a convenient or even a necessary break. There is much more concern these days about the mental health and wellbeing of carers but there is still a feeling that stress related issues will provide a long-term barrier for carers, most especially single carers. As a single male Foster Carer there has never been a moment where I have not been aware of the insecurity of being a Foster Carer. Over the years, I have seen so many Foster Carers leave the service because of feeling unsupported in times of crisis. It continues to be one of the flaws of our profession that despite all the fine words to the contrary, one placement that ends badly, through no fault of the carers can destroy any trust or confidence that the carer has in Social Services.

It is difficult for couples that foster, but at least they usually have their partners for support in times of crisis. I say usually because foster families are not immune from marital problems and break-ups, so it is not always straightforward. Being a carer, as a single man is very different indeed. There is usually nobody else in the house who can step in to give you even a momentary break from a difficult situation. If a night's sleep is missed and the child or children need caring for during the following day then there can be no respite and little, if any, chance for rest. In theory, the carers social worker will offer support but that can be conditional on other factors. For instance, is there a good enough working relationship and mutual trust between carer and Social Worker for the carer to be confident that there will not be difficult consequences later on? Will the Carers ability to continue to care in the future be questioned? Asking for help often leads to questions about competence. When you are under continual and unrelenting scrutiny, as most carers are, then the straw that breaks the camel's back is often supplied by the Social Worker, rather than any badly behaved child.

As a carer, you are often made to feel that you are only as good as your last placement and if that ended badly, then there is little margin for error. As a single male fostering, it has often felt that no matter how many steps forward I make, some people are just waiting for me to trip up at the next one, rather than say well done! Expressing doubts about a placement, whether a current one or a potential one, does not always play out well. Ending a placement by giving 28 days' notice on it can also be a risky strategy for a carer. When a service is continually overloaded, then a carer can be made to feel very bad for giving notice and it is not uncommon for that carer suddenly to find that they are left without a placement for some time afterwards. That is fine if the carer needs a break, but all too often it feels like a punishment. The sudden drop in income can be more stressful than anything else, but of course as we are all too often reminded, fostering is not about the money. Try telling that to your landlord or mortgage provider.

For me, back in those days that I was just leaving residential work, this was all a great unknown. It's true to say however that all through the entirety of my fostering career there are some things that have hardly changed. The insecurity of the job, the often inadequate and inconsistent support, are reasons that have consistently been given over many decades as reasons for quitting fostering or failing to retain carers. I may have hesitated had I known more of this when I agreed to foster Wayne, but I doubt it somehow. Despite all the flaws in the delivery of the service, I have no regrets for making that choice. It was one of the best decisions of my life and I hope that the following pages demonstrate that.

Chapter 6

So it began! A Fostering career that was to span four decades, a career that had not even been a possibility a few weeks earlier. Back then, I had no idea where it would lead or even if it would last beyond the first few months. There had been no time to think ahead, such was the intensity of preparing to move Wayne into my house. In fact, my concern was more as to whether, despite the intense preparations, it might not happen at all. There was every chance that pending criminal matters for Wayne might scupper the whole plan if he were locked up again.

Until a few weeks earlier, I had shared my house with two lodgers, but now for the first time in years it was just me, about to get my first foster placement. Well, in truth, I wasn't totally alone as I had George, a Golden Labrador who was the canine equivalent of Wayne. Untrainable, manic and would grasp any opportunity to run if the front door was even momentarily left ajar. Whilst as friendly and affectionate as most Labradors, he did have something else in common with Wayne. A dislike of men in uniform. Up until then it had mainly been directed at the postman, but it soon became apparent that he had no love for policemen either. He was also very alert to approaching policemen, an added bonus for Wayne as visits from Avon and Somerset's finest often came without warning, soon after dawn.

More than once, their silent approach was met with growling, barking and a half-dressed Wayne disappearing through the back gate. Wayne was to bring a whole new level of excitement into George's life and into mine unfortunately.

My guests and visitors had long become used to the thundering sound of George descending the stairs at a pace to greet them with a leap that would often knock them backwards as they entered the house, followed by a slobbering hound offering his boisterous welcome. His manically wagging tail cleared the coffee table on many occasions. Male visitors knew to protect their Crown Jewels as George's front legs would often make sudden contact with their more sensitive regions of the male anatomy. Many times, male visitors were doubled up in pain by the time they escaped the hallway. Sitting on the sofa did not necessarily provide respite from George, as it could also prompt another leap by this rather substantial dog, who liked to sit on laps without invitation and was adept at removing food items before they reached mouths. The Labrador breed is renowned as retrievers and George could certainly retrieve food, especially from children. More often than not that invariably resulted in more food being offered. If not, George would sit drooling with his sad eyes, a look that would break the sternest resistance.

I sense George enjoyed the energy that Wayne brought to our house and his life. Here was someone who could get up the stairs as fast as George could descend them. They were well matched, although dog walking was not something that appealed much to Wayne, except on special occasions. One of those occasions was when Wayne acquired a pair of roller boots. George was an enthusiastic walker, one of those dogs that pulls rather than leisurely walks around the block. With his new roller boots, Wayne was up for the challenge. Wayne laid down the gauntlet by speeding away with George in tow. Not for long though, as George took up the challenge as they headed down the road, straining at the leash with Wayne now being pulled. They shot around the corner of the road, which was the point where Wayne was to regret the lack of a brake on the boots. It was several minutes later when they both reappeared with Wayne now moving somewhat more gingerly. The skin scrapes on Wayne's arms suggested that the brake had probably been the tarmac on the road. George was as usual panting excessively with tongue hanging out and headed directly for his water bowl. Wayne, despite the outcome, was howling with laughter. As long as it had wheels and speed then Wayne was in his element.

Unfortunately, the other residents of our cul-de-sac did not share George's enthusiasm for our new resident. This was to be one of my early indicators of the difficulties faced by Foster Carers. I expected a few things to change when Wayne moved in but nothing like the impact it actually had. We lived in a small cul-de-sac of just eight houses and had no problems with any of the neighbours previously. The problem with being a Foster Carer is that whilst you are aware of a child's history and behavioural issues, it is not something that you can share with neighbours or anybody else. Even if you could, then I doubt if many would either understand or sympathise. My own parents were as tolerant as anyone, but even they struggled to understand how I could work with some of the behaviours exhibited over the years by Wayne and some of the boys that followed in his footsteps.

It's an unfortunate fact that Foster children and Children's Homes bring out the NIMBY (Not In My Back Yard) attitude in people. Most just see these children as a threat, whether to their own security or to their own children, being worried that they may fall under the influence of these 'feral' children. Feral is exactly how many people view children in the Care System. They may use different and far less polite words to describe them, but their attitude is often open hostility to their presence in their neighbourhoods. Any applications to open Children's Homes in residential areas are inevitably met with complaints and protests.

Unfortunately, their hostility often puts a target on the back of any child in the care system living in the locality. Children in Care tend to be, 'Guilty until proven innocent,' rather than the contrary and will be blamed by locals for any damage, crimes or anti-social behaviour in the area. If a foster child doesn't come home at night, then the police are notified. More often than not there is an innocent explanation, but the presence of a police car in the street will be enough for some to allocate blame and confirm suspicions that the child is automatically a criminal. The majority of police visits to Foster Carers tend to be purely procedural and can also be if the child has themselves been a victim of crime. Neighbours rarely grasp this however, so any police presence merely reinforces their negative attitudes.

In those first few months of my fostering life, Wayne's impact on the neighbourhood was sufficient enough to earn countless and repetitive condemnation for numerous foster boys for the entirety of my time of living there. In terms of his capacity for criminal and anti-social behaviour, Wayne was a rare exception in my fostering career, but that matters little to people who have an agenda against foster children. For my own reputation, Wayne was the perfect storm. A hurricane that caused absolute havoc and who did himself, or me, few favours in our standing within our local community. For him, it was not just limited to our neighbourhood, but for me, it meant that I and successive foster children would be unfairly judged and targeted for many years to come. It is something that is not uncommon for Foster Carers, but it had not even been a consideration when I had taken Wayne on.

Bringing a charismatic fun-loving criminal into my relatively quiet neighbourhood was always going to be a challenge but was not in my worst expectations remotely on the scale of what it transpired to be. I had been working in Bathurst with all the support and back up that anyone could need and then suddenly I was flying solo and literally winging it, given my lack of Fostering experience. Added to that, for the first time in my life, I couldn't really turn to my parents for support because for all their life experience, they couldn't offer practical or relevant help or support. Moral support was given by the bucket load, which did ease the feeling of isolation, but I didn't want to worry them that I was out of my depth. I may have been out of my depth, but I was at least staying afloat and quickly learning about what was necessary to be able to navigate these choppy waters. It was probably the fastest learning time of my life, because there was in effect a simple choice. Making it work, or quitting and giving up on Wayne was never an option for me. I learned to fight like never before, I made mistakes, plenty of them, but the survival instinct that I had discovered in Knowle West was now part of me and getting stronger by the day.

I never did like dull and this fostering experience was never dull in those early days. I learned to savour the times of quiet that rarely lasted more than a few hours, but in those times, I could recharge and re-energise. A big factor in that was Patrick and Freshblood. That gave me another focus, a respite in a way and mostly something that I never really recognised or acknowledged for some time to come. This music connection with Pat had been key to my previous successful work with young people in Knowle West. Beyond his love of Jean Michel Jarre's music, Wayne was also well into Hip Hop. He loved some of the early rappers and through my connection with Pat and his boys, found an opportunity to develop his DJ skills. The events we were organising in those days gave Wayne scope for further opportunities and Wayne never turns down an opportunity.

What I didn't truly appreciate at the time was just how much Pat's influence and support made my work so much easier. Of course, I realised that the music was a great tool in working with young people, but there was a difference between Eagle House and Fostering. From a purely selfish perspective, my Foster Children were my responsibility alone, my work. The isolation of being a single carer made me naturally defensive about my role. I felt that I was under constant scrutiny from the moment Wayne moved to my house and I probably was. Initial results with Wayne won me considerable plaudits and I was not inclined to share this newfound acclaim. I would always reference Pat's input, but only as a music mentor to Wayne and others that were to follow. I was the carer, I was the one who would stand or fall by my work, so I was very protective over my perceived role. Crediting Pat on Fostering issues was just like watering down my input and for some years, I selfishly guarded my growing reputation and was reluctant to share the credit.

From the moment I started fostering, my relationship with Pat changed. I was happy for him to take the lead in all things musical, but the moment that Wayne or the following children leaned towards him for advice or guidance, I went on the defensive. This was my world, not his and was something that was maybe reinforced by Pat's more cavalier attitude to rules and regulations. I had become one of his sidekicks, figuratively speaking and that was fine. Music was his world, not mine, but Fostering was mine and in the early days I was probably over-protective and somewhat possessive over my Foster kids. Despite my friendship with Pat, I resented Wayne initially getting closer to Pat, as there was always a competitive element in our relationship. There was certainly a little jealousy on my part at the ease with which Pat breezed through difficult situations with young people, a jealousy that I couldn't acknowledge at the time. He made it all look so easy, whilst I had to go through all the day-to-day crap without getting such joyous moments as he seemed to experience on a daily basis. He was a bit like the 'Disney dad' who visits his kids and gives them treats whilst mum goes through all the day-to-day hassle without the fun times.

That competitive streak between us led to many arguments over the years and occasional walkouts and splits on my part, but the fact that we had an undefinable chemistry that worked so well inevitably brought us back together. It was during one of those splits that I went off to work with some other people who were putting together a Country Music event in Bristol, musically poles apart from the stuff with Pat. The event featured an American guitar player, Chet Atkins. His name meant little to me until I researched his history.

Chet was, in fact, a legendary guitar player and music producer, but not exactly one that most in the UK public were aware of, despite his successes. He had worked with Elvis Presley, playing guitar and co-producing his first million-seller *Heartbreak Hotel* as well as many other tracks with many famous artists. He discovered the Everly Brothers, Dolly Parton and Jim Reeves, amongst others. Arranging the concert got me a trip to Nashville to meet Chet and a weekend escorting him around when he came over to Bristol for the show.

For me personally, meeting and spending some time with Chet was fascinating. He was idolised by the likes of Mark Knopfler, Paul McCartney and George Harrison, all idols of mine. Years spent working in Rap music and I had never met anyone that commanded that sort of respect from my idols, so this was exciting on a whole new level. He was quietly spoken, easy going and yet an assertive man just past his 70th birthday. I can so relate to him now, having reached the same age. He attracted many guitar lovers over his weekend in Bristol all seemingly carrying their own guitars so they could play him a few of their own licks. I could soon see that he was bored with this incessant need for validation that so many of his fans had. In the presence of a guitar legend, they preferred to discuss their own limited talents rather than gain any valuable insights from a living legend.

When his press interviews and 'meet and greets' were finally over he asked me to take him to a golf course where he could get some respite. In occasional asides to his young PA, I could see that his patience with numerous sycophants was wearing somewhat thin. Once out on the golf course, he came alive in surprisingly relaxed conversations, with humorous tales of his much loved friend Dolly (Parton), Elvis and various other legends. He told me how, after making a few recordings with the young Elvis, everything changed. Elvis was catapulted to worldwide fame and Chet was asked if, rather than daytime sessions, he could record overnight sessions with Elvis to avoid fans. Chet politely refused as he didn't work nights. He went on to great success of his own, always on his own terms ,whereas poor Elvis, for all his success, became a slave to fame and fortune and the infamous Colonel Parker.

I was somewhat unexpectedly, completely in awe of this old man by the end of our time together. Old Man? You see, that sums up the perspective change in me from 30 years ago until now. I saw an old man then, whereas now I would see him as an Elder with all the respect that goes with that. I respected him, but not his age, so I should not be surprised that people now can dismiss me because of my age. What goes around comes around. Not once did anything he said about working with various legends or his career come across as even remotely boastful. He was merely an elder looking to pass on little gems of knowledge to an eager recipient. He had grown tired of demonstrating licks to people young and old, who only sought his technical know-how and who had little interest in the man, just what he could do with a guitar. He had taught and inspired countless people over his lifetime and had been paid homage to by some of the greatest guitar legends ever, people who had enjoyed far greater commercial success than he had himself. He dutifully did the press and PR rounds that weekend, because he was not the sort of person to let people down and, as I learned that weekend, fame doesn't mean you can just do whatever you like. It was excruciating to watch him have to answer respective questions from journalists who were largely unable to awaken his interest beyond polite answers. He no longer wanted to hold court for his followers but was too respectful to say so and too hamstrung by contractual obligations.

What he wanted, other than getting back home to Nashville, was to enjoy the simple things in life and the sweet memories. Late on the first day after a tribute evening to honour him, he looked tired and drained. I was about to take my leave when he turned to me and said quietly, "John, I like you and do you know why I like you?"

Surprised by his remark and question, I just responded with a shrug of the shoulders.

"It's because John, you don't play guitar."

He then looked around. We were momentarily alone after an evening of hangers on, followers and sycophants. Quietly as if not to be overheard he asked, "Do you walk John?"

I took a second to think what he meant by this and he saw my uncertainty and laughed, "Walk John! I like to walk a mile or so of an evening."

"Would you walk with me?"

"My pleasure," I said and he quickly banished his entourage and PA and said to them, "Don't worry now, John will be with me."

Here was the man who sent Elvis away because he wanted peace at night, asking me to join him in his personal time. It was quite a surreal moment and so I felt truly honoured. I was almost 30 years his junior so walking with him would be no problem I thought. We left the hotel on College Green next to Bristol Cathedral and he proceeded up Park Street, a steep hill of shops leading up towards Clifton. I knew that Chet had experienced some health problems with cancer in recent years and was suddenly struck by the frightening thought. What if this legend were to pass out climbing one of Bristol's steepest hills.

I could be the man who killed the legend. Saying that it wasn't my idea may not hold much sway, I would probably be hunted down by his followers. As it was, however, I very quickly discovered that if anyone was going to pass out on this walk it was more likely to be me. This dapper 70 year old had probably read my mind and set off at a rate that completely took me by surprise. The grin on his face suggested he was enjoying this exercise and at the same time defying his companions expectations. Before we were even halfway up Park Street I was feeling the pace and he knew it. This man had a wonderful devilish side to him, something that had no doubt endeared him to Dolly in their long friendship, as well as countless others no doubt.

All the way up Park Street he was telling me funny tales of his and Dolly's wonderful relationship. They fortunately only required mostly minimal responses from me, something I could manage on the out-breath between my desperate gasps for breath. On reaching the top of Park Street I guided us in the direction of Whiteladies Road, a much less physically demanding route before turning around 10 minutes later to retrace our route, thankfully downhill. He started asking me questions on the return leg, no doubt realising that I had recaptured the ability to breathe again. Drawing his attention to a Georgian building as we passed by, I explained that it was where my mother had lived in Bristol during the Luftwaffe's blitz in the Second World War. Luckily, we were proceeding downhill, so I still had enough breath to answer a few questions regarding my family history.

It was probably only a thirty minute walk, but I felt so blessed to have shared that special time with him. Inspiration is something that can happen in the briefest of moments and the time spent with Chet was just one weekend, but so very inspiring. This man who had looked so tired before we had left the hotel had sprung to life and given me a very personal and precious snapshot of his life but more than that he had shown real interest in me and my life too. I got the feeling that he enjoyed our walk and our conversation about our respective lives. I am now a similar age to what Chet was that weekend and I understand more fully now why he wanted to walk, talk and share. Conversation really is the most precious of things, and the best ones we can treasure for life, long after people have passed. I wish so much that I could have walked with him once again but it was never going to be. Two worlds briefly met before once again going on their own respective paths. He left me with an unforgettable memory and I gave him a few moments of peace and a break from guitar talk.

He was indeed a very special man. A true legend in every sense. RIP Chet x.

Back in Yate meanwhile Wayne was busy blazing a trail himself. He too had his followers who yearned for the sort of notoriety that he was rapidly gaining. It didn't take long for the local police to have our address as one of their favourite go-to places. It wasn't just that there had been a spike in juvenile crime, it was also that he had no problem with drawing attention to himself. Keeping a low profile would never be Wayne's way for long. He borrowed a BMX bike from one of his followers one day and just fancied an opportunity to add to his growing status among his followers. A popular pastime amongst the local kids was to ride their bikes at speed through Yate Shopping Centre, where security guards would bellow instructions to dismount.

Winding up security guards would hardly enhance his reputation, so seeing a police car parked up, he rode the BMX straight at them before bunny-hopping onto the bonnet of their car. He then headed off with the police in hot pursuit. He knew all the local lanes and shortcuts by then, so their chase was pointless and just added to his reputation amongst the local kids. He would be sure to remind the police officers of his feat the next time they came across him.

Wayne had developed quite a passion for DJ'ing thanks to Pat and his crew. It was something that wasn't criminal and mostly not anti-social. I say mostly because Wayne did like a bit of volume with his music. I wanted to encourage his new passion so bought him a set of technics, (record decks to the uninitiated). They were the most sought after decks of the time by DJ's but brought their own problems with them. First off was New Years Eve and we met up with Pat and the boys for a party. When we got home in the early hours the front door was wide open. George was gone and so were the technics. Wayne located George returning from the park a short time later. As usual, George had not missed an opportunity for a run. He tended to be loud when anyone came to the door, but clearly not loud enough to act as a deterrent. At least he had a good night and was safe.

The police were called and probably had a good chuckle later that the source of so much grief for them had been robbed himself. Wayne didn't hang around to see the police as with George safely home he was straight off to make his own enquiries. I certainly didn't think that locating Wayne's property would sit very high on the police to-do list. Wayne was gone for the night, not an unusual occurrence. It was the first time that I had been robbed and seeing my bedroom, with contents of my drawers and cupboards strewn around the room, left its mark. I had nothing of much value, but it was the fact that someone, a stranger had been through all of my personal possessions and invaded my private space. It was to be a long time before I got back any feeling of comfort and security in my room or in my house.

This robbery was a good eighteen months into my life as a foster carer and I had recently been cleared to have a second foster placement. The new lad, Martin, had quickly gained friends in the local school among pupils who knew of Wayne's reputation. It gave him some very much welcome 'street cred'. Wayne had been struck by the coincidence of us all being out in the evening, which rarely ever happened. His first reaction was asking who knew that we were off to a party. He had told nobody as he had only decided to go at the last minute. He knew a few of the kids Martin was hanging around with and decided that they were the prime suspects. That had been his thought process before leaving, ahead of the police visit the night before. Martin knew that I was keen not to broadcast our absence, partly because I distrusted a few of the boys that came home with Wayne and Martin. Martin was trying to establish himself amongst his new friends and Wayne and I suspected he had inadvertently let slip too much information.

Wayne returned soon after dawn with news. I was still up partly due to the adrenaline rush from the nights events and partly because my bed did not feel a very safe or comfortable place at that moment. Martin was however fast asleep.

"I know where my decks are," he said.

"I know the house."

"It's one of Martin's mates' houses so don't tip him off please".

"How did you find that out?" I asked thinking, "it takes a thief to catch a thief".

"One of his mates gave the kiddie up," he replied.

"Willingly ?" I enquired.

"Well sort of when I put him up against the wall. You don't need to know the details"

"Probably best that I don't then," I replied.

I then called Chipping Sodbury Police Station and spoke to the officer dealing with the case.

"We'll check it out," he said and a while later called back to say that they would be paying the house a visit.

A couple of hours later, they called back to say that they had checked the house and found nothing. Wayne naturally was not a happy bunny and shot off out again on another mission. He returned with more detailed information on where exactly in the house the decks were hidden. A further call to the police and off they went again. A while later, they called back to say that they had located the decks on their second visit. Wayne was positioned close to the house before they arrived to make sure that they hadn't been tipped off. I knew the young lad who had been arrested and bumped into him a few days later. A black eye indicated that someone else had also 'bumped' into him and a degree of retribution had been taken. He was quick and eager to apologise for his actions. We knew that he wasn't alone, but I think that his associates had been made aware that actions have consequences. That would be the end of the matter and lessons were learned all round, I think.

Wayne soon got back to his DJing which included a few guest appearances on a Bristol Pirate radio station that Pat was involved with. Those were the days when pirate radio stations were appearing across the UK in response to the bland output that most legal radio stations were broadcasting. He was sat at home one night saying that he had started his own pirate radio station in Yate. Unwisely, I ventured to ask where in Yate he had set that up.

"In my bedroom," was his response.

"Are you mad?" I asked. "They will be organising a dawn raid on our house again."

"No, they won't," he said.

"But they might be visiting our neighbours in the house on the other end of the terrace. I put the aerial on their roof."

My reaction contained a few expletives, to put it mildly. Yate FM had to close the next day, although I suspect it just moved to another location.

Chapter 7

When I became a Foster Carer, I discovered that being alone was a lifestyle choice and not something forced on me by circumstance. I was single and used to living alone. As a child, I liked being alone and I enjoyed studying people. My father's job as a salesman meant we moved often. By the end of Junior School I was already on to my third school and about to start my fourth. Senior school lasted a year before another move and another school and only then did I finally settle in one school for the rest of my school years before my restless streak, now well established, took over once again.

The constant moving of schools meant that I was invariably the new kid in school, having to make a new set of friends. From Staffordshire to Worcestershire, then North Bristol and onto South Bristol. By my mid-twenties, I had added Bath, Hampshire, London and Chipping Sodbury to the list. Moving was no hassle, just another new adventure. The almost nomadic existence left me reluctant to put down roots in any particular place. It also confirmed that I was averse to following the expected societal norm of finding a wife, having some kids and settling down. Even in my mid-twenties several friends had married, divorced and remarried. I could never get this urge to sacrifice one's independence to satisfy society's expectations. Of course, I felt the expectation and pressure through teens and well into my twenties, but the great thing about becoming a single male carer was it made a statement. I was one of the first single men in the country to become a Foster Carer and I wasn't in any hurry to pair off with anyone and give that up.

The whole idea of single men becoming Foster Carers appealed to my pioneering spirit. I was never a follower and certainly not a leader, but pioneers, at least in essence, were intrepid lone explorers. There was no template to follow, which pleased me and within the structure of Foster Caring I could pretty much carve my own path. Occasionally, in those early years, I would get into a relationship that was doomed to failure. I recall one first date that had gone pretty well and I was feeling optimistic. We stopped off at home to check on one of my boys. My mistake was to make introductions and then leave them together for 10 minutes. When I came back into the room the boy was grinning and she was looking most uncomfortable. I never did find out what had happened, or what had been said, but excuses were made and the rest of the night was cancelled as was any idea of further contact.

I have never met anyone who I felt would have been able to adapt to my lifestyle choices or my foster boys. Most of the boys that I took on had come from broken homes. Playing mum off against dad or vice versa had become normal behaviour for them. When they were put in Foster placements it would often seem like replacement mums and dads. They would resort to learned behaviour of choosing sides, sometimes putting pressure on Foster Carers own relationships, such was the intensity of their behaviour. When boys were placed with me, I was effectively mum and dad. They couldn't play one off against the other and I wasn't there to replace either parent for them. I had already become more of a mentor than a traditional parent, although that was as a result of my working methods, rather than by deliberate design.

My fostering, mentoring and all the projects with Pat suited a single man, so much more than if I had a partner. I had evolved into someone who was immensely comfortable as a single man, being able to enjoy my peace and solitude when the kids were not around and recharge, ready for the next burst of activity. Maybe it was and is selfish, but it's my life and it's my choice. Although I have never really felt lonely, what I did feel, especially in those early years as a Foster Carer was isolation. At Bathurst, with a strong team to support one's every move I had never felt isolated. As a Foster Carer it was to be very different.

We have support, of course, from Social Services, but it's very hard to actually feel part of a team despite the constant reminders from them that we are part of their team. In saying that we are part of their team, then it only serves to demonstrate that we are not, as they just don't understand how it feels from our perspective. We are literally on the frontline, whilst they are more like wartime generals, very much in the rear, usually at a safe distance from the action and often from the aftermath except in terms of judgement. The fallout from any problem generally falls upon the carer, who will then be scrutinised, reviewed, investigated and possibly suspended, depending on the severity of the problem. If it gets to an investigation then that is often the beginning of the end for the Foster Carer, irrespective of the outcome. Investigations almost inevitably leave their mark on carers who mostly feel unsupported throughout the process.

Whether it's fostering in the 1990s, or fostering today, the buck tends to stop with the carer at the first sign of trouble. At that point we find our own Social Worker or Support Worker has three functions. A duty to the child, a duty to Social Services and a duty to the Carer. One can argue about which, in effect, comes first, duty to Social Services, or duty to the Child, but whichever way it goes. we foster carers are number three in terms of consideration and support. We are the easiest to jettison and the easiest to hold accountable. This is never more apparent than when there is a complaint made against a foster carer. That is when the feeling of isolation becomes ever-present and for some never goes away.

Complaints and how they are handled cause many foster carers to leave the service, irrespective of the outcome. Most complaints are found to be not justified, but for many carers, the stigma and the damaging nature of the investigation process and its procedures leave them totally disillusioned with the service. Guilty until proven innocent is how many of us feel that we are treated, rather than innocent until proven guilty. In my career there has only to my knowledge been one serious investigation.

I was looking after two lads, one of whom was a fifteen-year-old schoolboy. I was renting a house at that time and the young man apparently found some pornographic videos in a loft space that we had never previously accessed. Left there by a previous occupant, he and his friend neglected to tell me of the discovery, unsurprisingly. By coincidence at the same time our local police were apparently looking into the distribution of hard core snuff movies. For those of you that don't know, 'snuff movies' can show actual killings or murders.

Having enjoyed his discovery of some porn films, they both went to his friend's house. Unfortunately, the boy's mother overheard them discussing snuff movies (a subject of much discussion among teenagers at the time) and also that they had discovered pornographic material in my loft. The mother put two and two together, made five and called the police. As is the way of these things, Social Services were of course notified and an investigation launched in association with the officers already investigating snuff movies. I was blissfully unaware of any of this until my boy failed to come home from school one day.

Instead, I had a visit from my support worker who informed me that an investigation had opened into the allegations and my boy had been taken in for questioning after school. At that point, the boy would be allowed to return to me, providing nothing in his interview or the wider investigation would require that he be removed from my care. The boy returned home, angry and shaken by the whole experience. He had been asked a good few embarrassing questions, many relating to me. Full of apologies, he said he knew I was innocent, but he felt that they were trying to get him to say something against me. His explanation of how it went gave the impression that he had been purposely defensive with his answers, as he thought that they were trying to stitch me up. I admired his loyalty but suspected that it had actually done me few favours. He explained that what he had found was porn, but nothing like snuff movies and nothing I heard then or since ever contradicted that.

A nervous few days followed when I was expecting a police visit with a search warrant but it didn't come, not that I had anything to worry about if it did. Interestingly, the day before I found out about the investigation, I asked the boys if they had returned to the house during the day as several things in my room had been moved. Had someone been in the house? It certainly felt like it and everywhere I had been in the days preceding, I had noted police cars parked nearby. Working with Wayne for so long had made me naturally over-vigilant.

Eventually, I had a return visit from my support worker. His words have stayed with me. "John, I am pleased to tell you that following an intensive investigation, no evidence could be found against you in relation to the complaint."

There was no use of the word 'innocent' nor the word 'cleared' in relation to the allegations. I neither felt cleared nor found innocent and I was supposed to accept that as satisfactory. I remained angry for a long time to come, but in the years since then, I have spoken to so many carers who have received similar treatment. I know of many who have quit following unfounded allegations and unsatisfactory investigations. It really doesn't matter how successful a foster carer you have been because you are only ever one bad placement or experience away from a career-ending moment.

That is part of the massive insecurity that foster carers experience. In almost any other line of work, if you experience problems with your employer, then you can quit and get another job. If a carer wants to remain a carer it's different. They have to apply for a transfer to another local authority or agency. The transfer process takes many months and, in the meantime, you have no income, so most people in that position will just leave fostering. If your employers felt that they had any dispute or problem with you, then it can become impossible to get approval with anyone else. Even if your record is outstanding over many years, then the process still involves fresh assessment and fresh checks, duplicating information that your current employers already hold. It's a senseless and time-consuming waste of everyone's time and adds undue pressures on already stressed foster carers. If checks and references are already up to date and current, then why is there a need to do them all again? I have transferred several times in my career and every single time it feels that you have to constantly repeat already known information. It really is time for instigating a new, more efficient system, but the appetite for change seems as always to be merely with the foster carers and not with social services.

After a couple more foster boys, I moved out of Yate to Kingswood, on the edge of Bristol. Wayne had pretty much exhausted everybody, the neighbours, the police and the house was also looking tired. My mum and dad had sold their own house and moved into mine for a couple of years before moving into a retirement bungalow. They used the time to improve it immeasurably before my return. The neighbours were so happy to see my parents move in and Wayne move out. Wayne stayed on with me for a while but soon moved to independence. The top dog had left the building but made sure that nobody else took over the role. Rob the lad who was to follow Wayne under that Glastonbury fence moved in and life became generally less stressful. Like Wayne before him, Rob was close to Pat but lacked Wayne's criminal leanings and became one of my most likeable foster lads. He was a bit of a party animal, loving the rave culture, but apart from a liking for weed and pills, did nothing to upset neighbours and was usually fun to have around.

Next up was Richard and he was certainly a character. His problem was sniffing gas which he did daily. He would break into cars just for handfuls of loose change to fund his dangerous habit. Richard was a large, round-faced and generally cheerful lad. He was polite, caring and very respectful, except when he was 'away with the fairies' after sniffing a can of gas. He was prone to depression at times, but he absolutely loved Wayne. He did break the glass on my front door one day when 'on the gas' but was full of apologies for his behaviour. I suspect Wayne had 'suggested' an apology but I never knew for sure.

Richard, bless him, is one of my boys who has periodically come back into my life over the years. He had serious mental health issues, but he always found a way to get the best out of a situation. I bumped into him in his hometown of Bath a couple of years later and he was homeless and yet as cheerful as ever. He had found himself a discarded box that had contained a fridge-freezer and it had become his temporary home. Best place yet, he said and was very appreciative that the lining in the box meant he was, 'as snug as a bug in a rug' in this upmarket box. Fortunately, the council eventually found him a flat that he has shared with various cats and the occasional girlfriend over the last 20 years, broken only by a couple of months, where as a result of handling stolen goods, he was offered alternative more supervised accommodation.

As a foster carer, I measure success in different ways. People like Richard rarely have good outcomes, but when I see him in his flat, he is rightly proud to have generally kept his life together and now has a life that gets him through the occasional depressive episodes. That, I think, is a major success and I am proud of him. Several more young men passed through my care before I was to move back to my Yate home, which had been made more homely thanks to Mum and Dad's care. The same neighbours were still in residence, so not surprisingly, I was not welcomed back with open arms. This was a new era though and Wayne only appeared when things needed fixing, whether my car, plumbing, electrics or the computer, now that the internet had appeared to transform our lives. Back in Yate and life was a lot quieter and bridges with the neighbours were slowly rebuilding. A succession of nice teenagers without criminal inclinations certainly helped things get better.

Life remained settled until I had a call from a team manager, Anita, who was aware that I had a vacancy coming up. It was November 1996 and I knew if a team manager called then it was likely to be someone challenging and probably with a history of failed placements.

"We're looking for a placement for a young lad and I think it might just suit you John," she said, which sounded a little ominous.

"He needs a bit of nurturing and I think you'd be perfect for him."

"Nurturing? Me?" I asked.

I may have had some successful placements, but I didn't recall the word 'nurturing' ever being used to describe my work. I had never thought that car thieves and numerous anti-social boys had been placed with me because of my nurturing skills. I don't nurture, I thought to myself. Do I?

Maybe others saw an aspect to my work that I had never recognised. If I had to use a word to describe most of my work, I would say 'containment'. Children that couldn't settle in successive placements, because of their behaviour would be passed to me to hold for as long as possible. Regarding local authority foster carers, I was usually the end of the line. From me, they would either move on to independent living, to the private sector, or custodial. I was by then very well experienced in having regular contact with the Police and the Youth Justice system and I was effectively becoming an alternative to custody for some young lads.

"David just needs someone who can stick with him John, so I think that he would be a good match with you".

Stick ability? Yes, I recognised that as one of my traits. Wayne had set the bar on that one.

"David is 11, nearly 12," she quickly added to soften the shock and has no criminal history. He just needs some love and attention.

'Love', I mused, another word that perhaps was not the first word that came to mind regarding my caring style. Single man, teenage boys and love were not a comfortable combination when used in conversation in my male-dominated household. Whilst I was naturally reluctant to use the word love in describing my work, it would be hard to argue that I had not shown these boys the love that many of their fathers and mothers had failed to show them.

David had been placed with another carer that I knew well, alongside another boy of a similar age. Placing any two boys of similar ages together usually only happens when alternative placements are in short supply, or if they are siblings. I knew Mo, his carer very well. She had provided respite breaks for several of my lads when I went away for breaks and was a brilliant Foster Carer, along with Terry her husband. People who are not carers, often fail to appreciate the need for carers to have breaks without their foster children. Foster Caring is 24/7 and however much you care for a child: I believe that it is important to have occasional breaks to recharge. One argument is that you should treat these children exactly the same as your natural children and take them with you. That argument can fail when one takes into consideration how stressing and unsettling foster children can be on your own children. They usually adapt and welcome these foster children into the family, but it's often not easy for them. The constant demands for attention can leave your own children feeling neglected. They deserve their breaks too and their own time for some extra attention.

Before I agreed to take David, I spoke to Mo. She had just returned from Tescos; where David had experienced a temper tantrum. Not getting what he wanted and maybe wound up by the other lad that Mo looked after, he had started grabbing melons and smashing them on the floor. Mo explained that he was hard work, but a lovable lad. She was not the sort of person that failed to give an honest assessment.

Everything was agreed with Anita and the social worker brought him later on that day. A short, slightly chubby, dark-haired boy with a suspicious glare, arrived with the then customary black bin liners containing his possessions. One of the worst aspects of the care system in those days was that children moved placements with all their possessions thrown into refuse sacks. Dave has never forgotten that to this day, a memory shared with countless other former Children in Care. Despite his initial nervousness and suspicion, he was soon tucking into a plate full of food. As Mo had said David certainly had a healthy appetite. One trait that I noticed straight away was his apologetic instinct, constantly saying sorry, even when he really had done nothing wrong. If there was a need for a reprimand, his hands would be clasped to his chest with fearful eyes peering up to me. I was not used to this at all from previous boys, apologies were not often so easily offered.

It took a few days of exemplary behaviour before David had his first temper tantrum. In what was to become his usual reaction. "F*** OFF YOU BALD C***!"

He stormed out of the house and went just across the road but didn't go out of sight. His middle finger let me know that his temper had not calmed, but he stayed, almost expecting me to chase him. I gave him a few minutes keeping an eye on him through the net curtains and then called out to him that tea was ready. Without hesitation he came straight back, very tearful and hands clasped to his chest. By the time he had cleared his plate the beaming smile had returned, especially once he knew that he was not going to be denied 'second helpings.'

Looking after such a young lad was very different for me. He was 11 but had learning difficulties and was young for his age, totally unlike any of the boys that I had thus far looked after. My mum and dad took to David from the moment they met him. Here was a boy that they could understand, rather than a manic teen who could cause all sorts of grief to me. During their time living at my house, they had installed a large garden shed with a porch where their younger grandchildren would come for tea once a week. The shed was now largely neglected, but their tea sessions continued at their new bungalow. Two of the grandchildren were close to David in age, so they quickly added him to the weekly tea invitation. They rarely witnessed even a hint of David's temper tantrums, as he knew better than to put this weekly treat at risk. Food always won his heart and he quickly took on the mantle of the new grandson. Nan and Pops quickly became the most dearest and loved people in his life and remained so for the rest of their days.

David attended a special school in Bristol where he could exhibit the full range of his behaviours. Whilst his behaviour was erratic at best the support he got from the teachers at Warmley Towers was exceptional. It had been a constant factor in his life despite his numerous placement moves prior to coming to me. His reading skills were, not unexpectedly, well below his age and his attention span was very short, except at mealtimes where he would be at the front of the queue every day.

A couple of weeks into his placement with me I decided to take him to a football match with me. I was a lifelong Bristol City supporter, so I hoped he would enjoy it. We had seats in the stand close to the halfway line so he could get a good view. There followed 90 minutes of incessant questions. Who is number 3, who is number 9 and on and on with every question repeated again and again. It was hard to concentrate on the game and I was a little frustrated that he seemed to forget every bit of information almost as soon as I gave it to him. Otherwise, why would he repeat every question numerous times? As I said, I had never looked after a lad of his age with learning disabilities, so unfortunately, at that point I just didn't understand it at all. When a goal was scored, he appeared mildly interested but more so in the crowd's reaction. As we left for home, I really wasn't sure as to whether he had got any enjoyment out of the game at all, although he was still asking incessant questions. My conclusion on that day was that he was interested, hence the multitude of questions, but his level of understanding seemed to match what school had said about his inability to learn. His most used word was probably 'Why?' Most questions were met with that response rather than an answer.

"What time is it?"
"Why?"
"What's your favourite food?"
"Why?"
"What do you fancy doing today?"
"Why?"
"Who is your favourite teacher?"
"Why?"

Questions were responded to with questions, and usually just the one word 'Why?'

I couldn't work it out at first and put it down purely to his severe learning difficulties, which had already been diagnosed. Going to football and indeed doing pretty much anything at all with this little lad was likely to be very challenging. Now, what I should have been doing was putting myself into his shoes. Having bounced around more placements than most in the system over the previous six years, then what was it like to move in with me? He had been moved around placements so many times that even someone he spent a weekend with he counted as his foster carer. I guess technically he was right, because they were carers but he had so many short placements that he couldn't distinguish between them. He was always on the move so coming to me would seem no different, probably a few weeks with me and then off again. How could anyone concentrate on learning whilst they were continually in transit between placements. The only constant in his life was his school, which was why they were such a good source of information for me in respect of David. They had some great teachers at Warmley Towers, but one in particular, Deputy Head Mike Fotherby, had a brilliant way of working with David. Watching him work with kids was an education in itself for me.

He had a wonderful way of engaging with David, as with all the children. Outwardly he had a booming voice that could get the attention of any child, but he was not a person who would just bark out an order. Having got their attention, he would then engage with the child, reason with them and convince them to either calm down or moderate their behaviour. With David, he would give him the space to act out often by means of a bugle that David could take out onto the field and make as much noise as he liked without disrupting the rest of the school. What was so impressive was the way that he commanded attention, but at the same time could work with multiple children at once, all with their own special needs. I was learning to adapt to working with David but the thought of having to manage multiple David's all at the same time was on another level. Mike was loud when necessary, but not angry, always calm and controlled, like he was in the eye of a hurricane surrounded by mayhem, but able to ride out the storm and restore peace and control. I only looked after two children and to have both causing problems at the same time was very rare indeed. Patrick and I used to help coach Mike's pupils in football occasionally, children with a wide range of complex needs. Even with our combined talents and experience I think we would have struggled without Mike's input.

Chapter 8

A few weeks after taking David to the football match he had settled in well to my house and was quickly establishing himself into the role of a new lovable Grandson for my Mum and Dad (Nan and Pops). We were off for a trip in the car, just me and Dave, the way he always preferred it. He loved trips, especially when they were one to one. Trips, (as with school) involving multiple children usually went awry for David who tended to be abrasive with his peers. Sat in the car, he started talking about Bristol City and the match we had attended. He started naming the players and to my surprise started describing one of the goals in great detail.

"Darren Barnard to Tinnion, then over to Greg Goodridge on the other side who crossed for Shaun Goater to score. What a Goal," he said, pumping the air with a clenched fist just like 'The Goat' had done.

It was at that moment that I realised just how naive I had been to assume that his multiple repeated questions meant that he wasn't understanding. He was merely seeking confirmation because he was putting the pieces together in his own way of learning. What he needed from me was not irritation at having to repeat myself, but pride that this boy was proving people wrong. When you have spent most of your life to date being made fun of and being put down by both peers and adults then of course you need patience and reassurance before speaking up. Constant reassurance was apparently needed, for him to even start to gain a little self-confidence, something that I had never seen until then.

How remarkably stupid I had been. With all those teenagers that I had mentored I would first seek out their interests, whether music, football or whatever. Finding their interests, anything they loved to do, well, that was the key to gaining their attention and their interest so as to enable me to work with them. Why had I treated David so differently? Why had so many adults in his life failed to find the key to David. It wasn't the 3 R's as they were called (Reading wRiting and aRithmetic), it was the 3 F's (Football, Food and Family) the latter being something he had largely been deprived of since coming into care, apart from at Mo and Terry's. His absolute love of Football and Food and his new Family too (especially Nan and Pops), has never diminished since those early days. Still with me 28 years on, I can testify to that. His beloved Nan and Pops have sadly gone, but not his love for them or for me or my family.

In the car that day, he recognised the joy that I had shown in his description of that Goater goal. It was one of those moments when two people make a connection, just like that moment with Wayne in Paris. A brief moment, when you know that you have a special connection that will endure. It's hard to explain and it doesn't happen often, which in no way disrespects other young people that I have fostered. As a carer, that moment of connection is magical. It makes so many other problems seem much more manageable. It's like switching on a light in your heart that will never switch off. Whatever happens going forward, from that moment two people are connected like one and are stronger for the connection. Fostering by its nature is about temporarily caring for a child, maybe until they reach adulthood but always knowing that the placement will end, hopefully with a positive outcome. There is no lifelong expectation and for most children, we are just a safe and secure resting place between a troubled past and future dreams. Whilst the dreams may not become reality, the seeds that we foster carers plant can give life to the future.

Sadly, although settling so well into my family David had to move on from Warmley Towers school the following year. It was deemed by the powers that be that he should move to a special residential school. You can rightly assume that it was not something that I either agreed with or was comfortable with. I felt that they risked undoing so much progress that had been made. Whilst it's always painful to admit that financial concerns affect foster carers and their placements, it was a fact that financially I could not survive with David as just a weekend placement. Fortunately, someone in authority realised that he would need a stable placement at weekends and holidays and that would be unlikely if he were removed from my care. The decision was made to maintain a full-time placement with me, perhaps in anticipation that he would have multiple weekday exclusions adapting to a new school. They were not wrong.

He would be picked up by the school minibus on Monday mornings and returned by the same means on Friday afternoons. That was the theory, but I lost count of the midweek trips that myself, or his beloved Pops had to make. Often, he would be suspended on a Tuesday and then have to be collected and then returned to school the following day. Round trips of 80 miles each time, made twice in two days. It was, to my mind, pathetic and pointless and a complete waste of our time. David loved it all of course. A day at school, a fight with his usual adversary Philip, two half days with me or Pops. What was not to like? Usually, when I arrived at school to pick him up or to attend a meeting, he was not actually in class. He would instead be playing pool on his own and mostly unsupervised, despite the school being paid bucket-loads of money to look after him. It was not serving his needs; it was serving the schools. What a way to care for a child with learning difficulties!

From what I learned back then, all too often he was left alone after incidents to play pool until the next mealtime, rather than have anyone actually spending time and engaging with him. From the first day he arrived at my house, it was clear that he thrived on adult interaction, especially one-to-one. It was something that he was consistently denied at school. The excuse was that staff were needed to deal with the pupils who were still in class, but this was a special school for children who needed more individual attention. Controlling behaviour by isolating him was not a solution that benefited the child. If the lesson didn't engage him, then it was likely that he would misbehave and get sent to play pool. It was not an unpleasant outcome for David, but neither was it a response that would improve either his behaviour or his ability to learn.

From my very first visit to Kingsdown Manor, I was unimpressed. It was a converted old Manor House which provided accommodation and education for Bristol children who had either been excluded from mainstream schools, or that were otherwise not provided for. It was a school for kids with special needs who needed a different educational setting. To my mind, it was just a rather expensive way of containing these children. I would be surprised if many of the children had their educational learning stimulated or met. It was 40 miles from Bristol so it was out of sight and out of mind, I suspect.

As for the staff, well they mostly seemed a ragbag of rejects from social services and education. As if caught in a time warp from a bygone age, most of them probably wouldn't have fitted into mainstream education any more than their pupils had. They also, in my opinion, offered little of substance to many of their scholars. At my first meeting with the staff, I thought some of them looked rather scruffy and disorganised. That opinion wasn't to change over the following years.

The school's main function appeared to be justifying their existence to Social Services. In a service where it is notoriously difficult to get sacked, that was probably not too difficult. One of their methods seemed to involve blaming school behaviour on problems at home. Bearing in mind that was the reason why many were placed there, then that seemed an easy cop-out. Whenever I had to attend an educational review or disciplinary meeting for David, at the school they would invariably pitch the theory that David's behaviour was probably due to problems at home. Putting the foster carer on the defensive early on in any meeting seemed to be a consistent tactic of theirs. The social worker would then follow up by addressing David's care at home.

Their tactics, whilst transparent to me, were relatively effective. Professionals ganging up on Foster Carers in meetings was not that uncommon. It was itself a type of bullying experienced by many carers in my experience. All too often, meetings ended up like inquisitions for me and for many other carers I suspect.

David's behaviour at home was exemplary and an absolute pleasure. Calling me a bald c*** was now a rarity and tantrums, on the rare occasion they occurred, quickly subsided. David's ADHD diagnosis was used by the school to justify their degree of difficulties faced along with his very low reading age.

"He can only read like a five-year-old" was one teacher's quote. "Engaging him in reading is almost impossible".

When I queried the ADHD diagnosis, it was dismissed as being made long before he came to the school. When I insisted that they find out who made the diagnosis they just put off the discussion to the next meeting pending further research and then the next meeting and so on. Out of sight, out of mind, as I said. Eventually, David's records were checked and no recorded diagnosis was ever found. There was simply a statement by someone years earlier at a meeting saying that they suspected David had ADHD. By the next meeting it was repeated and so on until nobody checked anymore as to whether he had actually been diagnosed. David was easily distracted, so it must be the case. Almost every child I looked after for years was said to have ADHD. Assumptions that became accepted as 'facts' were all too common and rarely challenged.

As regards his poor reading skills, I queried as to why it was then that David, on weekends at home, would read the Saturday football paper from cover to cover and could repeat multiple results from all four divisions of the Football League, involving 92 clubs. I suggested that it was not that he couldn't read or digest information, but rather that they had failed to engage him in reading anything that he was remotely interested in. David was not someone who couldn't learn, he was instead someone who traditional teaching and education provision could not teach, unless they could capture his interest. My remarks rarely went down well and were usually carefully edited in the minutes of the meetings.

Several complaints that I had made of abuse and bullying were never officially addressed, although one child, who was the subject of my allegations was dealt with on other similar historic matters by the courts when he became an adult. Not long after David left the school, it was in fact closed down, although probably due to cuts in Social Services and Educational budgets rather than poor performance. It had improved somewhat, after a poor Ofsted report resulted in a change of Head and a new regime. Apart from a lovely support worker, a guy called Harry, it was not in my humble opinion a great loss to Education, Social Services or Children in the Care System.

Whilst David was enjoying his school days, Pat and myself, along with Mike from Freshblood, had taken over one of Bristol's best known record shops. It was a venture that neatly fitted in with the events and music that we were producing. Pat and his boys had continued to have a very positive influence on the young lads that I fostered and it had not gone unnoticed in Social Services, especially in the local Youth Offending team.

They were based in Kingswood not far from our record store. Leading up to Christmas one year, the team manager of the Youth Offending team, a guy called Peter called me about a lad who they were struggling to find a bed for. He knew that I had no empty placements, having David and another lad at my house, but he wondered if Pat and his crew could help in some way. Pat and I had recently taken on some daytime mentoring of young people and were already trading under the name of Elevation. We offered three-hour mentoring sessions, which mostly involved Pat or the boys taking young people excluded from school out on various activities.

Peter asked if it would be possible for one or two of our staff to supervise the boy over the Christmas period, if he were accommodated in a registered B&B. It would mean at least one of them staying in the same B&B overnight. The boy was yet another car thief and the service that we would supply would be an alternative to custody for him over the Christmas period. It was an odd request, but an interesting challenge that we considered might also get us in a favourable position for getting more mentoring work from Social Services. It also meant that a couple of our Elevation staff could earn good money over the Christmas period. Elevation was a new venture and we employed people that we knew through the music and record store, mostly young men in their early to mid-twenties.

Mentoring was to become a growing business in the following years, with numerous companies sprouting up, eager to tap into a new source of revenue. It usually involved them being contracted by Social Services and Education departments around the country. Staff had to be police checked, but with the high numbers of young people being excluded from schools, the demand was increasing. With Elevation, we challenged the traditional concept of mentoring with our unique approach of employing young mentors, but not volunteers. Mentoring was being seen as something that college and university students in particular could do for a few months to add to their CVs and it was not seen as paid employment. The emerging companies, often trading like we were as not-for-profit were often run by former Social Work, Education and Youth Work professionals, who had spotted a lucrative opportunity that would make use of their contacts. Nothing wrong with that of course, except the mentors who were at the very core of the business were not usually employed, but instead were volunteers. It was a great way to gain work experience, but inevitably led to a high turnover of mentors, who at best could only possibly ever earn a little in expenses.

With Elevation, however, we looked to reward the mentors who were so essential to the business. Other businesses were more inclined to reward their management, as mentors did not need to be paid. They could always find a plentiful supply of young mentors who would be thankful for their plaudits and certificates. Voluntary work can be very good for young people, but, in our opinion, when that work is the core of that business then the people who perform it should be adequately paid for their services. Our work at Elevation was all about motivating and inspiring disenfranchised young people. Those young people loved being picked up for their sessions by fashion-conscious and music-loving role models in nice cars. Some of our rivals were cynical about our approach, but there was nothing wrong with demonstrating to young people that hard work can give you a good lifestyle. Most of them knew plenty of criminals, trying to prove otherwise.

We successfully completed the Christmas work with the young lad, Kai, which was to lead to plenty more work from other Local Authorities. My court experience proved invaluable, as we could help support young people throughout the court process. It soon progressed to us supplying court reports for some of the young people and we were invited to meet magistrates who had been impressed by our contributions. They were well-received for being more balanced in real expectations, rather than desired ones. For instance, the magistrates asked me if they thought giving a particular young person another chance would mean that the young person would not reoffend. I replied it was unlikely to happen and that he would almost certainly reoffend. I backed that up by saying the results of our work indicated that offending would reduce gradually, but consistently and that he would be taking up much less of the courts time in the future. The young man was then given another chance and indeed it went exactly as I had predicted.

The contract we had for Kai was extended in the New Year. It also led Pat and I to make the decision to expand our work into providing residential accommodation, establishing small children's homes, accommodating two or three young people in each house. A few months later, we opened our first Children's Home, having completed a lengthy application process. Before that happened, my second placement moved on to independence and Kai moved in to join David. My labrador, George, had sadly reached his final painful days and I had to make the heartbreaking decision to take him to the vets. I found it incredibly hard walking into that surgery and looking into his sad eyes. Luckily, Wayne came with me and offered to take George in for that final injection. As always, he was more practical, but certainly no less caring in saying goodbye to that ever-present joy in our lives.

Wayne had already started to repay my commitment to him as regular visits were required to make repairs to my car and to my house. I had endured more than I should have from Wayne in those early days after Bathurst, but he was to more than settle the debt over the years and decades that followed. Of course, I would be occasionally called upon to extricate him from a difficult situation. One of the most unexpected was soon after his then partner gave birth to their first child. Within a few months and absolutely exhausted, she asked if I could look after my little 'granddaughter' Tia overnight. After the initial shock of the request, I agreed. Yes, that was me with zero experience of ever having looked after a baby. It was probably not the most well-thought-out decision that I'd ever made, but what else could I do? Me and Dave filled the boot and car with all sorts of essential supplies and equipment needed by a baby, even for an overnight stay. We then took baby Tia home with us. There were more such occasions over subsequent months, but as with Tia's father, when I started fostering I just jumped straight into the deep end and got on with it. How many single, childless men ever get to look after a baby. Fostering certainly has its blessings, although I didn't necessarily feel that at the time. It was more likely the fear and trepidation of being totally out of my depth again, but at least Mum was nearby for plenty of advice, once she got over the shock of me looking after a baby. Her childless son suddenly had a baby granddaughter and she couldn't wait to meet her.

As for young Kai? Yes, well, he turned out to be one of those poor souls who just could not help himself. He was a lovely lad but just couldn't help stealing when the opportunity arose. Planning wasn't his strong point and he rarely evaded the police for long. He is the only car thief that I know who tried to steal a car that was missing an engine. Of course, he didn't know it was missing, but numerous attempts to start the vehicle may have been a clue. Poor Kai sat in the car, trying to start it with increasing desperation, as the owner of the car approached. The owner was quite an impressive man in respect of his size and proceeded to pull young Kai from the car in order to suitably admonish him before calling the police. It was a somewhat battered Kai who was handed over to the police when they arrived.

When it came to court Kai's defence crumbled quickly. He argued that it couldn't be TDA as the car couldn't be driven away. Well, I guess he had a point. However, Courts are not inclined to respond favourably to such attempts at humour. He was also charged with going equipped to steal cars, which he also denied. The prosecution statement mentioned that he was carrying a screwdriver. Kai answered that he had fixed a plug earlier and forgot that it was still in his pocket. In response to his denial, the screwdriver was then produced in evidence and was about the length of an average hammer. Even the head magistrate had to suppress a smile when the screwdriver was brought out. Kai was indeed lucky that day to avoid another prison sentence, but it was only a temporary delay of the inevitable. A few weeks later Kai took a shortcut through the grounds of Southmead Hospital. Quite by chance, as he was passing the A&E department, he noticed an ambulance with its keys still visible in the ignition.

"It was asking to be stolen", he remarked. He naturally jumped in and drove off. He was driving down the nearby Gloucester Road with the blues and twos on by the time he was apprehended.

Lovely though he was, his time with me was short and his placement was soon over, thanks to the local magistrate courts. There were some good memories, all the same. I guess his lasting legacy was that his emergency placement the previous Christmas led to Elevation becoming a registered Children's Home supplier and that became the most successful business that I was ever to be part of. Just as with our mentoring work, we were well ahead of our time in operating very small children's homes, long before Local Authorities realised their potential.

For me, Fostering and Mentoring have worked hand in glove, but that does not mean a foster carer necessarily makes a good mentor or vice versa. They are different skills and different roles that can work together, but not for everyone. As foster carers, we sometimes get to work with mentors and we can really benefit from their insight and their support for our young people.

It also depends very much on the needs of the individual child. The priority for many is having the opportunity of having a normal family life, something they may not have ever enjoyed. Just getting that sort of stability can get them through so many of their problems and day-to day-issues. Quite often, however, it must be said that those young men who have been placed with me have either not taken or not wanted that opportunity. Trying to fit them into a traditional type family may have either exacerbated their problems or even triggered other ones. Many struggle to adapt to other children in the foster home, often the carer's own children, who they can see as rivals.

Whatever the reason might be, then clearly something has not worked in previous placements and I have then been chosen as an alternative. As a mentor, I might see something in the young person amidst the chaos and anger. An interest maybe, or an undeveloped talent. For me that is the key to intervention. It's not always there and I am certainly not always successful. There has to be a chemistry that works for both him and I to work together, rather than just coexist in the same space. There have been young people that I have fostered successfully without mentoring and some that I have mentored but never wanted to foster. Again, it might come down to the chemistry of others in my house.

There are all sorts of mentors with all sorts of skill levels, from young people to elders like me. There is no rank or title that demonstrates the mentor's abilities; we are all just mentors. This is of course part of the problem, as to why mentoring is rarely seen as a profession. All too often the public perception is of a 'willing helper' rather than a professional, as there is no acknowledged process to evaluate one's credentials other than one's experience. I know only too well, as a foster carer, that the absence of recognised qualifications can lead to us being undervalued.

In the business world, mentors tend to be successful business people, mostly men for all the usual stereotypes. Having a successful business does not always mean that one understands people and therein lies a common problem. Being successful, whether in business or maybe as a creative (a musician or artist for example), can be inspirational to others who desire such success. The ability to inspire is one of the qualities of a mentor, but all too often successful people have massive egos or just a lack of people skills. Their egos also come with the prerequisite that they have to be the best at what they do, which can be somewhat limiting in helping another person develop their own skills. The determination and maybe arrogance that made them successful means that they struggle to work with a young person, who one day might become more successful than their mentor. For some it's more about talent spotting for their own business. The mentoring can be good in helping the young person initially, but a rising star can potentially become a rival which is not always so welcome.

Part of my success is down to wanting to help young people be far more successful than I have ever been. Too many so-called professional mentors are just looking for another validation of their own success, a willing disciple, but not someone who could potentially eclipse them.

I maintain my belief that a good mentor does not need to have all the answers nor prove how clever or superior their knowledge or experience is. It is about providing an environment where a young person can thrive and can develop their social skills and their life skills as well as their career. It's also about developing their ability to trust another person, invariably an older person. If that mentor is averse to trusting people because they themselves have succeeded in a very competitive environment, then it just does not work. It's also important to challenge ideas, not necessarily to prove those ideas wrong, but in order to show a young person that rather than just accepting a theory, an idea, or a philosophy they should make sure that it can stand up to scrutiny.

We as mentors are not always right and it's so important to acknowledge sometimes the ability to discuss rather than to argue. Arguments have been a constant factor in the lives of most children in the Care System and consequently, they have become defensive rather than open to other views. We should not expect them to listen to us if we are too defensive about our own beliefs and ideas. As I said, it's not about always having the answers for young people, it's more about having the right questions for them, because in their lives, they will often have to find the answers for themselves.

Chapter 9

In the early part of the new century, Elevation Child Care became a successful company. We did so by utilising and rewarding the talents of our young mentors who went on to become residential staff in our small children's homes. We had one of the lowest staff turnovers of any organisation in the sector, because our philosophy was built on mutual respect between staff and young people and between staff and the company, with a zero tolerance policy on disrespect. Residents and staff were part of the Elevation family and for many of the young people, we were the first family that they ever respected. Young people from local authorities across the country would often come to us with court cases outstanding. Many would lack any kind of respect, so that often would be the first battle for us to win and it would be won.

We made sure our young people were dressed in the latest fashionable clothes and best trainers, just like their peers and our mentors. Some critics would argue that we were effectively bribing them. Absolutely not, as it was all about improving their self-esteem, self-respect and self-confidence. Too often, young people in the Care System stand out for the wrong reasons but ours did not. Increasing self-respect helped them to show more respect to others. Having their peers envious of them for positive rather than negative reasons was a new feeling for many. We didn't burden them with too many rules, but those we did have were all about mutual respect. Good behaviour and good school reports and attendance were rewarded as they should be. Mealtimes at our homes were taken together and with staff as much as possible. Sunday lunch would be around the table, as in most good caring families, a perfect place for discussion and socialising together.

The young people knew from day one that Patrick and I were the heads of Elevation, but Pat was the figurehead, the man who ultimately made the decisions. If they had a problem they would go and see Pat, usually without the need for an appointment. He was always accessible and would resolve problems one-to-one without undermining any of his staff. Pat would take them clothes shopping himself often and to restaurants on a regular basis. After a while, my house was added to the Elevation houses and was officially made a registered Children's Home. Any children that I looked after, like David, automatically became part of the Elevation family. This meant that my boys could go clothes shopping with Pat or one of the mentors rather than the least fashionable member of Elevation, namely myself. The trade-off for that was if they did anything seriously wrong then Pat would deal with it and I never met a young person who would get the better of Pat in an argument. They had too much respect for him and potentially too much to lose for that to happen. Not one young person ever wanted to leave Elevation or asked to do so.

We would take everyone away together with Pat, an ever-present. Fishing trips to Devon, Team building weekends in Dorset, or Holiday Villas in Lanzarote. Just like any good family, everyone together. They were good times for all of us, but most importantly special times for our young people. When new boys arrived, it sometimes would take a while for them to understand, because we were also tougher in some ways than standard children's homes. I recall one time when a new placement arrived and he was on court curfew and could not go out between certain hours. The local shop was only 50 yards down the road so he decided to break the curfew.

"What are you gonna do about it?" he said, grinning as he walked out the door.

He returned two minutes later and was arrested within the hour. In an unusually swift conclusion, he was in court that same afternoon. He was bailed back to us with a stricter curfew which he didn't break again. He respected our advice from that day on and enjoyed several years with us.

Elevation quickly built a reputation for successful placements, often at a fraction of the cost of other Children's Homes in the private sector. We invested in people rather than expensive infrastructure and we got results where others had failed. When our young people left us, they either went home or to independent living, but never to other Children's Homes or Carers. What made Elevation special for me was that I could input my fostering experience and ideas without having to run them through Social Services for approval. So, what was it that actually made our care methods and our care homes unique and so loved by the children that we cared for? You could call it 'Fosterdential', a mix of Fostering and Residential children's homes, neither really one nor the other. We rarely employed experienced residential staff, or apart from me any actual foster carers. We took a core of our own young, trained mentors and put them to work in the homes and it worked brilliantly.

The merging of mentoring and fostering was something that I had unknowingly done for many years as a Foster Carer and was, I think, core to the success of Elevation. Our Elevation homes were neither Children's Homes nor Foster Homes but instead homes mainly run by mentors. It's what made them unique and is not something that I have ever seen anywhere else. Looking at them as maybe a Children's Homes/Foster Homes hybrid does however miss a key component that made them work. It was not me or Pat so much as the staff, our mentors. None of the staff, aside from myself, had been Foster Carers and only a couple of others had any experience of working in Children's Homes.

I was still officially a Foster Carer and yet my home also became a Children's Home. Initially, the extra support that I received from the Elevation team seemed intrusive. There were many more checks (some due to the Children's Homes regulations), many more staff visits and younger staff and mentors involved in the care of my foster children. After so many years as a single carer, I was naturally protective and certainly, with hindsight, too defensive in respect of addressing care issues within the home. The bottom line was that the quality of care and quality of life undoubtedly improved for the children that I looked after, even though the extra supervision occasionally highlighted my personal insecurities.

Our children were not, in the main, looking for replacement families in the traditional sense. Of course, they needed love and care, but so many of them came from dysfunctional families. Playing mum off against dad or vice versa was the norm for many. Without any real intention, I had become a father figure, especially to David. I had become somewhat over-protective, which caused friction when anyone appeared to usurp my authority. It was so ironic that I had unknowingly myself become somewhat arrogant in my reluctance to accept support, having had so many years with inadequate support. Elevation was not about adapting Foster Carers or Residential workers to our ways, but more in developing a new model, a new alternative system of looking after children by employing people less rigidly invested in different systems. I had started Elevation with Pat and yet in some ways I had become the dinosaur.

We had developed a wonderful way of accommodating disconnected and disenfranchised children, which was not necessarily compatible or workable with either traditional foster carers or residential staff who were used to different ways of working. It was, I guess, revolutionary, but as is often the case with leaders of revolutions, in some aspects I was a little left behind with the changes that evolved. My passion for Foster Caring blinkered me to the possibilities that Elevation was developing a viable alternative to the current provision. Maybe my own situation was a snapshot as to why Foster Carer recruitment consistently fails to deliver. The Foster Care system has long struggled to attract enough potential Foster Carers. Maybe using the Elevation type model, then what is actually needed is a new type of accommodation, a Third way, using mentors rather than foster carers in two to three bedded units. Neither foster care nor traditional residential homes these homes could work together as hubs sharing staff and identity. The majority of the staff would be mentors and for young people that have exhausted both residential and foster care provision it could be a viable alternative. In doing so, you open up employment opportunities from untapped markets and thus recruit staff using a different template to fostering or current residential provision. Could it work? Why not. We did it successfully with Elevation over 20 years ago and recently many Local Authorities are changing their residential provision to similar sized houses.

For the whole of my career in Fostering there has been a shortage of Foster Carers, a shortage that has only increased in recent years. Recruitment is still mainly along the lines of, "Have you got a spare room and some love to give?" and has never reached satisfactory levels. As a result, the Private Sector has filled the gap with increasing dominance and monopoly. Costs to Local Authorities have multiplied to a point where the only real beneficiaries are not the children but the investors, shareholders and hedge funds that now dominate the market. It's hard to see how it can be sustainable and, in my opinion, once the market is saturated then profits will be less and we will see these investors quickly disappearing off to new projects, leaving local authorities to pick up the pieces with insufficient resources and carers.

New ideas and new initiatives are needed and often those come from the smaller businesses as Elevation then was. Unfortunately, these are exactly the type of companies that have been squeezed out by mergers and takeovers from the private sector heavyweights. The Care System has become a Profit System, as it's now led by profits and not by care. Our first duty should be to the Children not to Shareholders and until that changes, we will see public money continue to be drained by the private sector. Successive Governments have let this happen, but Local Authorities share responsibility by reducing in-house resources, especially their own Children's Homes.

Since the introduction of the commissioning process, councils have clearly become increasingly reliant on the big beasts of the private sector, who have hoovered up the smaller companies. Meanwhile, local authority Foster Carers have continued to be the most crucial sector in the system, despite being underfunded and poorly supported. It is so often the case with the 'cheap option', absolutely essential to service delivery, but badly neglected. It's always been the same and will continue until there is a major overhaul of fostering and children's homes provision.

The Foster Carer recruitment processes are not fit for purpose as they do not address the shortages or the lack of retention of existing carers. Too many are lost through poor support. The same factors, poor recruitment, poor support, lack of recognition and insufficient financial packages have existed for decades. Local Authorities have consistently failed to invest in their core services blaming financial constraints. Yet, they pay vast sums to the private sector to look after their children. It is inexcusable and inefficient management, which lines the pockets of hedge funds, but fails to provide carers with the necessary professional, emotional and financial support. They do a disservice to looked-after children, to Foster Carers and consequently waste huge amounts of taxpayers money.

Despite several very successful years with Elevation, I became restless, only fuelled by my feeling that the successful business that I had created was rapidly leaving me behind. I was in my late 40s and still young enough to want to make a difference to the lives of looked-after young people. At Elevation, we did that but it wasn't enough for me. I wanted to impact change in the system and, in particular, one aspect of the system that had never changed much. Respite care or Alternative Care as it's now called. I had an idea of setting up a residential centre in France primarily as a respite centre. I chose France for several reasons, but mostly because I wanted to leave England and France was accessible easily by road. The first reason was the overriding one, which in hindsight blinkered me to the more practical idea of setting it up in England.

After several failed attempts at locating the right place in France, Pat suggested Spain, which I agreed to as a compromise. We fairly quickly found a property that suited our needs and I moved with David to Spain in the Spring of 2004.

Buying a property in rural Spain was certainly an interesting experience, which involved making a substantial cash deposit, most of which would not appear in the official purchase. For the sellers, that would mean that they would pay less tax on any profit, as the official selling price was much less than the real one. Mortgages were extremely easy to obtain through numerous financial advisors. Finding a property and working out how much was needed and then getting one was all part of a mortgage advisor's work. Whatever was needed they would obtain in order to arrange a mortgage . When we (my financial advisor and I), went to the bank to agree to one particular mortgage I was amazed to see pictures of a swimming pool. Now, I may not have been that experienced at house purchases, but that pool was definitely not there when I had agreed to the purchase. A nod and a wink from my man was enough for me to realise that that inclusion of the surprise swimming pool had upped the mortgage valuation. The picture used to obtain the mortgage had been of a similar property but with a pool. The extra value meant that amount given for the mortgage (80%) was in fact 100% of the actual asking price. By the time I realised how it all worked, it was already done, amid reassuring words that this was normal practice. Normal and legal were not necessarily the same thing.

Completion on another property purchase involved a surprise 'local representative' (with no apparent legal standing) attending at the Notary. The mere presence of this man added a noticeable nervousness to proceedings. This surprise guest had alerted Wayne's criminal senses and he was immediately suspicious of him. Wayne had travelled to Spain to offer any practical help in moving out there and he was not about to let anyone take advantage of my good nature. This unexpected representative was a very small man with a walking stick (somewhat resembling a Spanish Danny DeVito). He waited until the notary was conveniently called out of the room before demanding an extra sum of cash in order to let the deal proceed. Possibly to avoid any culpability this 'friend' of the seller spoke no English but did manage to convey a substantial hint of menace. The agent working with both buyers and sellers clearly knew what was going on (as did the other parties present) but took no responsibility, other than to translate the 'proposal'. I suspected she probably was not in the least surprised and had been here many times before.

Thankfully, Wayne was in his element. He understood this sort of negotiation tactic. His lack of Spanish did not prevent him from spotting a con going on. Up until this point Wayne's fields of expertise had not been needed, but safe to say he then quickly came into his own. We had moved into Wayne territory. The clearly noticeable hint of menace from the little guy was then suitably returned by Wayne, only with some considerable interest. Although the guy apparently spoke no English whatsoever, I believe the phrase, "someone's going to get hurt in a minute," coming from Wayne successfully and swiftly concluded negotiations allowing the notary to return to the room to witness signatures. The notary then had to absent himself once more whilst other previously agreed matters of cash were settled before final salutations. Business done we all shook hands, although a few traditional English expletives were muttered by a smiling Wayne on exit. Our "Gracias" and "Hasta Luego's" were met by a very clear "Puta" from the man with the stick. I guess he had watched enough Hollywood movies to know when he was outgunned.

Unfortunately, for all sorts of reasons, but essentially my then deteriorating relationship with Patrick, my plan never came to fruition. Our business relationship had been floundering for some time and we both felt the move to Spain would give it new impetus. Within a few months, we both realised that was not to be and all the move had actually done was to hasten the demise of our partnership. Working successfully in a partnership for many years had made me somewhat blind to my own shortcomings, which were to become apparent once I was working alone. I was very much an ideas man who could spot an opportunity but could not necessarily dot enough 'i's' nor cross enough 't's' to bring the ideas to fruition or to implement them.

Just a few months after leaving England, my partnership with Pat was broken and the plans were mothballed. Dave and I were to enjoy our time in Spain, making some good friends along the way. It was a couple of years before agreements were reached to sell the property that I had bought with Pat, as well as my other property in Spain.

It was all too easy to explain away the reasons for failure in Spain, without having to accept that my own inabilities could be in any way to blame for not realising my dream. Almost three years on from leaving England, despite what was mostly an enjoyable experience, the part-owned properties that I had bought had become millstones, in so far as each property tied me to other people's dreams and plans. There had though, in the interim, been a massive property boom and the property values had rocketed. Cashing in, with the emphasis now very much on CASH seemed a logical way to go, as I suspected the bubble would burst before long and values would then depreciate.

Somehow, after much wrangling, I got my way and with it my exit route. Once more the transactions included what for me were pretty large amounts of cash, which whilst not exactly my choice did not present any obvious problems. How little I knew. Collect the money, put it in the bank with the various cheques and bank drafts and off to the next dream we go. It's easy, or so I thought! However, along with a box of cash came nods, winks and whispered warnings that putting cash into any bank would invite all sorts of problems in a country where money laundering was rife. No problem I thought just get a safety deposit box where I could keep it until I could get set up in my next destination, the Limousin in central France.

Whilst my bundle of cash seemed substantial to me, it was in reality but a drop in the ocean compared with many transactions that were happening all the time in Spain. When I inquired about safety deposit boxes, I was told that there was a considerable waiting list of some years in Spain, unless one was considerably wealthy or a Hollywood star. For the next few weeks until our departure from Spain we stayed with friends with the constant worry that locals accustomed to property deals would assume that we were sitting on a little nest egg, hidden under our beds. Every time I went out, I would return and rush to my little stash to check it was still intact.

With great relief ,me and Dave left for France in a hire car a few weeks later, with most of our belongings and a bag or two of cash. Other Brits had regaled us with tales of French border patrols stopping cars looking for laundered money. Explaining that it had come from a property sale would not hold much weight when the paper trail from the transaction was all but invisible. Confiscation would be the likely outcome. A two day journey with Dave where every coffee, petrol and toilet stop involved keeping 'eyes on the car' was not without stress. Neither was taking the A roads either side of the border to avoid toll booths and checkpoints. Selling property in rural Spain certainly made one feel uncomfortable, if not criminal. Wayne was long back in the UK by then and found it hilarious that someone like me who would feel criminalised by a parking ticket had to take the 'dodgy' route to France.

There followed several happy years in France, having bought my piece of land and Barns in the Limousin, with a wonderfully less complicated property purchase. I finally had a place that was my own and what I thought would be enough cash to develop my dream. I got as far as getting plans drawn up and planning permission before it slowly dawned on me that my financial resources were never going to achieve my dream. My plan, I still believe, could have been successful and financially sound. A respite centre for young people in the care system with a music studio, all for a weekly per-child cost less than local authorities were paying Independent Fostering Agencies in the UK. A week or two in the respite centre could prevent a placement breakdown in a local authority foster placement, rather than the all too familiar scenario of a placement breakdown leading to another expensive placement with an Independent Foster Agency. In a nutshell, a positive intervention in a struggling placement could prevent yet another damaging move for a child and also save an enormous long-term cost of an IFA placement. Foster carers and foster children often just need a break to avoid a complete breakdown.

Unfortunately, Social Services tend to see respite as moving the child to another carer for a few days or weeks, which often only amplifies the problem for the child. The child goes into school the next day having to face questions as to why they are staying in a different house, when in fact school may well be a big part of the child's current problem. That feeling of being shipped out to another family when nobody is really understanding what the problem is, just adds to the problem. As an experienced carer, I know that overworked Social Workers when beset by crisis after crisis involving multiple cases can often miss the early signs of a placement breakdown in a previously settled placement.

In most cases placement breakdowns could be avoided by better Social Work supervision and earlier intervention. Respite, by moving a child a few streets away or across town may take the pressure off the carers but does little for the child. For them, it just feels like a punishment. Having a respite centre where a child can go for a creative break, aimed at improving their well-being makes sense on so many levels, except the one that usually matters for Social Work Administrators, and that is COST! The problem as ever is that the assessment of cost only looks at the short term costs rather than long term savings, investment and planning. The constant fight to stay within any given year's budget means that long term planning usually takes second place in any decision. Suggest a respite centre to support foster placements and managers will say that it would see them incur a much higher weekly cost than would a temporary move to a standard foster carer. Using a respite centre two weeks a year to maintain a foster placement makes sound financial sense. The alternative is the placement breaks down and the child is moved to the private sector. The cost difference may be an increase tenfold in the price charged to the local authority and the child will likely then stay long term in the private sector.

My view has always been that Respite/Alternative Care should be a part of a consistent wellbeing plan for all children in the care system, rather than a crisis intervention response. Long term costs would then be greatly reduced, as less foster placements would break down. IFA's generally thrive, because the profit potential and opportunity in childcare for them is created due to poor management, planning and supervision by Social Services departments as a result of crisis intervention. Supporting Local Authority Foster carers better with well-planned respite can massively reduce overall annual costs. It would also reduce the unnecessary harm done to countless children from too many placement breakdowns and moves.

Admittedly the plan is based on improving the overall cost effectiveness of fostering provision in the UK. That is something that I've been campaigning for since the last millennium, so I won't hold my breath, but I do live in hope that the penny will drop one of these days. A peaceful haven where young people could briefly leave behind the daily chaos of their lives, have a lot of fun and be creatively challenged on lifestyle and wellbeing issues is a dream for others now. Teaching children to cook, creatively and more healthily, was part of the plan. Using fresh ,rather than frozen produce, without an over reliance on microwaves whilst meeting the crucial requirements of young people. It would work for fostered children and those moving on to independent living.

After decades of caring for teenage boys, I had learned that teaching them to cook was not an easy job for any Carer, never mind one like myself whose signature dishes were either Quiche or frozen pizza with oven chips. Why would any of my boys have time to spend in the kitchen for anything more than a brief microwave blast or a pot noodle stop? My consolation in the now buried dream in France was that if I had succeeded in setting it up then I would have not returned to fostering and thereby missed the opportunity of looking after some incredible young people.

My undeveloped French property has finally been sold, but my respite centre for young people in care will need a lottery win and another somewhat younger dreamer to emerge. The dream in fact died very slowly over a couple of years ,but the death of my father was the turning point. Initially I had wanted to dedicate the Respite Centre to him, but I was drawn back to England by the thought of my mum being alone without Dad. It didn't happen overnight, but one week's visit to England became two weeks the next time and carried on increasing until without actually making a conscious decision me and Dave were back for good. Mum had other family around her, but I was the one best able to support her with mine and Dave's continued presence. Life moved on and there was no longer room for my European dream, Mum's needs became my priority for her remaining years just as I had promised Dad

Chapter 10

Life-changing days don't come along that often and most often they tend to be unexpected. As we set up the recording equipment for our music workshop in the rather dour community centre, I certainly wasn't expecting anything special. A room that reminded me of my old junior school was hardly inspiring. The building we were in was in fact an old Victorian workhouse, so it had no doubt seen its fair share of misery. Just a few tables and chairs scattered around the large room with a very high ceiling, which would not be great acoustically. The windows were too high to see anything at all outside, except some grey clouds. It reminded me of childhood days spent longing to get out of an oppressive classroom. Hopefully, the children about to arrive for one of our music workshop days would not feel that same sense of boredom and confinement that was triggering such negative memories for me.

Whilst my colleague Steve set up the sound equipment, my boy David was having flashbacks to his own schooldays. In his case though, they were happy memories of often misbehaving during chaotic lessons in his boarding school. It was behaviour that most days resulted in his banishment to the headmaster's office. He always loved to see the headmaster for a chat and an apology. The head would invariably send him to the quiet room in the old Manor House, where he could play pool until lunchtime. He would then be nicely positioned to get to the front of the queue for lunch. First to be served food and then first to return for seconds made for a good day for Dave. He didn't get any qualifications, but his tearful apologies for tantrums and fighting were A-level standard and generally got exactly what he wanted. A classroom fight with his adversary Philip (aka 'squid-eye'), followed by a chat with the head, then some time on the pool table and a nice bit of lunch. A perfect day for Dave. If it got out of hand, he would get a day's suspension and my dad would drive 40 miles to pick him up. A drive home with his beloved Pops, knowing that Nan would have a nice, cooked tea waiting for him was adequate compensation for a day's suspension.

Back to the workshop and Dave was eagerly awaiting today's students. His infectious optimism, as usual, dispelled any negative thoughts that I was having. The mission for the day was to work with a small group of young people from Foster Care. Our, by then tried and tested, formula involved helping the children write some words and then recording them with musical assistance from my colleague Steve. By the end of the day, we would have a rough edit for them to listen to and then in a few days, we would deliver a final edit of their own music track to them. All was designed to inspire the children and hopefully help raise their self-esteem.

Myself, Dave and Steve Redman were collectively known as 'The Musicworks' and delivered workshops in both the UK and Germany, where Steve had enjoyed musical success as a singer in the 1990s. Over our years in Spain and France, Dave had adapted seamlessly from foster son into the role of my wingman. The children who were about to arrive at our workshop were the first fostered children that I had encountered since leaving fostering when we moved to Spain. Dave had already been a foster brother to some particularly challenging children and survived them all. He, like me, had missed my time in Fostering and relished the opportunity to meet some more foster kids again.

As for my colleague Steve, well, what can I say? Singer, songwriter, producer and performer. In the 1990's as 'Sir Prize' Steve had a successful chart career in Germany. Having moved back to the UK, he had linked up with my former music associates Freshblood, Together we set up The Musicworks project in 2007. From the day we met I don't think we've ever argued, so collaborating has always been a joy.

We had plenty of workshop experience, so on that day I think it was safe to say neither the participants nor the extremely dreary venue would be likely to phase us. My role in our workshops could be likened to a learning support teacher. Basically, I was there to help any young people who were struggling or potentially disruptive. Amongst this group my initial observations were that there were two potentially fractious individuals, Leslie and Marcus. Leslie, fair-haired, smiling and personable, was the dominant one and very keen to participate and ingratiate himself with Steve and myself. Marcus, on the other hand, presented with a face half hidden behind a wild thatch of hair and with eyes as wild as his hair. He looked fiery, inquisitive and unpredictable and was most certainly irritated by Leslie. First impressions, as they say, can last. His eyes seemed to never stop moving, as if he were assessing everything and everyone in the room. He constantly fidgeted and I occasionally caught his gaze. His response each time was an angry glare that screamed "f*** off". Eye contact was apparently not his thing.

All went pretty much to plan in the session until Marcus had a proper meltdown and stormed out of the building. The attention that Leslie was demanding was just too much for him. One of the social workers then went outside to offer some calming support for Marcus. Sadly, it was not the sort of attention that Marcus needed. Attempted hugs and platitudes just fanned the flames of his rage. She was responding exactly as he had expected, thus allowing him full licence to vent his anger. The situation quickly moved to an end-game scenario insofar as his workshop participation was concerned.

As an experienced mentor I could possibly have rescued the situation were it not for the social worker's well-intentioned, but so typically textbook social work intervention. This boy probably had too much previous experience of such interventions. The irritation and annoyance caused by this textbook approach was something that I absolutely identified with. All too often in my career, the use of instinct and unpredictability have worked for me in difficult situations with young people who had been brought up in the care system. Over the decades, I have come to appreciate the importance of training, but in my most humble opinion, applying it too literally can often be exposed by care-experienced young people. Many have grown to be adept at recognising, outmanoeuvring and overcoming this social-work style approach. Social workers, however well-read on the latest social work theories and practice, would do well to remember that whilst social work may be their nine to five jobs their young clients have a lived-in 24/7 experience, which can outrank and often outwit them. For me, a 24/7 lived-in experience is one reason why a Foster Carers approach can often work better. It can make a Foster Carer a stronger adversary in coping with a child's challenging behaviour as well as a stronger advocate for helping a looked-after child. Unsurprisingly, for me on that day in Yate, the textbook approach meant that Marcus's participation in the workshop was at an end.

Personally speaking, I was unaccustomed to such sudden and abject failure, so I decided to stay outside with Marcus until his carer arrived to pick him up. In his eyes I could see the resignation and frustration of a young man who was clearly accustomed to days like these. If Marcus's eyes could speak, then the angry "F*** Off" had now been replaced with a desperate "For F**ks Sake". All I could do was to try and give him hope that there might be another chance sometime and let him spill out his frustration. Sometimes, just listening seems wholly inadequate, but it was all that I felt I could offer. I really sensed that we shared a mutual feeling of helplessness and disappointment as he was taken away by his carer that day and in that moment a real connection was all too briefly sparked and then quickly extinguished.

I have certainly learned after decades of mentoring that sometimes the briefest of connections between mentor and mentee can spark a flame. Inspiration, as I have mentioned, can only take a moment but can last a lifetime. Sitting on that uncomfortable stone wall, looking at this forlorn, isolated child being removed, though did not come with any positive thoughts or reassurance. Only years later did I realise that I had left him with a lasting impression as in fact he had also left me. I wish I had known at the time, although I doubt that it would have made any difference.

After he was driven away, I returned to what was to be an otherwise successful workshop. His departure though left me with a real feeling of disappointment that day. I don't like giving up, especially when it was not my decision to do so. Despite whatever good feelings those kids got out of the day, for me, it was clouded with a sense of disappointment. Young people do tend to be conditioned to certain behaviours when familiar adults, such as Social Workers, are around and Marcus was no exception. With all due respect, I often found that workshops went smoother when the participants were not inhibited or influenced by the presence of those familiar adults.

I will admit that the lost look in the boy's eyes had taken me back to my days of Fostering. I did miss those days. The feelings of disappointment and frustration that stayed with me after that workshop in Yate led to me deciding several months later to return to Fostering. In fact, I was to join the very same Independent Fostering Agency that had commissioned our workshop on that day.

Maybe it was fate and was meant to be. Who knows? It had never been in my plans to foster again after returning to England. I suppose though that my plans for the 'Respite Centre' in France were not that far removed from Fostering. For all the massive disappointment of not fulfilling my respite dream in Spain or France, the knowledge that I was now able to spend the last years of my mum's life being ever closer to her easily outweighed any regrets about returning to the UK. There again, in the years that have passed since returning to fostering, there have been countless adventures, memories and special people that have enriched both mine and Dave's lives. This book will share a few of those experiences, but more than that, will I hope, show some of the joy and love that a life in fostering has blessed me with. Maybe it will even convince a few readers to consider fostering themselves. Simply put, it can be a life changing experience for both carers and children.

Getting back to my story and as all Foster Carers will know, the process of becoming a foster carer takes many months with endless checks, reports and interviews. A full 15 months had elapsed from the day of the music workshop in Yate before I actually became a Foster Carer again. It was like I had never been away and within three months of once again dealing with curfews, courts and the Youth Justice system a referral came my way for some weekend respite for a young man. I have to say that I was far from disappointed when I realised it was to be young Marcus. I never did like 'unfinished business' and this was a rare opportunity of a second chance for both of us.

A few days later, a considerably larger version of Marcus, with those wild eyes and an even more substantial mop of unkempt hair, literally exploded through my front door. Seeing me, totally unexpectedly, he was momentarily taken aback and, although not fond of surprises, was not able to contain his excitement. This time, there was no Leslie and no place in the world that he would rather be. Marcus had been told that as a season ticket holder at Bristol City, I would probably be taking him to a football game that weekend but I had made other plans. Excited though he was at the prospect of seeing a game, his disappointment was extremely short-lived however when I told him that we were going to Gloucester to attend a Graffiti and Rap event that some friends of mine were organising.

Now Gloucester, whilst not perhaps the first place that springs to mind regarding Graffiti and Rap, had a healthy scene itself going, albeit on a much smaller scale than its close neighbour Bristol. The spectre of Fred West remains as Gloucester's most famous recent citizen unfortunately, although on a more positive note, it is now home to John Nation, the Godfather of Bristol Graffiti and his other half Cath.

Two inner city Youth Centres in the late 1980s had been responsible for my introduction to the Hip-Hop culture that has been core to my life ever since. Many years later ,on that day in 2013, when Marcus reappeared in my life that enduring connection led me and young Marcus to the 'Known Rhymers' event at Teague's Bar in Gloucester.

In 2013, 'Known Rhymers' was in fact a Gloucester Music and Graffiti day for local street artists and rappers. Dan and Darren, stalwarts of the Gloucester scene and their 'Cold Case Records' were the organisers, as always, trying to put on a day to remember for local artists and rappers. They must have had many successes over the years, but looking back could never have expected to put on an event that would be life-changing for a neglected and frustrated teenager with Asperger's. A boy who had recently started writing down his thoughts and observations on life, but who on that day walked into that pub in Gloucester with me in search of some fun. When Marcus left a couple of hours later, he was empowered with a dream. Despite many personal setbacks for Marcus. in the following years it was a dream that just would not die.

A trip to McDonalds and a graffiti and rap event was probably close to the perfect day out for Marcus. He came alive, surrounded by all those talented people, although for all his enthusiasm, I too could never have imagined that it was to be such a significant day for this unique young man. The Graf guys kicked off the afternoon session and Marcus was enthralled, although a little disappointed that it was not an interactive event, as he was itching to spray some paint. Close observation was needed on my part to make sure that he didn't acquire any free samples of spray paint from the participants.

Later on, that day the rap took over and for Marcus, the real inspiration began. Happily telling all and sundry that he should be allowed to go on stage, there were one or two casting irritated looks towards him. On the whole though, the rap guys were welcoming to Marcus and happily shared advice and suggestions. It's fair to say that he was more than a touch reluctant to leave that evening, but I was also there to introduce a young Bristol talent B-Dee to the Gloucester stage. Once B-Dee had performed it was time for us to leave despite Marcus's pleas to stay.

It took at least an hour to get home that evening, Just me and Marcus in the car having the sort of conversation that in my experience tends to be the norm when dealing with a youngster with Asperger's. My experience of Aspies was not extensive however, but it was a conversation that neither of us would ever forget. In the following years, other Aspies were to come my way, each utterly fascinating to me, but, at the same time, regarded as disconnected loners by the majority of people that they encountered.

For those that don't know about Asperger's, it is said to be a high-functioning type of Autism, something that has often been identified in successful people and unique talents. Asperger's has been linked with people such as Einstein, Beethoven and rapper Eminem. Aspies often find an interest that they are able to focus on and develop to a high level, from Mathematics genius' to Musical virtuoso's. The Aspies that I have had the pleasure of caring for have provided me with amazing conversations, usually about their interests. They tend to develop an extensive and specialised knowledge of their favoured interests and pastimes. As with Marcus, they can often be loners, who with little encouragement, can talk on favoured subjects endlessly in the most intricate detail. Be warned that if you express an interest, you will unlock a Pandora's box of Knowledge that in most cases you will probably think you really never needed to know.

On that journey back from Gloucester, we had an extended conversation about the exciting events of the day, but also about time travel, an interest that had evolved from his fascination with the TV series Dr Who. He started quoting Doctor Who speeches from years before he was even born and talked enthusiastically of his favourite Doctors. Ten was his favourite and remains so. Mine too! I guess many people would yawn at the prospect of a long conversation about a TV sci-fi programme, but for me it was an opening into his understanding and his interests and was a real opportunity to engage. For his part, I later discovered it was the wonderment of meeting an adult who would not only listen to him and admire his knowledge but who could challenge some of the theories that emanated from the Doctor Who storylines. To then take those theories and expand on them or challenge them was exactly the type of conversations that Marcus had always longed for. For my part it took me into the head of a young person with Asperger's which was stimulating and enlightening in equal measure.

For me, at that time it was initially just a fun conversation that became something more. For Marcus, after being blown away by the event I had just taken him to, it was a confirmation that here was an adult who maybe, just maybe, could actually understand what being Marcus was like. Not for one moment did I realise that I had just made a connection with this unique individual that would convince him that I would play a big part in his future. For the next five years, he would continue, (despite numerous setbacks and personal problems) to hold on to the dream that was born that day in Gloucester. I never considered that this quirky, awkward young man would play such a significant role in my future, but he had no such doubts.

It was during our conversations that Marcus suddenly changed tack and announced that he was bisexual. Although totally unexpected, I gave a very low-key reaction as I suspected it had been announced to gauge my reaction and possibly shock me. My suspicions have more recently been confirmed and made Marcus much more at ease with me. With no great reaction from me, the conversation returned quickly to time travel and we didn't revisit the subject of his sexuality that day or for some years after.

I was a mentor, fairly skilled at probing and questioning, at motivation and occasionally inspiration, but on that day, I was inclined to let the conversation go any way Marcus chose, as maybe selfishly I was enjoying him talking excitedly on so many different but fascinating subjects. In hindsight, I can see why this boy was to become so interested in me because rather than trying to shut him up, I was actually encouraging him to talk and talk and talk. Marcus knew the journey back would soon be over and it was like he was rushing through seemingly random subjects. As with our first meeting 18 months earlier, Marcus's eyes gave him away. Gone was that dejected and despondent look. This time they were clearly happy eyes, almost dancing with pleasure it seemed, as he rushed to impart reams of knowledge to this willing listener.

Had I been Marcus' full-time carer, I would probably have probed a little more on his sexuality and talked about his current situation, but as he was only with me for the weekend, I decided to leave questions for another time. Another time turned out to be five years later, but a lot was to happen before that. When the Gloucester day was over, what followed was a relatively quiet Sunday. Marcus was visibly still buzzing from the previous day's excitement. Aside from actually being allowed to get on the mic or spray some paint, it had been almost a perfect day for him.

Life at his Carers would sadly never be the same again. I had inadvertently unleashed a lyrical beast who would, over the following 18 months, grow increasingly resentful of his current Carers. He did have a few weekends of respite with me over that time, which probably held him together, but that day in Gloucester was when the clock on the end of foster care started ticking for him. Unbeknown to me, he dreamed of being permanently placed with me, so when I left the Fostering company 18 months later, his hopes were dashed. Before that however there would be more weekends and experiences that would only reinforce his desire to become a master of words.

How little I knew or realised at that time of the effect that I had on him. I am used to imparting pearls of wisdom from my life experiences to young people, whether useful or not. The difference with Marcus is that he made a memory necklace out of those pearls and kept them for constant reference and reassurance. In hindsight, I do feel for his Foster Carers who really did their best for him. Ultimately though, they just could not compete with the magical world that I had now opened up to him.

Marcus had been totally inspired by the Saturday event. Inspiration is something one hopes to give but can come from any source. It's very much one of those 'right time and right place' things. Sometimes a person just needs something to give their life purpose or hope. For some it is finding God for others it is finding another passion. Marcus had found his passion and nobody and nothing would come between him and his new love for many years to come.

Compared to Marcus, it had been so much easier for me as a young man because my parents were always my safety net, something Marcus had never had. My good fortune was having a father who was always there for me, with advice and support on any big decisions that

I needed to make. There was never any criticism or judgement, if he thought I was wrong and he never said, "I told you so" when I messed up. Until I started to foster, I had never appreciated just how important that was or how lucky I was. My dad showed me such a perfect example of how a father should be. Never having my own children, I would probably never have been able to use what he taught me had I not become a Foster Carer. Without my parents I would never have had the knowledge or ability to foster. Fostering became my raison d'etre. It has made my life meaningful and worthwhile and given me so much. It was effectively my parents gift to me.

After Gloucester Marcus had found a faith, just as his foster Carers had hoped, but unfortunately for them it was not the God that they hoped for, although they had planted that seed which would flower many years later. His god was now Eminem and that could never sit well with such devout Christians. Not unsurprisingly, they would do all they could to divert and discourage this music, as it was so much at odds with their beliefs. At least that was how it seemed to Marcus. He had found something to love, a place where he could do more than merely exist. He had a new self-belief and self-awareness that gave him the freedom to grow. In me, he saw someone who believed in him, encouraged him but most importantly someone who, in his opinion, actually listened to him. His carers had become like parents to him but he had probably outgrown them through no fault of their own. If anything, unwittingly it was because of me.

I have always found Marcus a fascinating character, but it's probably fair to say that few other people have really stopped to listen to him. His demeanour doesn't encourage people to linger or get too close. Foster Carers like me have to deal with all the daily teenage trauma which can sometimes distance them from their troubled teenagers. As his respite Carer, I had a very different role, where conflict was mostly absent and his visits to me were like holiday breaks away from all the day-to-day issues and problems. I had a massive advantage over his full-time carers, but that in itself is part of why respite can be useful. Ironically, although my respite centre had failed to materialise, my home had now become Marcus's own little respite centre.

Chapter 11

Marcus had spent much of his life gathering information without any real processing of it. On occasions, his brain would be like a personal Google with a massive database of random information just waiting to be shared. More often than not, people would be bored rather than impressed with his outpourings of random facts. It was like having a library in a world of illiterates. When I came into his life, he at last had someone who he felt was worthy of sharing it with. For every bit of advice and philosophy I gave him, he would return it ten-fold. He had a depth of knowledge and ideas that I would expect to hear from a University student, rather than an angry and disconnected child in the Care System. His ability to dissect and analyse arguments, discussions and theories made for some very interesting conversations.

Getting back to that first respite visit and Marcus was to be with me until Monday morning when his school taxi was due to pick him up. Before that we still had to navigate a Sunday without any plans. A typical Sunday back at his full-time foster placement would mean being, in his words, "dragged off" by his carers to the local church. Today was to be a church free Sunday and Marcus was savouring the prospect. Any fears I had that Sunday would be a massive anti-climax for him were quickly dispelled. He had my total attention and that was everything that he wanted.

Whilst Marcus was still reliving the previous day's activities, I was more taken with the multi-layered conversations that I had experienced on the journey with him. Conversations that seemed to awaken long-dormant parts of my brain. It was like a light being switched on for me, suddenly finding myself introduced to an Aspie's personal world, so different from my own.

Stepping into this Aspies world was an interesting new challenge for me. It was like discovering a new game, where I needed a new skill set in order to play it. In the years since then I have learned to play the game with Marcus, progressing through different levels of awareness. There is no comfort zone because by nature Marcus doesn't exist in comfort zones, as his brain can't stop and turn off his thoughts. He likes to stay on the front foot and conversations with him are more like duels. Occasionally, I can catch him off guard, but that invariably brings a quick riposte, denying me the opportunity to follow up. Mistakes are rare though and Marcus could challenge Boris Johnson for effective distraction techniques in fending off difficult questions or counter arguments.

On occasions, his excitement and impatience when talking with me has revealed more than he intended. He has a speed of thought that can however effectively change the direction of any conversation as soon as he becomes uncomfortable. His years of isolation have made him reluctant to trust anyone and I became the guinea pig in his social interaction experiments. Actually, I think probably more of a lab-rat from his more arrogant viewpoint.

Back then I was still learning much of this. I had spent the previous months working with a severely criminally inclined young man. Life, it has to be said, had become somewhat mundane and predictable, even with regular police visits. The young man in question had been curfewed by the court and then electronically tagged. You might think that this would actually make things easier for his foster carer, but the reverse was true. I had unsuccessfully tried to convince the court against tagging him as I was a single carer. The magistrate really didn't get my argument as a single carer and was happy to effectively tag me for the next few months, as I had to be home constantly in order to monitor the situation. Being single, I had no partner to carry the load with me. That lad's placement did eventually come to a sudden end a while after the tag was removed. He went through my room one night and found the spare key for my car. Lipstick on the passenger visor mirror and a major adjustment to my car seat position alerted me the next morning that others had been in my car overnight. Justice was unusually swift. It was actually justice for other misdemeanours committed in the days prior to his late-night speed-dating in my car. By the next evening, he was locked up in a secure children's unit in South Wales, never to return to me. A charming lad, but one that fortunately was taken away before damaging my relationship with a new set of neighbours.

As with many of the young criminals that I have encountered, he had run rings around an all too lenient youth justice system. The last chance saloon finally closed that day after so many visits. The absolute shock on his face was palpable when his fate dawned on him. Unfortunately, all that his incarceration ultimately achieved was to return him to society a more hardened and far more capable criminal. He was undoubtedly a menace to society, but for those months with me he was 'my menace'. Nicos was an immensely charming young man, with an unfortunate penchant for crime. He thus became one of the 'ones that got away' in my Fostering career and I understand he went on to become a career criminal. After three months of living under what seemed like house arrest, I was finally able to leave the house between the hours of 6pm and 6am without worries. My social life briefly returned. Then Marcus came back.

This respite weekend for Marcus interrupted a brief spell of no foster boys. It had though, reawakened my mentoring instincts. When he left on Monday morning in his taxi, I was already wondering as to whether he might return or not. My empty foster beds could be quickly filled thus making more respite weekends unlikely. As it worked out, I was to get a couple of fairly short placements in the following months, so opportunities arose for more weekend visits from Marcus.

He next returned to me about six weeks later carrying a bulging backpack stretched to its limit, a beaming smile and wearing a velvet jacket and bow tie. He looked as if he had just stepped out of the Tardis and promptly announced that he had something to show me. Wasting no time on pleasantries, he proceeded to remove numerous exercise books from the aforementioned backpack. The books contained his raps, his 'writtens' as he called them along with numerous scraps of paper. I laughed to myself thinking about how his teachers were probably thinking that he was busying himself with schoolwork when in fact his focus was on writing rap lyrics. Yes, it was English of a kind I suppose but not so much William Shakespeare as Slim Shady.

John Lennon had been the inspiration for so much of my life. I loved his honest and direct way of putting a point across, whether lyrically or politically. The sheer rawness of his first solo album and the brilliance of Imagine. So often Lennon seemed to express an emotion exactly mirroring a feeling within me. In that way, I could relate to Marcus and his Eminem fascination. The two of us were from different era's and different worlds and yet just sparked each other's imagination and intellects. Our conversations constantly probed and challenged each other. Over the years, I'd had many young adversaries trying to outwit me and occasionally doing so with streetwise cunning and stealth, or on a rare occasion with a violent response. This was different, this was not about a boy trying to gain some advantage by deceit or distraction, but a boy who had an armoury of knowledge that he wanted to display and test with a worthy challenger.

This was education in a way that schools could not hope to achieve. Knowledge was the power that interested Marcus, but no school or teacher that he had encountered up until that time had gained his respect, nor aroused his interest like me . He was like a sponge absorbing information and yet school was passing him by, seemingly without any recognition of his learning abilities. How many young people like Marcus pass through the education system unnoticed except for their behaviour? Too many I fear.

Their talents are neglected, because the young person cannot and will not conform to a system that blatantly ignores them. How ironic that we search the solar system for aliens when all the time they live among us, invisible to our perceptions. For these young people are like an alien culture that our society spends little time trying to understand. Yet among them are fascinating and spectacular individuals, who could really benefit us all, if given the opportunity. For every Asperger success story, there are no doubt countless others that remain in their own worlds devoid of human interaction.

It was six weeks again before Marcus returned, bursting into the house like an Exocet missile. The warhead on this targeted missile was undoubtedly the box file full of lyrics that he was clutching as if his life depended upon it. The intended target was naturally me. The target was acquired within seconds of entering the building. The next hour of my life was duly cancelled whilst Marcus described and demonstrated how his lyrical ability was developing. "Eminem your days are numbered," I thought to myself. "Step aside now or get swept away by this new phenomenon."

If I had any doubt about how long Marcus would retain his interest in Rhymes and lyrics it had been dispelled by this third visit. This I now knew was not a passing interest for Marcus. It was even overtaking his beloved Doctor Who and Harry Potter as his top interest. He, of course, continued those interests with a passion, but this was different. This was for him a way forward that would not involve abandoning the pleasures discovered in his childhood. At the same time, this new passion could satisfy the demands that his journey into adolescence demanded. His love of Doctor Who, Harry Potter and indeed Lego had marked him in the weird and geeky category for his peers, but Rap was a medium that gave him a whole new standing in the world.

He was under no illusion that his vast knowledge and interest in Wizards and Time Lords alone would never enable him to compete on a level stage with other teenagers. He recognised the challenge that puberty brought forward, that he had to walk out of the shadows of fantasy adventures and prepare for a battle of his own. A battle of his life and for his life and a chance to, once and for all, dismiss those sneering, arrogant and dismissive peers that had caused him so much pain growing up. He had been no real threat to them, but they had appeared to be a constant threat to him. Now he could rise and challenge them and lyrically destroy them along with anyone else that had ever doubted him. Marcus was preparing himself for war. No prisoners would be taken and no mercy shown. Like a young Luke Skywalker, his time was coming and he had absolutely no fear of confrontation or the fight ahead.

I recall taking Marcus out to lunch with my mother and family one day. She was quite taken with him, if a little confused, partly due to her deteriorating hearing. He thrived on being in this social setting with other elders of my family and a chance to impress these elders with his knowledge.

When talk turned to religious beliefs, Mum asked as to what his religious persuasion was. "I'm a Jedi," he exclaimed to my mum. Her long and eventful life had certainly not involved watching a single moment of any *Star Wars* film. After a short pause she replied with "Jedi, well I haven't heard of that one".

Mum turned to her younger sister Eileen for reassurance. Eileen, with her own hearing issues, looked equally bemused by this talk of a new religion. As the food arrived a puzzled look was exchanged between them, and a mutual shrug of the 'Woodrow girls' shoulders as other family members struggled to contain their amusement at the two sisters discussing the 'Jedi' religion. A religion that had somehow evaded their combined 170 years of knowledge and experience.

The Woodrow girls, Nita and Eileen, had survived the worst that Hitler could throw at Bristol during the Blitz. Early mornings they had emerged from the bomb shelter after nighttime air raids to see neighbouring properties raised to the ground and fires raging across the city. Day by day the city surrounding them was being reduced to rubble. Their family's home was in the upper rooms of Chilcott's Jewellers, a prestigious Georgian building in Park Street in central Bristol. The upper rooms were for the building's Caretaker, my Grandfather Fred Woodrow and his family. The Woodrow girls including elder sister Rene had watched as their young brother John ran around the rubble picking up spent incendiaries in the manner that today's children sit in front of screens picking up trophies for completing levels on Xbox games. Different times that bred a generation of the most resilient people. Our modern day anxieties of Low Battery, No signal and Food fads, pale into insignificance compared to a generation where being alive in the morning was not a given.

Had Mum or Eileen ever had an opportunity to watch any of the *Star Wars* films, then I suspect that they would have immediately rushed off to the kitchen to put the kettle on for a cuppa and a chat, well before the opening credits had finished rolling. I guess, in their own way, their generation were the 'Jedi warriors', refusing to be intimidated by an evil empire. I never once heard any of them talk about having anxiety issues, despite living through the darkest of times. Growing up in war times defined that generation and gave them an appreciation of life that would be sadly lost on today's generation.

Meanwhile, for Marcus, the lightsabre, which his carers had bought him had now been replaced by the pen and pad. Obi-Wan Kenobi had no doubt evolved into 'yours truly' as this young Jedi was ready to announce his assault on the Empire. The Empire, at that time of course, was controlled not by Darth Vader but by Alice, his Foster Carer and her Stormtrooper husband, Andrew. Behind them was an army of Social Workers, enough to quell the challenge from any disruptive looked-after child. Marcus though, was not to be easily deterred nor diverted from his lyrical dream, no matter what the strength of the opposition. His carers were to become acceptable collateral damage of his quest.

A third respite was completed with a mixture of Minecraft and Doctor Who, but all things naturally taking second place to his lyrical doodling. For me it was more of those unusual conversations, full of ideas, theories and opinions, where Marcus loved to joust with me. Dave and Marcus really got on well too, in a totally different way, but with a strong mutual respect. Dave of course was crucial for distracting Marcus at times where I had to do other things or just needed a break from the intensity of Aspergic conversations.

Dave would be ever vigilant and skilled at avoiding socially embarrassing situations with Marcus and always confident of not being challenged.

On one of our regular morning visits to Costa Coffee, Dave had felt compelled to give his customary look of disapproval at Marcus, who was collecting as many sugar sachets as possible before proceeding to empty them one by one down his throat. Dave would thereafter see to it that sugar sachets were always quickly moved away from Marcus on future visits to any coffee shops. Anyone else doing that would likely have witnessed one of Marcus's meltdowns, but Dave was always excused from such criticism.

That particular July visit subsequently turned out to be the final one of the year for Marcus, as just days later another permanent resident was to be moved to my house, ending any chance of further respite. The next six months were to be an extremely turbulent time in my household, as was also the case in Marcus's placement, as he grew increasingly frustrated and angry.

I was talked into accepting a placements of two 16 year old boys, who already had some history together at school. Their school was shocked to learn that I had taken on two of their most troubled pupils. Taking two children of the same age usually brings added complications and this certainly did. David was marked out as an easy target by them, as they started working together. He became increasingly uneasy as it was all purposely done out of sight of me. Despite expressing my concerns to the fostering agency, all I got back was a dismissive get on with it attitude. That my concerns were ignored was disappointing, but other carers were expressing similar reservations about the support given by the agency, as well as behaviour that we felt was bordering on bullying towards us carers. I became increasingly concerned that a more intimate relationship had developed between the boys and how they were working together was becoming intimidating for David. It was almost Christmas and I was insisting that they be split up and one of them moved. I was told to get through Christmas, which resulted in the most unpleasant Christmas I have ever experienced. By New Year they finally agreed to move one of the boys and the whole thing became far messier than if they had acted sooner.

Early in the New Year with a placement now empty Marcus returned and was able to realise the first part of his dream. As a Christmas present, I had promised him a visit to our newly set up recording studio and the chance to record his first track. His excitement probably registered on the Richter scale and suddenly the six months of frustration melted away.

The day duly arrived and went smoothly, considering his excitement. He was new to the mic but not at all overawed by the situation. He savoured every moment and handled everything without a hint of a meltdown. A track 'It's my life' was recorded and the plan was to have it ready by his next respite. Recording his first track was a major milestone and gave him confirmation of his abilities. Unfortunately, being a looked-after child in the care system brings with it certain restrictions and obstacles that other young people do not encounter. For a first effort it was good and my music project, The Musicworks, wanted to put it on our website as well as Facebook and other social media. Whilst it was never intended to release it commercially it was an excellent example of our work with young people. Being in the Care System it was deemed by the Social Worker not appropriate to publish his track ,so he was only able to demonstrate his abilities to a few people close to him. Over two years were to pass before Marcus reached 18 and we were finally able to release the track to the public, by which time much had changed, especially for Marcus.

Back in 2014, young Marcus was flying off the back of the studio session and another successful weekend of respite. Following on from the weekend, Marcus did make another couple of weekend visits, but clearly all was not well in his foster placement, although he was still somehow hanging in there.

On one of the final weekend visits, we took my iPad and made a video to accompany the track he had recorded with us. The location was a local private railway station, complete with cafe and a Tardis which had been converted into a toilet. The Tardis was of course the main attraction and Marcus naturally was keen to sample the full experience of this Tardis before commencing the video shoot.

Considering the limitations of the equipment, myself, Dave and Marcus had some fun and got a passable video from the day, although like the track itself, it would be a long time before anyone other than close friends could watch it. It's good to look back on now, but I still feel the frustration watching 16-year-old Marcus and thinking how nice it would have been to have shown it to more people at the time and, most importantly, how good for his self-esteem. Sometimes the Care System can be so unwieldy and discriminating and incredibly inflexible. For Marcus, whilst he loved having made the video, the frustration of doing something like that but then to not be able to show it off must have been immense.

We did however make a return visit to Gloucester that summer with my amazing friend Liz Wilson. Probably the nearest to a true soulmate that I have ever known, Liz was a larger than life character, known throughout the world of Social Work. She was more fun and more widely loved than anyone I have ever known. She had I think retired a few times but was talked into coming back each time. She could mediate any dispute and she was a trusted confidante to many more than just me. As a foster carer, there had been so many occasions when I needed her advice to negotiate the minefield of Social Work procedure.

Back then I had seconded her to join me at a new foster agency I was joining. They were desperately in need of someone with her experience. She had been training University students in Social Work for some years but had many years' of experience prior as a Senior Social Worker. In the early days, Liz would have been one of the few black women to rise through the ranks of Social Work. She was a groundbreaking, earth shattering, trail blazer who took on all adversaries with a gushing charm but steely determination. Liz didn't take prisoners but her victims often ended up becoming supporters. Anyone at a meeting where Liz was present would expect her to turn up with carrier bags full of homemade cakes and treats, which would dissolve even the most resolute opponent.

The foster agency in Gloucester was newly set up by Neil, a lovely man who had made his money in property and had recently diversified into Foster Care with hedge fund backing. That backing was ultimately to cause its demise. Unfortunately, his experience in the social care field was non-existent, so he had quickly recruited a couple of Social Workers who had no experience of the private sector. It's a very different animal from the Local Authority, where however hopeless you are you can seemingly never get sacked for being useless. Even the totally useless can survive in Social Services, but when they pop up in the Private Sector they tend to get found out.

For those two Social Workers here was a golden opportunity to jump on the latest gravy train where money had become king. Neil for all his good intentions was out of his depth in Social Work and they knew it. This particular gravy train was out of control, long before Liz and I got on board.

Of course, when Liz blew into the building carrying her customary cakes and goodies, she charmed everyone, except those who's self-centred self-interest was threatened. They had no doubt stolen a living in Social Care for years, where the biggest challenge was to work out if they had taken all their available sick leave. Then along came Neil to offer them the golden ticket. They blinded him with paperwork and procedure and ran this agency like their own private business. In order to cement their positions, they were already planning to employ a collection of, probably equally useless, former colleagues and friends.

Liz in contrast was just the best person ever to have on your side. She tended to be the first name on every party or event invitation list and for anyone that needed a voice to stand up for them. What Liz did better than anyone that I've ever met, was to tell you off without an obvious lecture or reprimand and always with plenty of understanding and humour. As you munched away on her Millionaire Shortbread or Choc chip cookies, she would deliver her 'helpful' suggestions. Occasionally though, of course, there would be that poor misguided or delusional soul who perhaps lacking a sweet tooth would decide to take on this Boadicea of Social Work. Those two Social Workers must have worked in some far flung outpost of the Social Work empire to not know of her reputation. Liz came in with charm and cakes and they were left literally sweeping up the crumbs of their plans within a few short weeks.

That second trip to Gloucester was for Marcus so very different, although he absolutely relished his first meeting with Liz. Marcus knowing little of her history or career, suggested to her that she would have made a very good social worker. This drew the customary howls of laughter from Liz and Marcus, like many before him, was completely entranced. Liz made people feel good and she certainly made quite an impression on Marcus. He loved knowledge and especially elders with knowledge. He had probably never met anyone quite like Liz before. As he joked with Liz on the way home, he was unaware that her charm offensive had hidden the real purpose of the day. two bags of cakes and two social workers were effectively dispatched that day in Gloucester. Liz had made her usual first and lasting impressions.

The gravy train left Gloucester station shortly afterwards, as did two misguided and bitter Social Workers. They were at least safe in the knowledge that they probably wouldn't ever encounter an adversary of Liz's abilities again. No more golden tickets for them, but surely plenty of social work departments where they could hide for a few more years. They are probably even now ticking endless boxes, in never ending Social Services structuring reviews. These reviews often change nothing but are merely part of a well-used distraction technique that avoids exposing any serious issues that could otherwise be highlighted in a more independent review. As one review ends, another one usually begins keeping everybody too busy watching their own backs to worry about more serious issues.

The agency in Gloucester only lasted a year, before the Hedge Fund decided, without warning, to pull the plug. I had to up sticks again and decided to move back to working for the Local Authority again in Bristol. It was time for me and Marcus to follow different paths and it was over a year before we met up again.

Chapter 12

My transfer to the agency in Gloucester had taken almost a year and, within a few short months, it was over. I had been taken on, not just as a Foster Carer, but also as a consultant and with Liz had helped them through their Ofsted approval. As a foster carer, there is no route open to progress career-wise, so this had been a rare opportunity. Apart from voluntary contributions, there was little opportunity to use the wealth of expertise I had acquired to either better myself or help improve the service. This new job had finally offered me a way to make better use of my experience in Fostering, so it was doubly disappointing when the agency folded.

Owning my own Children's Homes with Patrick Hart before moving to Spain, had shown me how my skills and experience could be utilised beyond purely being a Foster Carer. It was something few Foster Carers would be able to experience and emphasised one of the inherent problems for me, in that there was no career progression from fostering. There were and still are very few opportunities to progress beyond the role of Foster Carer, as it holds no paper qualification for career advancement. Whatever words or platitudes that prevail from senior Social Workers, we Foster Carers often feel like second-class citizens in the care sector. The lack of a recognised qualification or representation in management means that our voices are often ignored and largely muted by those in control.

The Social Work sector, or at least the Children's Services part of it, is very much based on preserving the status quo, however poorly functioning. Resistance to change prevails, unless forced upon them by Governments, budgets or scandals. Sadly, Governments and budgets rarely lead to positive change and scandals are usually managed as damage limitation exercises, so any improvements to the system usually proceed at a 'snail's pace'.

Whenever there is a demand for dramatic change, then it's easy enough to wheel out another Structural review or some fancy-named policy, that changes nothing except seconding a few pen pushers and social workers into setting up a whole new batch of training modules. It all seems designed to distract everyone from the 'nothing really happens' scenario. If bridge building engineers conducted the same review procedure, then Isambard Kingdom Brunel's Bristol Suspension Bridge would still be in the planning stage. Brunel, it is said, was the last guy that got anything significant built in Bristol before the City Council got involved in planning matters.

For me, the opportunity that I had longed for was all too quickly snatched away and, with my tail firmly between my legs, it was time to eat humble pie and return to being purely a foster carer. Now don't get me wrong, being a foster carer has been a joy and a privilege, but the chance to make an impact on the sector and its service delivery has always been a desire of mine. I was far from convinced that returning to a normal fostering role would be enough for me anymore.

Marcus, meanwhile, had somehow lasted at his foster placement and maintained writing as an outlet for his frustration. He had yet to find a way to contact me directly, so he just had to get on with his life as best he could, with the various distractions that adolescence had to offer. Unfortunately, one of those distractions was solvents, which did nothing to help address his anger and depressive tendencies. Fortunately, I was unaware of his problems.

We had given Marcus a copy of the track that he had made in our studio. The recording studio itself turned out to be a bit of a white elephant for us and we pulled out of the project a few months after saying goodbye to Marcus. The video we had made was left to gather dust as we took a few months out of music, something that became a much longer break. It was almost a year after the last respite that Steve re-visited the track and produced an edit which we were finally happy with.

Once we had the final edit, we started what were to be futile attempts to use it to publicise our work. Social Workers and innovation are not good bedfellows. At least the attempts did lead to Marcus getting a copy, which once again opened the door for him enough to make contact through Facebook Messenger. With that communication portal opened, then unsurprisingly with Marcus, a trickle of messages soon became a torrent with a stream of lyrics coming through for my approval.

For a boy of his age, his vocabulary was extensive, which made it all the more disappointing that the lyrics were littered with 'bitches' 'hoes' and numerous expletives. I knew that most young rappers expressed themselves in a similar vein, but in my opinion any originality is totally decimated by this urban slang that sits so uncomfortably with an English accent. It was nonetheless pleasing to see that he still had the passion to write and the last thing I needed to do was find fault with his lyrics, when he quite clearly had enough negative voices in his life.

It was late Summer 2015 when, with renewed contact and receiving his video, Marcus asked me to help him produce an album. I have to admit that I didn't give it serious consideration for all manner of reasons, so I think a standard "we'll see" was my way of not letting him down. It was enough though to give Marcus something to hang on to for a while.

Marcus had by then left school and was due to start college in September. It was a residential college, so he would be leaving his Carers too. As often happens, that particular placement ending did not go well. Marcus had a lot of pent-up frustration towards his Carers, despite a lot of positives over his time with them. Moving on from a long-term placement is often a difficult time and, with Marcus, anything difficult provokes a hostile reaction.

Ironically, I had recently experienced a very similar placement breakdown myself, with one of my long term foster placements. It's easy to apportion blame, whether to the child or the Carers, but the reality is that is a very tense time for all involved and it's not unusual for a placement ending to feel like a bomb about to blow. Everything and everyone appears to move too slowly as the fuse gets shorter and then it just all just goes off.

With some young people, it's easier to deal with the feeling of rejection by triggering the rejection themselves, like a self-destruct. They hope that may make it less painful but invariably it does not. What it can do however, is momentarily give the child the feeling that they can control their destiny, even if it is inevitably destructive. Whatever the reasons, a successful placement can sadly end abruptly, leaving lasting disappointment and regrets for all. Foster Carers are of course trained to deal with this, but for the child it, just reinforces negative feelings, emotions and experiences. Often the anger in the child makes it impossible to ever find any acceptable form of resolution. In my own experience, time can heal the wounds, but usually in years, not months.

As autumn arrived, both Marcus and I were beginning new journeys. Marcus started college with fortnightly respite at another Carers, whilst I joined Bristol Social Services and almost immediately had two new placements. The first was a local Muslim boy, my first Muslim child and another with Autistic traits, albeit not yet diagnosed. Here was another fascinating boy from whom I would learn so much, both about his culture and his autism. Having worked with Marcus, I relished the challenge, whilst accepting that while these boys shared certain traits each was distinctly individual. Initially conversations were sporadic and sometimes days went by without any verbal communication whatsoever. He had a form of selective mutism when he decided not to talk at all. However, as the months passed, he found his voice and, as with Marcus, we had long fascinating conversations.

Those conversations tended to be about TV series such as Gotham and Arrow or Spider-Man films but then drifted into religion and his childhood years spent in his family's village in Pakistan. It was a place so different to where we now lived in my end terrace house in Bristol. He painted a vivid picture of an idyllic life, surrounded by loving elders, home-made food and peace, so very different from media portrayals of life in Pakistan that we get to see.

His favourite pastime when he moved in was playing on Minecraft, where he could recreate an idyllic village that he could control and defend against all those that would seek to challenge his domestic security. For Marcus, Minecraft was all about building urban landscapes with incredibly tall buildings that had all the trappings of wealth and success, but for this boy it was about recreating his long lost village, where peace and serenity were king.

The other boy that arrived in early September 2015, was an unaccompanied Asylum seeking boy called Ali, who had made his way across Europe in search of a better life. Having spent my entire Fostering career looking after young English boys these two lads were to be a refreshing change. They were not the usual Care-Experienced teenagers full of negativity, gathered from being left too long in the Care System. The latest arrival probably had more negative experiences than any of the lads I had previously encountered, but he did also have a resilience and determination that is sadly absent from boys well versed in the workings of our care system. It reminded me of my Mother and her generation that had survived hard times growing up but had never used it to excuse or demonstrate any lack of effort.

These two boys were each in their own way interesting new challenges, which in turn meant that they were great opportunities for me to widen my experience. The work with Marcus had been likewise and now it was all wrapped up and neatly put away, with few thoughts on my part as to whether there would be a chance for taking things musically any further. Music generally was still very much on the back burner and was to stay that way for far longer than I could have imagined.

For Marcus, it was more about writing than harbouring too many thoughts about becoming a performer. September and college brought exciting new discoveries for him. A social life, friends, weed and unchallenged access to food and the internet. These were mostly things that had been denied him during his foster care years. There would of course be new rules and disciplines required for survival at college. Talking about those days recently, Marcus' view was, "free food and internet what's not to like? That alone made it worth putting up with all the shit". Marcus may be a boy who has the wildest imagination and an incredibly complex mind, but his strategies for coping with the day-to-day routines can be relatively simple and basic.

Sleep when you can't stay awake, eat when there is nothing else to do, but even then, enjoyment is rarely required. It's purely a necessary function that more often will be secondary to whatever he is engrossed in at the time. A meal was merely an accompaniment to Minecraft or YouTube. Food could be left to get cold and eaten later when bored.

Marcus is in fact, more likely to discuss his bowel movements in the most excruciating detail than the merits of the food on his plate. Food only usually gets a mention when he storms out of a restaurant having a meltdown, because the food was too hot, too cold, too late, too spicy or delivered by an unsmiling waiter or waitress, unless the server is cute of course. Now that's when food goes right off the menu, as I've recently discovered, but hey, back in September 2015, this was not something that Marcus chose to share. Discussing bowel movements at the dinner table, however, was always on the menu.

The sudden appearance of a social life and friends at college proved to be a welcome distraction from his music dreams. Whilst he still harboured musical aspirations, there was little time to dwell on losing his contact with me as a result. At that point, it was probably more of an inconvenience than a major disappointment. He would have liked to have continued to develop more musical ideas with Steve and myself, but Marcus rarely worries about obstacles when he can just change course. At the time, new freedoms, new friends and a social life that increasingly involved weed, far outweighed any loss musically. There had been a connection made with us. He felt a part of The Musicworks, but the connection was far from essential or unbreakable.

It was late November when Marcus got back in touch. The musical flame had not died after all. He had adjusted to college life, but just like the latest drug, the effects were not long-lasting. A few verses appeared on Messenger along with a question.

"Will you buy my album?"

"Of course I would," I said.

"It will be £5 and will you help me produce it?"

Planning ahead as always, I thought. More lyrics quickly followed, less jumbled and random than most of his previous efforts and he was pleased that I had noted that.

"Will you sign me ?"

I managed to avoid giving answers to the last two questions and he didn't push for them, possibly to avoid more disappointment. Yes, Marcus was back! This was also very much part of his current lyrical theme. In his view it was emerging from his 'solvent times' and returning to music dreams. The writing continued through Christmas and into the New Year and I sensed a renewed optimism in his life. The placement breakdown still angered him, whilst choosing to ignore his own part in that. Unfortunately, that renewed optimism took a big hit in early 2016 when one of his closest friends took their own life, returning him to a lot of negative emotions and attitudes .

College days during term time meant little contact and no doubt more distractions. It was quite understandable that contact would be mostly holiday time, when boredom crept in with more time on his own. As with Christmas, Easter came and went without the hoped for visit from myself. Sadly, it is only looking back and summarising those times that I realise how lonely he probably was and how disappointing my non-appearances probably were. Looking back maybe I should have made better efforts to meet up, but I didn't appreciate then how much he still wanted my help. Unquestionably, a lesson learned on my part and once again the words of Liz Wilson echo in my thoughts.

"Analysis and Reflection John. Keep hold of that and remember to address it to everything you do." Liz was still very much around and guiding me back in 2016 and fortunately I can still draw on her wise words now.

On reflection, I suppose, however experienced at our work we are, there is always room for improvement. Being good at something means that sometimes we can move into a kind of auto-pilot mode and miss the little things that can make such a big difference. Being a fairly modest person, I tended to underrate my abilities so would not have considered how much effect my words could have or just how much pain my failure to keep an appointment could give.

I do believe that I have generally been a successful mentor. However, thanks to reviewing our many conversations on Messenger in 2016 I have had a good chance to analyse and reflect on my performance. The words 'could have done better' spring to mind. If anything, my performance has in some degree suffered because I doubted my own abilities. That in itself is a little ironic. I am a Mentor, who spends much of his time convincing young people to believe in themselves and yet didn't always believe in my own abilities. Maybe, just maybe, the whole reason it's taken 30 years to write a book is that I had to wait until I did believe in my own abilities in order to do so. Marcus, for all his problems is well ahead of me on that.

Assuming I'm right, then I would imagine this will not be my last book. The words of a now dearly departed soulmate and a young Aspie have together convinced me at last of my own abilities. 'Could have done this,' 'Would have done that' are largely irrelevant now. No time for regrets because having taken so long to get to this point, I need to get a move on now. Retirement is no longer an option which is fortunate as due to my lack of financial planning I need to keep working. Everything happens for a reason as they say.

When the summer holidays arrived in 2016, Marcus was back in touch. Plenty of messaging throughout the summer, Marcus talking about making an album, starting his own label and designing a logo. That summer we talked often about meeting up, but once more for various reasons it did not happen.

My car broke down on one attempt, then I missed him with a surprise visit and had to change plans when Mum became ill. For his part, he was coming to visit but had an altercation with a support worker that changed his plans and then family demands thwarted his next attempt. Before anything happened, September arrived and college began again.

Meanwhile, the saddest days of my life were about to unfold as cancer was finally to take my Mum at the end of September. Dave, Ali and Wayne were there for me, as were Steve and Liz consistently through difficult times. None of them were my blood, but I could not have had better family and friends. There were, to be honest, some very dark days that autumn and another failed attempt to meet up with Marcus, before finally just before Christmas me and Dave got ourselves down to Bridgwater and met up with him. It was a relief to finally meet up, even more so for Marcus I would imagine.

After an awful few months, just seeing Marcus really lifted me. He was in good spirits and with the year coming to an end there was real reason for looking forward to 2017 with renewed optimism, for all of us talking about getting some music going at last. Naturally, every New Year is greeted with high hopes and fortunately, neither Marcus nor I, knew what was around the corner, that all the optimism would be cruelly wiped out over the coming months.

It was February that it went wrong for Marcus. He had been working on his music at college but the plans never materialised and it all went downhill. By March, college was over, due to his behaviour and then boredom and disappointment led to increasing experiments with drugs as his life fell apart.

Later that month Dave and I met Liz for lunch, a regular treat before we went off to France for a few days. Liz was a little less than her usual ebullient self and was due to have a few hospital tests whilst we were gone. She had not seen a doctor in many years and just seemed indestructible.

When we came home a few days later, we were shocked to hear that she was in hospital. As soon as we saw her, she told us it was Cancer, but it should all be dealt with within a few weeks. A few weeks later and treatment was apparently done and she would be off for recuperation in a week or so. A few days later a call from her daughter informed me that Liz had gone home for her final days and then, just like that, she was gone. I think she had known and probably decided to shield me from having to watch Cancer take another precious soul. It was so very hard to grasp that there would be no more late-night calls exchanging hilarious escapades in Social Work. No more 'Suppers', no more 'Coffees' and no more analysing friends, family and colleagues and situations. When she walked in a room Liz took it over no matter who was present, whether for work or socially. In recent years she had become my rock, my guide and my dearest friend.

The enormity of losing both Mum and Liz within seven months took a long time to grasp. They were the two women in a very male-orientated life, two absolute rocks. Mum and Liz brought balance to my life and provided a family influence for the boys. As happens at times like these, bad times bring people closer together and with it the realisation of one's own mortality that comes with age. I realised that Wayne, Dave and Ali were all in their own ways looking out for me, even more than before. Once the grief had subsided, I decided not to waste time anymore with people that didn't matter to me or to delay in doing the things that I still wanted to do. It's actually alright to still have dreams, even as an elder, but the one thing I don't want is regrets for what I could have done or for wasted time.

Marcus wasn't far from my thoughts at that time, although there were plenty of things much closer to home to address, and unbeknown to me, he had his own demons to face. I was sadly oblivious to his situation but in all honesty his mentor was himself a little lost. Whilst grieving it's so easy to make bad decisions or over-react, so it was probably just as well that I was otherwise engaged.

I did however get down to see him a couple of weeks after losing Liz and he said about the changes, losing his college place and getting into drugs more. Too much of it sadly went over my head at the time, as I was too wrapped up in my own grief. It was only much later that I realised how bad a period it had been for him. Grief can be a very selfish emotion and I forgot for a while that others around me were dealing with it in their own way. Dave in particular had to process losing Mum and Liz too and I was too wrapped up in my own emotions to be of much help to him. His life had become so dependent on me and suddenly he realised that I too was vulnerable and that in turn made him feel vulnerable for the first time in his adult life. For most of the remainder of the year it was a case of making arrangements, then breaking them with Marcus. Plenty of excuses, but putting it simply, it's hard to deal with anyone else's problems when your own are constantly at the forefront of your mind. Grieving changes everything and everyone. It just takes over and never really let's go, but the bit that holds on most is full of love and memories albeit permanently tinged with sadness too.

The thing about grieving is spending time thinking about what might have been. Amongst her many talents Liz was a great storyteller. There was always a new story that would reduce her audience into tears of laughter. Over later years, we often talked about the books that she would write when she was finally not working anymore. I think that she had retired three times, so the thought of her sitting in a Care home, writing her memoirs was always amusing although hard to imagine. Liz could find humour and use it to lighten even the darkest of days.

Her own mother had only died a few years earlier and Liz took her ashes back to her native Italy, to the Bay of Naples. Once there she was to scatter them in the bay. Of course something like this could not pass without incident. Not with Liz.

She had told us how, once out in the bay of Naples, standing on the front of the boat the time had arrived for her to say goodbye to her Mum. As she began her task a sudden gust of wind appeared blowing her mother's ashes back over the boat. The other passengers were unaware of Liz's task, so when they were suddenly covered in ash one had suggested that their proximity to the Mount Vesuvius volcano was surely the reason. Another hilarious story to tell over dinner. There really was never a dull moment with Liz.

Sadly, now though, her books will never be written and it made me think how sometimes the years and lives pass before we actually get to do long planned things. With encouragement from Steve, I resolved to write a book, although still not quite ready, despite the best intentions. Grieving doesn't have a time scale, but

I suspected I would begin when the world felt right again, as surely it must.

On reflection, there I was with my world turned upside down and without a doubt I was struggling to maintain any sort of balance. So, looking back now, I imagine how it would have felt if I were Marcus. Here is a young man who is having a great day, but the merest of irritations can send him plummeting into furious anger and despair. Imagine your world falling apart due to something trivial, so much so that it really could happen at any time and any moment without warning.

I knew that for me the real intensity of grief would pass, even if it took some time. That empty, lost and lonely feeling can return of course, now and then for me. That's how loss is but for Marcus, that can be every day. Something as trivial as not being able to find his cigarettes or lighter or his laptop not responding fast enough, can trigger a meltdown. Once begun it has to reach a conclusion usually by causing damage to himself or his possessions. Almost a Hulk-like loss of self-control, visibly fighting his demons, fighting himself. Headphones, phone, laptop all flung away, ripping his top or T-shirt off and holding or punching his head. It's like watching a person self-destruct, and all you can do is stand back and watch in horror, because you know from past experience that getting too close or trying to comfort is not going to end well.

The first time it happened, I tried putting my arms around him to hug him, but his eyes flashed that "f*** off" look again and self-preservation made me back off. Trying to decide if enough of the caring Marcus was still in there at that moment was nearly impossible. Any move would be a gamble and an enormous risk. The feeling of helplessness is overwhelming, as you wait for the storm to subside. Deep down, I know, however scary the situation is for me that for Marcus it must be so much more so. This is emotion so raw, so out of control with furious words erupting like molten lava from a volcano.

Trying to find an explanation using logic just doesn't work. 'Losing my temper' for a mild mannered person like me always meant losing control, but seeing Marcus lose his temper is on another level. What I've experienced by comparison is not losing control, because there was always certain defence mechanisms that kicked in. Storming out of an argument with Patrick, or being held back by teammates after a particularly nasty cynical tackle on a football pitch. That was me 'losing it'. Never did I get so angry that I could risk everything that I loved and cared for. That concept was alien to me but certainly not to Marcus.

Chapter 13

It was back in September 2015 when Ali became the latest addition to my household. He looked more 14 than 16 when he arrived, with the Social Worker looking very sheepish. I had never looked after an Asylum Seeking Child before, so I really didn't know what to expect. He came from Albania, a country that I and probably most people in the UK knew little about. Wearing a horizontal striped T-shirt and blue jeans, he looked a bit like a rabbit in the headlights. Neither he nor I knew what to expect. I didn't realise it at the time, but this meeting of two different worlds was going to be a life-changing experience for both of us. These things do seem to happen to me.

His English was pretty good and he settled in very quickly. Within a few weeks he was signed up for a college course. We had been to the City of Bristol College Open Day the week before and from a selection of courses he had picked hospitality and catering. Like many young Albanians, he had, I discovered not been able to attend any school for a long time, so would be on catch-up. That catch-up was helped by sheer enthusiasm and he took to catering from day one. Within weeks, he was watching cooking programmes endlessly in his spare time. It was not in my experience unusual to find DVD's and books under the beds of teenage boys. What was different with Ali was that they were all about food and chefs. Gordon Ramsey and Jamie Oliver were his new heroes.

By the end of the college year, Ali had become the outstanding student in his year and was described as a natural by his tutors. Conversations at home revolved around food and chefs. He outgrew the college in the latter stages of his second year, by which time he was being mentored by a Michelin Star Chef who had invited him to work in his kitchen. It was during the summer of 2017 that Ali had received his letter refusing his Asylum and Leave to Remain. Only just 18 his success story looked to be coming to a premature end.

Without doubt, Ali had already become, at least from a work perspective, my greatest achiever. It was not through his college and work success that emboldened me to take on the Dinosaur that is the Home Office. It was, in fact, because unlike any other foster boy he had become such an integral part of both mine and David's lives. Perhaps the most surprising part of Ali's story was that a boy from a distant land and culture had actually evoked more of a paternal instincts in me than any other boy, with the exception of David, over the previous three decades. Everything about him fitted the criteria of what any father wants to see in a son. Although rarely mentioned, it was clear that Ali had known and experienced the love of a family.

My many years of fostering had taught me that sometimes one does not need to search out and explore too far into the traumatic experiences of children. Analysis is good, but forensic examinations of the past can risk exposing new trauma for children and young people and destabilise lives that have found stability for the first time. David was a case in point. Bad memories and experiences were neatly packaged up and filed away in dusty archives in one's memory and no longer a threat to the future. unless someone decides to bring them to the surface. Fortunately, Liz and her ability to balance maternal instinct with best Social Work practice had perceived as much with Ali, well ahead of my stumbling inquisitions when he first arrived. Those last few years of her life and her support for me, now seem to have been a preparation for me of challenges to come and greater achievements than I ever thought possible. That after all is true mentoring, even if I was unaware of much of it at the time.

Late summer and Autumn 2017 had been my first battle with the Home Office. I had throughout the 1990s and beyond dabbled in PR and at least locally had a good record of getting my press releases printed. I had always found it amusing back in my Elevation days, that they tended to appear in the press with minimal changes, but credited to various reporters. All of that was way back before my move to Spain in 2004, so I wasn't sure if I could make much of an impression with Ali's story, but fortunately the ability to present a story had not deserted me. I no longer had any contacts in the local press, except for Patrick and little in the way of support for a campaign so I was basically starting from scratch. The Brexit referendum had happened a year earlier and the anti-migrant feeling was becoming continually more visible, so I wasn't sure how Ali's story would be received. On the plus side it was a topic of interest so that gave me hope.

By August 2017, Ali was working with a leading chef in Torquay, less than two years after jumping off the back of a lorry in Bristol. That would be the main thrust of Ali's story and indeed of the Immigration Appeal that was to be handled by a local Immigration Solicitor.

I had little knowledge of the hospitality industry, but what I had picked up was that it relied heavily on a migrant workforce and faced a potentially catastrophic impact post Brexit. Fortunately, Ali's employer Simon, a Michelin starred Chef, had quite a reputation as an accomplished chef in the industry and his support and that of his considerable contacts would surely raise the profile of Ali's case and his story. The restaurant was in Torquay which gave me the added advantage of creating a newsworthy story for the local press, in both Bristol and Torquay. I didn't anticipate the story going beyond local TV and media, so the two locations at least gave me two chances of coverage.

With such a time-lapse since my last dealings with the press, the major change that had occurred was the growth of social media and online news platforms. Facebook had only launched a couple of weeks before I had moved to Spain in 2004 and Twitter was something that I had not even got to grips with by 2017. I had signed up to it in 2012 but never really posted anything with just a handful of followers. In all honesty I really didn't have a lot to work with in starting any sort of campaign, other than a hashtag and a slogan #Future4Ali.

My first #Future4Ali tweet went out on 10 August along with a Facebook post. Fortunately, Chef Simon was already mobilising the hospitality sector. The following day, as I launched a JustGiving page to help cover the anticipated £5,000 court costs *The Caterer* trade magazine was already featuring Ali's story. Patrick of course featured us on his local radio show and the *Bristol Post* featured us a few days later. By the end of the first week local TV and Radio got on it in Bristol and Devon and a leading food writer, Josh Barrie, had featured us in the *London Eater*. I didn't really expect the food magazines to impact much, although they were national, but that was down to my lack of understanding of modern media.

With the internet, stories can suddenly go viral and the story was picked up by the National media in Albania and various publications in the USA. In the United States, the story got noticed in New York by the charismatic Tiffany Hardin of the rapidly expanding WeWork organisation. WeWork were organising their first European Awards Event in London and they decided to give Ali a special award for dedication to his craft at the prestigious event. In the space of a month, Ali's story had gone national and international and he was a special VIP guest at the WeWork Awards in Battersea Park. Determined not to miss my boy's big moment, myself, Dave and Steve went up to London for the award which also came with a £10,000 prize, the sort of money that Ali could only have dreamed of as a child in Albania.

As part of the evening, Ali and Simon had to be interviewed on stage by well-known writer and foodie, Grace Dent. Foster Carers and their children tend to lead fairly anonymous lives, so for me this was quite unique and up there in my proudest moments. I fully expected Ali to be nervous, if not overwhelmed by the occasion, but on the contrary, he loved every minute and totally charmed the audience on his public speaking debut with his newly acquired Bristol accent. For the first time I realised that not only was he possibly destined to be a great chef, but also potentially somewhat of a celebrity. Posing for the cameras, it was hard to believe this boy in his smart suit had not been trained as a model, as it was only two years since his arrival in the UK with nothing but the clothes he was wearing. Yet here he was, dazzling an audience in his first ever public appearance. It was only a Primark suit, but he looked just as at ease in it as he did in his kitchen whites. Nerves were clearly not an obstacle to Ali and opportunity was not something he was going to pass on.

Any doubts that I had ever had about Ali's potential to be successful were blown away that evening, I just hoped that the court appeal would not destroy his future. It was hard to believe that in just four weeks, we had raised enough to cover the court costs, as well as establishing an excellent case with which to take on the Home Office. That night at the WeWork awards was when Ali was able to stop being a victim and be strong enough to move on with his life.

Whilst understanding that many, if not all, young people who come into care are victims in one way or another, I have long held the belief that the care system does not so much prepare young people for life after care, as provide young people with excuses for their life's journey after care. The expectations are usually low for Care Experienced young people and life outcomes are very poor in comparison with other young people. The number of Care leavers who end up in prison, or living on the streets, bears testament to that. In my opinion too much time is spent with young people in Care looking at their past problems. By all means address their problems and experiences and deal as best as possible with the traumas they have faced, but it's more important, I believe, to give them the support, motivation and opportunities to move forward with their lives. Less looking back and more looking forward. Of course, it's not easy for some traumatised young people but concentrating on their hopes and dreams rather than past nightmares can often help.

I have learned all too well, in recent years, that dealing with grief is not so much about moving on as moving forward. If you wait until you are ready to move on, it feels like letting go, so you keep holding on to the grief, whereas moving forward does not have to feel like letting go. Children in the care system grieve for the lives and families that they have lost and can be reluctant to let go.

However bad the memories are, help them move forward, give them hope to replace the shattered dreams, but don't let them believe that failure is okay, because of their past trauma in childhood. In doing that you are just giving them lifelong excuses for failure.

My feelings have been reinforced even more since I started working with Asylum Seeking children who have come late into the care system. Many of them have experienced awful traumas and events and yet in most that I have seen, they have grasped every opportunity of a better life. They have been committed and determined and have not used their poor life experiences as excuses for lack of effort or lack of success. The focus that most of these children have is impressive, even though many have lacked the basic education that we take for granted. They have often been shocked by the attitudes of young English people, especially those in the care system. They find it hard to understand the lack of engagement or interest in their futures and their lack of respect for their elders.

For me, the arrival of these children should be seen as an opportunity to inspire and motivate our own disinterested young people, by showing how to achieve in life despite adversity. They give me hope that there is a better way of helping young people who come into care. I believe that we can do that by focusing on the present and the future rather than continually revisiting the past. Writing life stories where children have to pick the few good bits out of a life spent in misery and lacking in love can be distressing and depressing. In order to select a few good memories, they have to mentally trawl through so many bad ones. It's the horrible parts left out of their Life Stories that reflect their lives better than any sanitised happy version they end up with and they know it. Their lives have effectively gone down the toilet. For me, it's better to flush the toilet and move on rather than to constantly make them look in the toilet bowl to pick out the good things. That to me, is what we seem to do all too often with damaged children. Children are amazing and resilient given the opportunity, so inspire them with what they can be and can do, rather than things that were never in their control. I am not saying that we should not help them deal with their traumas but first help them begin to enjoy life and get stronger. With more stable lives they can deal better with the past, but most importantly focus more on the future.

Right from that first day in the car coming back from Gloucester I told Marcus that Aspergers can be a blessing or a curse, depending on how you deal with it. Having an almost obsessive interest in something can help you specialise in certain subjects. I used his avid interest in Doctor Who as an example. His knowledge on the subject was way above most people's. That in itself demonstrated an ability for learning that the education system had failed to recognise. Basically, society's standard method of assessing intelligence is flawed. It's a system designed to produce sheep and not shepherds. It works for the majority, but not for those outside the mainstream of education. Marcus would never fit into their system, so surely it was better that he should work outside of it. That was soon what he was doing, as he had a vocabulary far in excess of most young people that I have encountered. The love of English, that J.K. Rowling's books had given him, could take him further than any school examinations ever would.

He took in my advice and believed it and believed in me, but most importantly, began to believe in himself. Now, although he has been through massively negative experiences in recent years, he has held on to that and pulled himself through, even when there was nobody with him to help. Despite regular bouts of depression, his dreams have survived with him. Having a reason to hope can do that for you and that is why I love mentoring so much. We are not there to change their lives, but we can help make damaged young people stronger, so that they are able to change their own lives.

Hopes and dreams, that's what life to me is all about. 2017 had seen me lose Liz, my soul mate and yet it turned out to be a truly significant year for other more positive reasons. Just a few days after Liz had passed away, a new joy came into my life. Wayne became a grandfather when his daughter Tia, (my eldest granddaughter), delivered the most beautiful baby girl Ava-Rose, my first Great Granddaughter. She was the first of the next generation for me. Even in the darkest of times something can bring light flooding back and the cycle of life begins again.

In the Autumn, we went to court with Ali to fight for his right to stay in the UK and follow his dreams of being a top chef. Patrick and I really worked together for the first time in many years on Ali's case. We had ended our successful partnership when I moved to Spain and had spent far too long apart, after a rather sad and acrimonious parting of the ways. Many years on and we had both mellowed and slowly rebuilt our friendship. Ali and his immigration fight had really brought us back together. As witnesses in the Immigration case, we were not able to be in the court for much of the proceedings, but Dave was there as ever giving Ali support and being warmly welcomed by the judge. Dave's the sort of person no one likes to disappoint, so I think (as does he) that his presence was indeed significant. After such a difficult 12 months and losing two amazing people in Liz and Mum the fear for me of losing Ali if we had lost was overwhelming. Patrick's calm and assured presence gave me and Ali strength and hope. Patrick and I working together again was an amazing feeling.

When Ali started college a few weeks after coming to me, he experienced a meteoric rise. He quickly became the best student of his catering course, was a runner-up in a Nationwide young chef competition and had been recruited by a Michelin Star chef. A young asylum seeker chef tipped for great things and threatened with deportation was very newsworthy both in the UK and beyond.

Ali's story appeared in National newspapers, on TV and in magazines. Thanks to the publicity we had raised the funds to fight his case when he was refused Leave to Remain in the UK by the Home Office. Fortunately, with having Patrick and a Michelin Star Chef supporting his case we were successful at that first appeal in court. Inadvertently, the publicity had shone the spotlight on myself as a Foster Carer and suddenly I was something of a Celebrity Foster Carer of sorts if only for a short time. That was quite a novel experience, which after a life of Foster Caring, without recognition was somewhat satisfying. It had basically all happened because of a press release that I had written. Putting a young person in the public eye does however carry enormous risks, so getting publicity can bring unwanted results sometimes.

Talking to one member of the press corps present when Ali's immigration case came to court was very informative. He explained to me how one of the most profitable means of obtaining information about a person who suddenly comes under press scrutiny is to trawl that person's social media. Many people for instance, leave their Facebook or other Social Media status open to the public. That can mean every embarrassing picture or political comment made to one's friends is suddenly public knowledge. A crazy night out or a stunt with a friend in the past can suddenly be exposed in the press. Even worse, it exposes ones friends and family to public scrutiny by association with the subject. Once in the public domain it cannot be deleted.

By the time we had won Ali's immigration case, another young Albanian had moved in with us. Samet was a couple of years younger than Al and was in awe of Ali's success. He was quite different to Ali and very shy and reserved, having suffered multiple traumas in his young life. Having another Albanian already in the same house was of great help to Samet. He had been forced to beg on the streets of the Albanian capital Tirana at the age of 12. His father had drink and gambling problems and had incurred substantial debts, so Samet was forced onto the streets to beg for money. Had he remained in Albania then Samet would have become liable for his father's debts. If debts are not paid in Albania, then the price can be paid in blood so his homeland had become very unsafe for Samet. After completing a year at school and becoming the top student on his carpentry course at college, Samet was looking forward to a bright future just like the one that Ali now had. That all changed two years later as he approached 18 and the bad news arrived.

It was August 2019 when a letter fell onto the doormat one morning, with the news that Samet had been refused Asylum and Leave to Remain in the UK, even though it was accepted by the Home Office that he had been trafficked to the UK. With the Government's attitude towards migrants, it was not a total surprise to be honest. What I didn't expect though was the way that this decision would transform our lives for the foreseeable future.

For Samet, the letter that put his entire future in doubt was naturally devastating, but I had been through this before with Ali and was reasonably confident that we could get the decision reversed. For young Albanians who come to the UK as unaccompanied children reaching 18 is a fearful time. Only one in every two hundred are granted asylum. Our Government did not turn away the children that arrived here, although it has to be said they showed no compassion for children in places like Calais and other EU countries even those trying to reunite with their parents in the UK. For those that do manage to get here, they are given the opportunity to build new lives. Most arrive aged 15 or 16 and are placed where possible with foster Carers like myself, or failing that in Children's Homes.

In my limited experience of working with Asylum Seeking Children most do well at establishing new lives. Hard work is something to be enjoyed rather than tolerated or avoided, unlike many of our own young people these days. For most young migrants, it gives them renewed hope and faith in their future. Sadly, that hope tends to come crashing down when they reach 18 and the Home Office inevitably crushes their dreams. The lucky few get to overturn the decision, but most are thwarted by a succession of obstacles that are placed to block their path to becoming the people that we have educated and trained them to be. I have yet to hear one good reason why we as a country invest in these young people and then just discard them like pieces of rubbish at 18. It is tragic and despicable!

These children have often experienced great trauma in their young lives before leaving Albania and other lands, only then to suffer possibly worse trauma during their journeys to the UK. Many are brought here by gangs to work in 'Grow houses', the cannabis farms where they are enslaved to pay off their 'debts' to the gangs. Countless children have ended up in places like Brussels or Calais. Places that are 'Honeypots' where evil paedophiles swarm from all over Europe. Rapes of young boys and girls were commonplace in the Calais Jungle, interspersed with attacks from rival gangs and French police. For impoverished and abandoned children, the cost of climbing aboard a lorry bound for

England was often sex. How many times have I crossed the Channel to Calais and briefly stopped for a croissant and coffee, totally oblivious to the human cargo of children going through a living hell in order to share my ferry back home after my French break. These days, when I return from holiday and walk through the car deck on my way up to the ships lounge and restaurant, I wonder how many battered and abused children might be secreted on the lorries that I pass? Others may be making the crossing in dinghy's in the darkness. How many have not made it this far, having been bought and sold to evil predators? How many just disappear forever?

The 'lucky' ones get to the Cannabis farms and are then held hostage for months until the 'grow' is harvested, before being deposited near Social Services offices to officially appear in the UK for the first time and begin their next journey through our care system and education. Until they are 18 they have opportunities to learn at schools and colleges, most often identifying a trade that they can learn and a focus upon, in order to build a new life. For them this is where life and their future begins. Reaching 18 is unfortunately for many where it effectively ends. Most of these young people will fall victim to an inhospitable Home Office and an Immigration policy underpinned by the Immigration Tribunals. The result is that they then choose to disappear into a hidden society that exists all around us, where they can hide from the authorities. Their other option is to wait to be taken to 'the camps'. These are the detention centres where they are held alongside serious criminals awaiting deportation.

Those that disappear underground are able to live a half-life unless discovered, often working for gangs and receiving a pittance whilst living in squalid conditions as virtual slaves. They will never be able to get health issues addressed or get tenancies, legitimate work or anything that requires proof of identity. As a nation we have borne the cost of educating and training these children as well as accommodating them within our care system. If they were given Asylum and Leave to Remain then they would be able to contribute fully to our society by their work and through their taxes. Driving them underground, aside from showing a complete lack of humanity, means that the UK will never be able to recoup our investment or benefit from it. That only serves to encourage those criminal elements that feed off these young people. We effectively keep the gangs supplied with young people who have no choice but to do their bidding.

Having been through the traumatic process of fighting Home Office decisions with Ali I felt much better prepared this time. I had since Ali's Appeal heard of many unsuccessful fights but I believed with everything that I had learned during and since that time that I could help Samet mount a successful appeal. It was only the middle of August, so I expected that we would have 4–6 weeks to prepare his case. With Ali, I had no idea what to expect with an appeal, as I had no previous experience in that particular field. By the time Samet arrived, I had learned much more so, I had been preparing his case since the day he arrived . I knew that it would not be easy, but I was nonetheless quietly confident. The following weeks were peppered with legal meetings and gathering support for our day in court.

Ali's case had been won by the strength of the bond that David and I had made with him along with his undoubted talent. By the time his case came to court Ali had been taken on by a Michelin Star Chef who was witness to his talent and potential. Being such a natural outstanding talent is rare and clearly made a difference in his appeal. Unquestionably, with Samet the appeal would likely rest more on the ties with my family and his obvious vulnerability. I have always felt that it must be difficult for Samet in comparison to Ali. Success came quickly and easily to Ali and Samet clearly felt the weight of following in the shadow of his success. I was constantly conscious of trying not to make comparisons, for fear of them overwhelming Samet. I so wished that we didn't have to enter another battle with the Home Office, but in all honesty, I never expected anything else.

Remembering how difficult it had been to win Ali's case, even with him being a quite exceptional talent, it was a daunting task ahead to win for Samet. The facts are that by the very nature of their situation young, trafficked migrants are almost always vulnerable and likely to be extremely traumatised by either their upbringing or by their journey to the UK or probably by both. The facts were also that most young Albanians have their appeals rejected. To win like I had with Ali, was a rare event and highly unlikely. Imagine for a moment the public outcry if it were to be announced that only one in every two hundred child victims of abuse in this country would be given safety and protection. Yet that is the reality for young Albanians trafficked to the UK. It is scandalous, it is inhumane, it is cruelty beyond words. It is the hostile environment that we have to work with, that young migrants have to live with and it is so very wrong.

Chapter 14

The memories of a successful #Future4Ali campaign really counted for little as we approached Samet's court appeal. This time around, I felt better prepared with a victory behind me and all the experience that I had gained from it. I saw no need for a public campaign as Samet's life here did not have the necessary wow factor for press exposure and I really felt that we had enough evidence to win the day without it. I never assumed that success was a given, but my confidence was such that I felt defeat unlikely. I was probably overdue for a wake-up call. A day in court was coming soon and the most settled family unit I had ever been blessed with in 30 years of fostering would be at risk once again. Having been diagnosed with severe PTSD after a traumatic childhood and journey to the UK, I expected humanity to win the day. Was that a foolish or unrealistic expectation? Most child migrants are severely traumatised and yet are still refused Asylum or Leave to Remain. The expectation of humanity from the Home Office and from many of the Immigration Tribunals was not really backed up by the evidence of the many refusals that continue to destroy young migrants' lives.

The court day came and compared with Ali's it seemed very straightforward. I did have a nagging feeling that it was all too easy, as it was much shorter than Ali's had been and my contribution surprisingly much less on the day. I had supplied written evidence, so maybe I had covered all the bases in that, but I will admit that my second day in an Immigration Court was something of an anti-climax. A complete contrast to Ali's case, which had felt much more of a battle. The day over fairly painlessly, it was now just a matter of waiting a few weeks for a decision to arrive and once again, day after day, I was awaiting the postman's morning delivery. Ten days later, Mr Postie got a break from my daily doorstep vigil when Dave and I took a three-day trip to Bologna, Dave's first visit to Italy.

Three days and a fine selection of pasta dishes later we returned home to be met by a smiling Samet. That smile was making its last appearance for many weeks, as amongst the letters just delivered was one from our solicitor notifying us that Samet's appeal had been unsuccessful. I can't remember a moment in my life that so dramatically flipped from happiness to despair in literally a heartbeat. For a second, as I read the short letter, I paused thinking I can't do this to this smiling boy so full of hope.

"I really can't do this. This is just so wrong." I so wanted to preserve the moment of joy and delay giving him the devastating news. Being welcomed home by a young boy who was about to be told that it would soon not be his home anymore. The shock of the letter however, was etched on my face. It was too late to pretend all was okay and he had seen it. Fighting back tears, the news just destroyed him. Never in all my fostering career had there been such a soul-destroying moment. I summoned up the words of reassurance, "we'll appeal, this is just a little setback," but they were hollow words uttered almost remotely from my mouth, as with my brain in panic mode, it was all I could do not to scream with anger. There would be calls to make and plans to cancel and change. All my years of training were kicking in to help me stay calm if only for Samet's sake. The trouble is that nothing can prepare someone for a moment like this. The feelings of sheer helplessness and hopelessness were overwhelming both of us. Meanwhile, Dave was just standing there, lost for words, desperately looking for reassurance. "God, I wish Liz was here," I thought. There was no one to lean on, no shoulder to cry on, just a massive void of emptiness engulfing the three of us. Moments ago, as we had arrived home, I had given Samet a hug, but now I just put an arm around his shoulder, knowing another hug would be too much for either of us. Someone had just pulled the rug out from underneath us. Every part of our lives was suddenly in turmoil.

A shell-shocked Samet went to his room and it would be many weeks before I would even see the semblance of a smile from him again. I had constantly reassured him that we would win this case and now I was racked with guilt for giving him false hope. I am old enough to know that the human spirit has amazing powers of recovery, but also old enough to know that some experiences leave permanent scars and that everyone has a limit of pain that they can take. In that moment, I might have felt broken, but Samet really was broken and with the fragility of his mental state, I knew it would be an enormous task to rebuild him. Once again, 'It's the hope that kills you,' phrase that comes to the fore. The insane cruelty with which our immigration policy tortures young people has to be witnessed to be believed. How many young people's lives have been and continue to be destroyed by this hostile environment? When did our society lose its humanity? It is the only explanation for such cruelty and detestable practice. Such punishment of victims should have no place in a civilised society.

By the next day, Samet was gone, unsure whether to return. His life had collapsed and it was so hard for him to see anything positive in his future. I sensed that he would go, as he had friends who had been through this and gone underground to live permanently in the dark depths of our society. I knew he would probably have discussed this painful eventuality and I had, in better times, discussed the scenario with him. I had told him that whatever happened, he should find a way to stay in touch, to let me know that he was okay. I told him that wherever he went, even to Albania that I would find him and help him somehow. When he went off the next morning I wondered if I would see him again. The only need he had was to feel safe and secure. I was heartbroken that my house, his home, was no longer a place where he could feel safe. My anger at the way the Home Office and the Immigration courts treat these victims will never leave me until the day comes when they show humanity. I fear that I may not see that day.

These young people in Samet's situation understand their duty to help each other, far better than those who terrify them, traumatise them and hunt them down. Is it any wonder many are recruited into gangs? They run to evil from evil, it's hard to tell the difference for them. Their friends are often the only people they can trust, the only people that truly understand just how they feel.

This was to be a crucial few days and knowing Samet had friends that he could trust made it a little easier for me. I was worried of course. Would he just give up and run, or would he take some time out to think about his options? Fortunately, it was the latter and he let me know he was okay and after a couple of weeks, he came back home. There was still no sign of anything resembling a smile, but he had realised that for now it would be best to fight on.

In some ways Samet's absence probably helped, in that it let me calm down, talk to a few people and plan our next move. We had the right to appeal so there was never any doubt that I would use it. I knew that it could be expensive, but as with Ali and his fight, I was not going to let money be an obstacle. After all, we had enough obstacles already. Another round of meetings with legal representatives followed on, but the appeal would be more a matter of lawyers arguing over legal technicalities and no new evidence would be allowed. Whereas I had to write and gather statements for the original appeal, my main involvement moving forward would be rebuilding Samet and paying the legal bills. For that, I needed a plan.

I had raised £4,000 to fight Ali's case in 2017, so I figured that would be a minimum financial requirement, but probably more as we may have to go to a higher court. The publicity we generated with Ali had helped raise the funds but what had kick-started that story was Chef Simon getting the story out in the hospitality press initially. I had then followed up with local press and some national coverage and it all neatly coincided with severe labour shortages in the hospitality trade. This all gave the story some topical relevance. Samet's case would be very different. Ali was an exceptional talent, whereas Samet was just a normal teenager, and a very shy one at that. To make an impact with Samet's story looked like being much more difficult. Since Ali's success, another young Albanian had made the news in Bristol. A young lad, Stevan, who again was a star student and had attracted 90,000 supporters to his petition asking the Home Office to reverse their decision to deport him.

Two young Bristol Albanians in two years had been newsworthy, but that could well be a disadvantage for Samet who had not until then displayed any exceptional skills. I couldn't help thinking that the deep well of sympathy in Bristol may have dried up by now. A third story on the same theme may not be very newsworthy at all. Some of the PR that I had done in my younger days related to events, record releases and sales offers, basically advertising on the cheap. Creating a newsworthy story around a product was like free advertising but must include the necessary hype to get attention. Writing about the troubles of a young migrant would be a very different proposition. Facts would be all important. With Ali there had been a very supportive industry behind the story, but there was no such commercial interest this time. It really was a daunting task. If I could generate some local news interest and if the story picked up some traction, then maybe, with luck, we could get some national coverage in a few weeks. Sadly, relying on luck seemed to be my best chance, so I was thinking that the bulk of the legal fees would probably have to come out of my own meagre resources. My plan was therefore about as detailed as the roll of a dice and gambling had never been one of my skills.

Not for the first time, Patrick was looking like being my most likely starting point for publicity through his BCFM Community Radio Station. No matter what personal disagreements we had over the years, the one certainty I had was that he would offer his unconditional support for anything involving any of my boys. A quick phone call to Pat and the interview was set for his show 'The One Love Breakfast' on the following Monday. Well, I say quick phone call, but with Pat it's never quite that simple. Anyone that knows him will agree that getting hold of Pat on the phone can be a frustrating experience. For as long as I've known him, he has been the go-to person for so many people, but Pat answering his phone is like pulling out a winning lottery ticket. If there was a chart for most played answerphone messages then Pat would have been a chart topper for 30 years at least. To be fair, he shows no favour, whether it's a colleague, friend or a senior politician or celebrity. I've no doubt like me when most people see Pats' number pop up on a call then they quickly answer for fear that trying to return his call is like cancelling the rest of the day.

Monday 21 October would be the launch of #aFuture4Samet. Not very original but #Future4Ali had worked, so it was time for a sequel. I needed to set up the fundraiser before Monday so that I would be able to give out the details on Pat's show. Saturday morning and it was all done with a GoFundMe up and ready and press releases sent out the previous day. Had I not had the interview with Pat setup then I would probably have avoided releasing press on a Friday as they often seem to get lost over the weekend. I really wasn't expecting any immediate response, so I figured that I could always reissue the press release on Monday, if there was no positive response.

On that weekend, it was a fairly typical Sunday and I was out for an early morning coffee with Dave with a quiet day planned. That all came to an abrupt end early in the afternoon when I had a Twitter message from a guy at the *Metro* newspaper, which, according to Wikipedia, is the UK's highest circulation print newspaper. The reporter, Joe, was asking for my number as he wanted to do something with the story. I took a few minutes to gather my thoughts before replying as this level of interest was totally unexpected. I did some hasty Google research on the paper and Joe, as it was not one that I had previously dealt with. The bottom line was that this was national coverage and I'm not one for looking a gift horse in the mouth.

Having dealt on a few occasions with national media in the past, I did want to be cautious. A sensationalist story can do more harm than good to a campaign so I erred on the side of caution. What I did know from experience was that I would need, in some ways, to create and lead the narrative rather than just react to some random questions. The answers I would give in this first interview could well affect the direction and public understanding of the whole campaign. I needed at the very least to get some bullet points rehearsed so as to get the most important aspects of the story across. I had been expecting to gently ease into the campaign with a relaxed and friendly interview with Patrick the following day. It was a bit scary to suddenly have bypassed the usual local press filtering and gone straight through to a national newspaper.

The mere fact that I was now kicking off with national coverage left me feeling somewhat under-prepared. National press would undoubtedly stimulate more extensive press interest locally and probably nationally.

When a story goes out it is important to keep a little back, or have a follow up story planned, because one can very quickly become old news. Every media outlet would want their own little revelation or angle on the story, so as not to seem to be just regurgitating someone else's story. If, for one moment, I had expected any early interest from the national press, then I probably would have spent a few more days on planning press releases and follow ups. Any Tom, Dick or Harriet can get lucky with getting a story in the news, but keeping it there is a whole different ball game. To be successful with a campaign for Samet I knew that we would need momentum to keep it in the public eye for several weeks at least. A well-intentioned but misdirected opening story could derail everything from the start. Despite what many believe, reporters take pride and ownership in stories that they either break or develop. Getting a reporter invested in a story can be difficult, but when it happens it can be so empowering for that story and take it to another level. It's also important to listen carefully to the reporter, so that one can get an idea as to anything that might fit theirs or their publications agenda or narrative as long as it doesn't clash with one's own purpose, morals or ethics.

Sometimes, it's only in the course of an interview that a story begins to evolve. Stories are in some way akin to songs, in that they need a good hook. A musical or lyrical hook can make an ordinary song into a great one with the right production. A good hook, strapline or header can affect where the story is placed and how prominent it is on the page, or in the paper, or in the running order on a TV or Radio news programme.

When I got to speak to Joe from the *Metro* it felt like a good interview. During the call he asked me to describe how I saw Samet. We had talked about Samet's PTSD diagnosis, something soldiers often suffer from after battles and wars. It directly led to me talking of Samet as 'A Soldier' as his life, up until that point had been a constant battle, at home and on the streets of Tirana, on his journey to the UK and now with the Home Office. It seemed like a fitting description.

When the interview was over, I had a call from Steve with news of his own. He had written his first song in quite a while and it was something that he had wanted to write about for many years. It was based on his time serving in the British Army in Germany, where he would lead his troop in marching songs. When he said that it was titled 'I'm a Soldier' I proceeded to tell him of the interview that I had just given. It really was quite some coincidence and we both took it as a sign that it was meant to be. He sent me over the first demo and immediately I could see that it could relate to Samet and indeed to all the young people that had gone through similar situations and were now on the run and living off the grid in the UK. The song was about a soldier going into battle facing death and saying that he had done his best, fighting all his life and if he didn't survive then, "Box me up and send me home". The words seemed to echo Samet's situation, where if he lost the Home Office, they would effectively box him up and send him home. The timing of the song couldn't have been better and I knew that it could provide the campaign with its own anthem. The song itself immediately gave Steve a way of supporting us, so we agreed that he would concentrate on completing production of it as soon as possible, so that if we managed to get some momentum it would supply us with an ideal follow up story for the press in a few weeks.

Monday arrived and it certainly promised to be a momentous week. The *Metro* had the story ready for print on Tuesday and Samet and I were doing our first interview on Pat's One Love Breakfast show. The interview was the perfect way to start the week and by the time we had reached the car to go home just after 10am I had already had calls from several local papers and radio stations. I didn't want to get too excited, but starting like this was beyond my wildest expectations. On the show, I had announced both the petition and the GoFundMe and asked for support in reaching our first 100 signatures. Officially day one of the campaign and we were already approaching our first landmark on the petition. It had been Samet's first interview and it was visibly difficult for him, despite already knowing Pat. Pleased though I was with the interview, I realised that the pressure of interviews may just be too much for the boy. I would have to tread carefully. Before Monday was over, I had spoken to Tristan Cork of the *Bristol Post*. Tristan has a reputation as a campaigning journalist supportive of many community initiatives and good causes and he agreed to go with the story.

Day 2: Tuesday was the day that everything really started to take off. Tristan Cork's article was prominent in the *Bristol Post* and Joe's piece likewise in the print version of the *Metro*. Both the articles were really good pieces and had really helped kick the campaign off. I had tweeted out the stories and despite only having a handful of followers, there had been over 300 retweets and already the petition was into several hundred signatures.

Day 3: Wednesday was the day when everything changed. News broke about a lorry being found in Essex containing bodies of 39 Immigrants in the back. Along with the horror, was the thought that this could have been the fate for either of my boys, if things had been different. Children were among the victims. At that moment, I really hadn't grasped that this tragic event would have such a bearing on the campaign. Over the following days, there were many times I felt guilty that tragedy was clearly bringing the media attention headlong in our direction. A friend of mine, Paul, commented on Facebook that whilst on a train that morning reading headlines online he noticed that the tragic story of the Essex lorry deaths was placed next to Samet's story. The connection was obvious and Samet's story was inadvertently suddenly catapulted to a whole new level of public interest. Part of me wanted to put everything on hold, because I knew that publicity beyond my wildest dreams was about to come at the expense of 39 tragic deaths. For all the feelings of guilt, I knew that this was an opportunity to highlight the terrible situation that young people like Samet were facing every day. I could not turn away from that as, like it or not, we were part of the situation and part of the bigger picture. Opportunity seemed to be totally the wrong word to describe the media attention, but here it was and I would help nobody, especially Samet by staying quiet.

Within hours, representatives from the Victoria Derbyshire show were calling me along with various media outlets and the Press Association. On Sunday, the 'I'm a Soldier' connection with the *Metro* piece had seemed like it was fated to be. Now, once again, the

Metro story and another link seemed to be like fate playing its hand. Samet and I were asked to appear on a discussion with Victoria Derbyshire the next morning, but without hesitation, I knew that live TV across the nation would not be within Samet's capabilities. The risk was too high. However, a solution was found with Ali agreeing to appear to describe his experience of travelling to the UK inside the back of a lorry. By then we had many hundreds of signatures on the petition and a few donations on the GoFundMe too.

Thursday morning and Ali made his debut on live national TV and it was clearly emotional for him recalling his journey. The connection to Samet's campaign was not mentioned, which was actually something of a relief, as it still felt that we were benefiting from the tragic events even though there was no intent. I was proud seeing Ali on TV, but even after four years in England, it was easy to see the raw pain of the experience remained with him. It was a reminder to me that delving too deep into those memories could still be traumatic and not always advisable. As we reached the end of week one of our campaign, there had already been some success, although success did not feel like the right word at the time. We were over 600 signatures by Friday when the *London Evening Standard* featured our story, sparking a fair bit of Twitter activity. Saturday brought a welcome break after a manic week and a chance to meet up with Actor Joe Sims who had offered his support to Samet. Joe being a committed Bristol City fan like us met us pre-match at Ashton Gate (Home of the mighty Robins).

The meeting with Joe gave the *Bristol Post* the perfect opportunity for a follow-up story to the campaign launch, thereby giving week two an early boost. By

Monday morning the 600 signatures on the petition had become 6,000. One week in and 6,000 supporters was absolutely incredible. Thoughts turned to the possibility of reaching 10,000, now wouldn't that be something? Well indeed it was something, because by Wednesday signatures had doubled and 12,000 was passed. More media calls, interviews and regular tweets followed. With the petition, I tried to answer as many messages as I could. Just reading them was eating into my day but was also so uplifting. After difficult times those messages really restored my faith in humanity. I will admit that some of those wonderful messages brought tears to my eyes and energised me to press on.

Pleased that I was at this point (well that is probably an understatement), there was a part of me thinking that maybe we had peaked too soon. We already had local and national press and 12,000 signatures. Thursday of week two brought a trip with Dave to Taunton to meet up with family for lunch. Not unsurprisingly, given recent events, most of the talk before lunch was about our media appearances and interviews. It certainly livened up the lunch conversation too and brought back memories of Ali's campaign and my previous five minutes of fame. I was too long in the tooth to get carried away by a bit of media attention or naive enough to think that it would last beyond a few weeks.

The 13,000 mark had been passed before we started lunch and I hoped that would not be a bad luck omen. Forty minutes later and slightly stuffed after some lovely home-cooked food I sat down to check the figures. This was becoming my new routine, almost fearful to pull away from my screen for fear of missing a new development. I clicked on the petition and it said 27,000 signatures.

Numbers had doubled in the time that it had taken us to eat lunch. I suspected that this was an error or computer glitch. I put the phone down and asked Dave to check if it really was 27,000 on his phone. "NO," he exclaimed and as my heart sank, he said, "it's 28,000 now." "Oh wait a minute, make that 29,000". He was sounding like Jeff Stelling on Sky Sports Saturday giving out the latest score flashes. At that point we decided enough was enough and returned to more usual family conversations as it was taking over our visit. It certainly was an unusual family lunch.

I had planned to make a surprise visit to Marcus on the way home. His hometown of Bridgwater is just one junction back up the M5 from Taunton on the road back to Bristol. I had recently been in regular contact with him and was helping him build his catalogue of rap tunes along with help from some of my musical friends. It was a very long and arduous process, mostly due to his volatile and erratic outbursts. He had talent, but few of my friends could endure him for long. It eventually came down to me alone helping him put together what he hoped would be an album of music. Ultimately, he just craved any kind of recognition and a shot at fame. Ironically, after he had taken so long creating the music and waiting for some kind of recognition, it was suddenly me and not him that was all over the news. A surprise visit fuelled by such a successful day didn't seem like a great idea anymore. With today's events I would be distracted and giving Marcus anything less than 100 per cent attention is never a good idea. I knew that I would not be able to avoid mentioning the campaign and that would be just like rubbing salt into the wounds of a neglected young man, who was likely to be feeling a little envious. There was of course the possibility that my recent success was also making me a little above my station and even a touch arrogant and that would certainly inflame the boy. If I was only to be famous for five minutes, then I really should enjoy the brief interlude before deflating my ego. I was certainly experiencing a little adrenaline rush. For a man who had spent his life avoiding the spotlight, it was certainly surprisingly enticing.

By the time we arrived back in Bristol early evening, the scoreboard had gone well past the 40,000 mark. Almost 30,000 people signed in an afternoon and I was running out of superlatives. I had never experienced anything quite like it. The previous week I was wondering if we could make 1,000 and now this. Was this the effect of something going viral I wondered. I told Dave that reaching 27,000 had been the equivalent of a full capacity at Ashton Gate Stadium. Numbers mean little to Dave but change it into football terms and it all makes sense. We had now filled Stamford Bridge and Anfield was within our sights. We comfortably filled Anfield that evening and only Old Trafford and Wembley had any empty seats.

The next morning and we were into November. The news of the previous days' signing frenzy had made the press. Samet was front page news in the *Bristol Post* and calls were coming in from many media outlets. 70,000 people had signed our petition in the last 24-hours and Wembley Stadium was almost full in Dave's virtual reality calculator. We were right out of football stadium comparisons and from that point numbers were fairly meaningless to Dave. That Friday afternoon was like a countdown on my Facebook page as the tally passed 90,000 and then reached 100,000. Less than two weeks and we had 100,000 supporters. It was really hard to take in and comparisons like the football stadiums were all used up. With that kind of response how could the Home Office ignore our case for much longer. The euphoria of the moment had made us feel unstoppable. Unfortunately, humanity is not a valid reason for change by a faceless and unaccountable Government department or a Home Secretary clearly promoted well beyond her pay grade.

It was Friday, hopes had been raised and the weekend could be spent dreaming of potential victory. After all, Bristol's previous young Albanian campaigner had been granted Leave to Remain with 90,000 on his petition. I so wanted the agony to end for Samet and for him to be able to get on with his life. My hopes briefly soared on Saturday morning, when an official looking letter arrived, but it was not the reprieve that we had hoped for. Just when everything was going so incredibly well and we were daring to dream it was a notification that Samet's removal notice from the UK had begun. He was listed to sign on for bail at the Home Office near Bristol in a few days. He and I had heard the stories of young people being held when they attended to sign on and then being taken to the dreaded 'Camp'. The Camp refers to one of the Immigration detention centres that migrants are held in to await deportation.

I believe that we are the only country in Europe that has unlimited detention. It is said that the difference between prison and detention centres is that from your first day in prison you begin counting down the time left on your sentence, whereas from your first day in the detention camp you start counting up with no known end in sight. The previous few weeks had slowly dispelled some of Samet's negativity following the Court decision, but once again his world came crashing down. The timing, once again, could not have been more painful or cruel had it been planned by a master of torture. As with the earlier decision it took me some hours to take it all in. Samet, having done everything right since the day he arrived, was to be treated like a common criminal. At 18 he was legally a man, but in reality, he was just a scared and desperate boy unable to believe in a future.

Chapter 15

It was Sunday and I was still trying to take in the momentous events of the previous week. Up until Saturday morning, it had been an exhilarating experience but then came the massive anti-climax of the Home Office letter. The adrenaline that fired me had faded and I really needed to lift myself for another week ahead. How can success turn sour so quickly? Lifting Samet again was not possible, not with a visit to the Home Office to answer bail looming on Thursday. My intention was to look at some of the many hundreds of messages of support that had come in on the petition, but I just couldn't find the motivation. I had probably the most successful week of my life and certainly the most newsworthy, but all I could think about was that letter from the Home Office and the cruelty that came with it. Late on Sunday, my cousin Sally messaged me to say how exciting everything was and about a Barrister offering her services by way of a message on the petition. It was just one of so many messages that I had yet to read but fortunately Sally directed me to it.

Having replied to the Barrister's message, I was impressed to get a reply followed by a phone call very early on Monday morning. I had by then googled Usha Sood, the Barrister and realised that she was one of the leading Immigration Barristers in England. The call from Usha was just what was required to lift the spirits on a Monday morning. We already had a Barrister of our own taking us to an appeal, but just hearing her warm and caring manner had eased my fears. She would for now remain in the background but would come in if needed further down the line. That Home Office letter had left me feeling very isolated and vulnerable. In a legal sense my experience counted for little to nothing. Usha's intervention was indeed reassuring for someone like me, who despite all the recent support was something of a loose cannon in the middle of a war. I had plenty of friends and family support but ultimately decisions were down to me and I couldn't afford to make too many mistakes to have any chance of success. Samet was depending on me and it felt like I had already let him down with the Appeal failure.

Our local BBC TV news programme, Points West, had sent a crew to film us at home. David and Ali joined me and Samet for the benefit of the cameras. Ali Vowles was the reporter/presenter and David was just a tad excited. When we lived in Spain, we used to keep up with the local news back home by way of Points West, thanks to a rather substantial satellite dish that Wayne had erected on our finca in Medina Sidonia. It had become Dave's favourite programme from then on and he had said many times that it was his dream to sit on the red sofa that the presenters used. Although he was slightly disappointed that we were not going to the Points West studio, Ali Vowles coming to us was more than adequate compensation. David had us laughing when he started reeling off the full names of all the Points West news presenters, concluding with "and Ian on the roof" mimicking the way the weatherman was referred to on the show. Ian the weatherman didn't have a surname in David's eyes, as he was usually introduced by way of ,"let's go outside to Ian on the roof".

This interview with Ali Vowles was to be my first TV interview for a long time and Samet's situation was for me a naturally emotive subject. I was keen to avoid coming across as emotional, which would do nothing for Samet's nerves. Samet was first up for an interview, but it was soon apparent that he was not in the least comfortable with talking on camera. We quickly agreed that his contribution would be visual only as it was to be in all interviews from then on. My Ali being an old hand at media interviews had no such fears and was happy to talk about me as his Foster Carer. That was the point where I realised I would be struggling to hold it together. I quietly left the room as I felt myself welling up with the affectionate sentiments that he was expressing about me. Ali V then decided to film my part in the kitchen, but emotionally the damage was already done. I started off okay but was visibly struggling to avoid getting upset about Samet's situation after just a few questions. To her credit she offered to stop the interview and start again if I so wished, although she was quite happy with how it came across. Taking a moment, I explained that looking after teenage boys over the years I had so often stressed that there was nothing wrong with a boy or man showing emotion. For me to then go and hide my emotions and to not, in effect, practice something that I had so often preached would have been so hypocritical.

We agreed to leave the emotion in the piece to be broadcast, which I later realised was one of my best decisions. Talking with Ali V, some weeks later, I had by then realised that her interview was one of those moments that a campaign can turn on. Sometimes, fine margins can make all the difference to a cause's success. Although this interview was only for a local news programme, I later shared it through Twitter, Facebook and most importantly on the petition in one of my updates to all those who had signed. A General Election had just been called and the country was very divided. Social Media was full of polarised views. With so much negativity and depressing news around, a story like Samet's that invoked so much sympathy and pulled at the heartstrings really hit hard with so many people in a very positive way. That certainly helped explain the explosion of interest in the response to our petition. In a world of fake and lying politicians, our honesty and raw emotion stood out. Ali Vowles captured the feelings that we were experiencing and the trauma we were enduring. In media terminology when the programme was aired on that Tuesday, she had nailed it. I couldn't have asked for a better piece to explain our plight and demonstrate the unity and strength of me and my boys.

We were into the third week of the campaign and I had developed another new pastime. Reading endless messages of support. Over 80,000 signatures had been added since a week earlier and many people had left messages of support on the petition when they had signed. There are two sections for comments on the petition, firstly on signing and secondly in response to my latest posted update. I had guessed that both sections would have a few messages but was not expecting anything like the numbers that appeared. I decided to take a few minutes to read them and answer a few and the minutes turned into hours at a time. The signatures were still growing rapidly. Trying to read them all was like treading water, albeit much more uplifting. I would read and answer a few only to find I was even further from catching up to the latest ones. There were literally thousands and not just from the UK, but from all around the world. I had almost missed Usha Sood's offer that had come by way of a good luck message, so at that point I had felt it my duty to read every single message. I had never in my life felt such an outpouring of love and support. So much love for us, that it was hard to take it all in. Signing a petition can be done with a click these days, but this was something else. Countless people had taken their time to write wonderful messages and it was just so incredibly moving.

Over the next few days as the petition spread. many more messages came in. Australia, Alaska ,South America, Canada and the United States. Trying to grasp the enormity of it all was breathtaking. The GoFundMe was growing too. It was always nice to see maybe a £100 donation. but it was moving that so many people were taking the trouble to donate £5 or £10 to help a boy, my boy. A few days earlier he was unknown, but now he had a following in excess of 100,000 people. I moved the reading and replying of messages to a late night spot before sleep, so that each day could finish with a good feeling. It was all very exciting but the reality was that there was no sign of a change of heart from the Home Office.

Thursday came and it was time for Samet's first visit to sign on for bail. A few messages had shared other Carers experiences of these fearful appointments. Samet already knew of one friend who had been taken to the Camp after attending to sign for bail. One carer had described how upon arrival at the building he was told to wait outside as the terrified young man was shown into the building, unsure if he would be allowed to return or sent to the Camp. The carer had asked to accompany his charge as the boy was very frightened. "Oh, that's alright they all are," was the reply from the security guard, as if being put into a traumatic and terrifying situation was quite normal and acceptable. Sadly, the more I see of Home Office practices, the more I realise that fear is a weapon used all too often and they see no need to adhere to any acceptable moral code. They are quite simply a law unto themselves and the law of the land is fairly meaningless when they are allowed to operate beyond any public scrutiny.

The Home Office building is a fairly anonymous-looking building on an industrial estate a few miles south of Bristol. Most people who have business on the estate would be oblivious to the fear that the mere sight of this building could have on young migrants. It was just under an hour from home, but the journey for me and Samet was especially quiet and as we got closer the feeling of trepidation increased. It reminded me of the nervous silence that I had experienced in youth courts with various youngsters, awaiting sentence and fearing the worst. Trying to make conversation to distract Samet from the approaching appointment was futile. His eyes were empty of emotion and he had long since given up looking at his phone as the dark fears overcame him. He was desperately trying to look calm and relaxed but failing miserably. Over recent decades Portishead has been transformed from a neglected harbour just down the Bristol channel from the industrialised Avonmouth Docks into the go-to place for those wanting a bit more exclusivity. Today though it was just a place of fears for us.

Footballers and celebrities have houses and apartments in the new marina complexes just minutes away from where some of the most unfortunate migrants have to attend such dreaded appointments. Neatly hidden away on a bland industrial estate, the great and the good probably never notice these migrants from the darkened windows of their luxurious 4x4s as they pass by. These poor unfortunate souls would not want to linger in the area one moment longer than necessary and rarely stop to venture into the town. The only migrants likely to frequent the coffee shops and restaurants in Portishead are millionaires, who's welcome from the community is the polar opposite to those visiting the Home Office on the edge of town. Those that have arrived in the UK by rubber dinghy probably have more sea faring experience than some of those drinking in the local yacht club, but they are unlikely to be found comparing nautical experiences over a gin and tonic in the bar.

We arrived at the Home Office a little early, so waited for what seemed like an eternity in the car. Fortunately, I was allowed into the building with Samet and having completed filling in various forms we were released back out into the fresh air and wasted no time at all in leaving the area and heading back over the M5 bridge into Bristol. The relief for Samet when the ordeal was over was palpable. For me it was relief, but an increasing sense of anger that we, as a country ,need to put young people through such a traumatic process. From the moment that they arrive in the UK, every step of the process seems dehumanising and traumatic and if anything it appears to be getting even worse, incredible though that seems. From that point on Bail signing would be once a month, although future appointments would be at a Police Station nearer home. More convenient but no less daunting.

Two days later and another interview with Ali Vowles, this time on her Radio Bristol Saturday morning show, by which time we had reached 120,000 signatures on the petition. The petition and media interest was carrying Samet's story around the world, so it should not really have been a surprise that we were making the news in Albania. Samet was impressed rather than excited by all the media interest but was amazed to be sent a clip of our story being headline news on national TV in Albania. Seeing the two of us sat on the bench outside my house on a foreign news channel was somewhat surreal. It was. as Samet translated. basically a rehash of UK media coverage. but the only two words that I understood were 'Samet' and 'Stokes' repeated numerous times. Any thoughts that the Home Office harboured that Samet could be quietly returned to a safe location in Albania were now surely gone. He and I were now known faces in Albania following the news report and anonymity would be impossible. In effect this had unintentionally made part of the Home Office argument for sending him back null and void. as they would be putting his safety at risk.

Week four of the campaign began with the news that the local radio station had playlisted 'I'm a Soldier' and hopefully more would follow. By Wednesday, the *Sunday Mirror* were booked in for a photo shoot and the *Metro* were updating the story with the news that

150,000 people had signed the petition. Another 10,000 were added by the weekend and the constant stream of well-wishing messages continued to dominate my late night reading. Sunday finally brought some respite and a chance to go out for lunch at Ali's restaurant. In just under a month, my family had become almost celebrities, with the amount of media coverage and it was showing no sign of easing off. It was good to just stop and take stock of how much we had achieved.

Another week of interviews followed, which included a request for an interview from the *Sun* newspaper. That was the point where I felt it necessary to draw a line. I had known from the start that it is naive in the extreme to seek publicity and then think that one can control it, or where it might go. World famous celebrities and politicians cannot do that, so I knew there would always be risk involved in a high-profile campaign. I have long held an opinion, shared by many, that the *Sun* will print anything for a story and using their coverage of the Hillsborough football tragedy as an example, they did not care who they hurt in the process with their lies. I have always admired the way that the people of Liverpool made their stand against the paper and banished it from their city. Coverage in the *Sun* would guarantee us even greater publicity, but for me it was never an option. Dealing with that paper was a step too far for me and not something I could entertain. It's possible that they would have given us some positive coverage, but deep down, I know that I would eternally regret any sanctioning or acceptance of their interest and it would be hypocritical of me to do so. Saying no to the *Sun* felt like a good thing to do, although I never really expected that to be the end of the matter. Things are never that simple with news stories.

The following week was mostly spent getting things ready for the release of the record. I've been too long working in music to harbour any hopes of commercial success, whatever the quality of the music. This release was more about supporting our campaign than seeking commercial success and also about highlighting the plight of the other 'soldiers' like Samet who have been forced into hiding. We had a few promotional T-shirts made as the record release would probably be our next story for the papers. Ross Arnott of the local *Gazette* had picked up on the story a week earlier and whilst they might pale into relative insignificance in relation to some of the other news outlets, they nevertheless did a really good piece which dominated their front page. Walking into my local Tesco superstore the next day and the first thing I saw as I entered the store with Dave was a newspaper rack filled with rows of the paper. To say the least, it was a little unnerving as my photo was emblazoned across the front page. Confronting one's own image and realising that one was in the gaze of multiple people walking around the shopping centre was a strange experience. Shopping was beginning to become a rather drawn out affair, being recognised so much and having so many people stop us and offer words of support and encouragement.

David, however, was very taken with his newfound fame, having been seen with Samet and Ali in recent local TV footage. Always a sociable person at the best of times, he would happily stop and engage in conversation with any willing participant. After appearing on television, he was now on a new fitness regime that involved constant circuits of the shopping centre on a personal 'meet and greet' until the call of food brought him home. The West Country ITV coverage that had sparked Dave's local celebrity status also brought contact from a few acquaintances of my own from younger days. One woman got in touch to say that her husband had spoken many times over the last 30 years about the guy who used to work at the local Eagle House youth club when he was a boy and the fun times he and his mates had to thank him for. When my face came on the news report, her husband apparently leapt out of his chair and said, "That's him. That's John from Eagle House, that I've always told you about". It was quite humbling to have been remembered with so much affection. An hour later after searching through a Cadbury Roses tin full of old photos, I sent her a picture that I had of her husband Martin and his mates when they were 16 at the very start of my youth work days. If I ever had any doubts as to validating my life's work then these last few weeks had forever dispelled them.

To start off December I wrote an update for the petition. My updates had become more personal and whilst naturally focusing on Samet had come to include all members of the household following so many messages wishing us all well. As with the Points West TV feature I think the personal nature of the story and how it was affecting all our lives, just gave it added momentum and interest for people who felt invested in it. The GoFundMe account had received £5,000 worth of donations and over the two days following my update another 50,000 signatures were added, bringing it up to 230,000 in total. My nighttime message reading and answering was taking me way into the early hours each night but was an absolute pleasure. There was still no word from the Home Office to suggest that they might reverse their decision, which seemed astonishing in the light of the public response, but I was convinced that it would happen as it had in the past when similar cases received massive public attention and support.

December 3rd was Dave's Birthday and it was the official release of 'I'm a Soldier' by Stevie D Red dedicated to the young victims of trafficking. Among Dave's Birthday cards was one from Ali Vowles inviting him to a tour of the BBC Points West Studios the following week. The Red Sofa was calling him and his dream was soon to be realised. The following day was another spent filming for BBC News this time at Samet's college where his tutor explained that he was the stand-out student on his carpentry course, something Samet had neglected to tell me. Samet, so shy and modest, had a much greater talent than I had realised, but living in a house where his foster brother Ali's exceptional talent was often talked about it had gone without mention. I really was blessed to be looking after two such talented young men.

The record release had given another boost to the campaign, which was all that we had intended. Musicworks 1, our own label was always going to be more about working with young people rather than record sales. Having owned the record store 'Soundsville Kingswood' with Patrick in the 1990s I knew a bit about record sales and how they are dominated by the major labels. Making even a tiny impact on them is rare indeed and extremely unlikely. Admittedly, my record store experience was in the days of Vinyl and CD's long before digital sales ,so some aspects were new to me. Late evening on the fourth whilst working through the latest mass of messages I decided to check out some of the charts out of interest.

Amazon seemed to be one of the main charts, so I took a look and was left stunned. Digital charts change every few hours but there it was. The fastest rising single was 'Soldier'. Number one in Amazon Movers and Shakers, Number two in Hot New Releases and Number five in the Amazon National Top 10. Blown away was an understatement. All achieved at nil expense, with no advertising budget and almost certainly on the back of my latest update to the petition. Alongside the likes of Ed Sheeran there was Stevie D Red. Getting over the initial shock I phoned Steve who greeted the news with total disbelief. His chart days were long ago and this was a totally unexpected return. We could imagine all the chart pluggers and major labels being totally bemused by this unknown track that had come from nowhere and gone high in the chart. "Who the f*** is that?" was probably echoing around the record industry at that point. With no promotion we had broken through the chart cartel. This was the power of having over 200,000 people reading petition updates and showing support. It could not be maintained of course, without continued promotion but that just didn't matter to us. We had just caused a little earthquake in the music industry and suddenly Steve's phone was ringing again from old music contacts. Those few days of having a chart presence were quite enough for us, the stuff of dreams.

For me personally, I began to feel a new power and self-belief. I had created this monster and it was down to me. To see Steve get recognised once more for his music was all the reward that I needed. Sometimes the good guys win and I just hoped that the roll that I was on could continue until Samet was safe and secure here in the UK.

By this time, I was probably almost immune to further surprises such had been the impact of the campaign, but another milestone was achieved shortly after with the petition reaching 250,000 signatures. A quarter of a million people had felt moved enough to sign our petition. From a handful of people a few weeks earlier, My 'soldier' Samet now had an army of a quarter of a million people behind him. The size of the support and the success of the record would give the media a few more weeks of coverage at the very least, so those weeks leading up to Christmas were likely to be as busy as the last few.

December 10th was quite a memorable day for Dave. First off, it was the promised visit to the BBC Bristol Points West News studios with Ali Vowles, where David finally got to sit on the red sofa. He was then taken out to the roof, where the weather reports were often broadcast. He also got to meet Geoff Twentyman, the head of Radio Bristol's sports team, another great favourite of his. Later in the afternoon, it was off with Dave and Samet to Ashton Gate to meet up with actor and supporter Joe Sims, who was our host for a VIP match day experience, gifted by the club. Included was a pre-match meal and half-time drinks and pies. Days don't come much better than that for Dave. Just seeing Samet get the VIP treatment was brilliant. There was at last a smile back on his face, after all the setbacks with his appeal.

The following days saw another round of interviews and updates. Russia Today was a surprising one, closely followed by Channel 5 News and another BBC feature, all carrying news of the record's success. We were heading for Christmas 2019 and yet another New Year full of hope. There is something about each new year that gives us new hope, which rarely comes to anything. At that period, just before Christmas, I was naturally optimistic in respect of Samet's campaign with the way that it had exploded into life. It certainly made me hungry to get going early in the new year. We had the momentum. What could possibly stop us?

Like most people, I was not taking too much notice of events across the world in China with talk of a new flu epidemic. How often the press liked to seize on some foreboding of doom to get our attention and rarely did they come to be anything serious. Would 2020 be any different to any other year? Probably not, apart from the approach of Brexit. It would be great to have something else other than Brexit to talk about I thought. Well, there you go I spoke too soon.

It was certainly into the New Year with a bang. I was somewhat surprised to see my name appear alongside some very worthy people in a list compiled by the *Bristol Post* of 25 people who had made Bristol a happier place in 2019. A bit of a New Year's honour without the gong. In that first week of 2020 we were off to Court in London with Samet, hoping for a good start to the year. It was a first chance to meet in person with our new Barrister, the wonderful Usha Sood, who exuded calm and confidence. The day over it was to be another one of those agonising waits for Samet before a decision would be forthcoming from the court.

Later in the week The *Sun* decided to publish an article about Albanian gangs and linked it with young Migrants. All press and publications had until then agreed not to print his name in full but as I had refused to talk to the *Sun* they were clearly not concerned and printed his full name. For Samet seeing his name in an article alongside convicted gang members was absolutely terrifying. Once again months spent rebuilding Samet's mental state were completely destroyed with an added pressure in that he now saw himself as a potential target for the gangs wanting to make an example of him. My only hope was that a favourable court decision would negate some of the damage the article had done and give him reason to look forward to the future at last. That decision unfortunately was still weeks away, so a new term at college began with more reasons to be fearful, rather than less. Month after month of pressure since his initial refusal was taking a big toll on his mental health and well-being.

Chapter 16

Samet's campaign had given me a lift with the amazing public support, but the breakthrough with a positive response from the Home Office was still not forthcoming. I was left wondering how much more I would have to do.

Reaching a quarter of a million supporters had made me think that a change of heart would be inevitable, but then the closure of Parliament prior to the winter General Election had given the Government the opportunity to avoid dealing with so many issues. With Parliament in recess for many weeks, almost all petitions to the Government became obsolete. All petitions on the Government site had to close permanently, no matter how many signatories they had accumulated and they would have to be restarted from scratch. Our petition, thankfully, was not affected as it was through Change. Org and not on the Government site. I suspected though, that the new Government was not ready to entertain conversations on any petitions at that time. We needed to give it a kick-start again and decided to follow the suggestion of Rima Amin (our liaison person with Change.org) and deliver the petition and signatures directly to the Home Office.

Using the strap line 'I Stand with Samet', the petition delivery was set for 23 January 2020 so as to give a focal point to the delivery and once again to highlight the campaign in the press. The 23rd gave us a renewed focus and once again unerring public support. On a chilly but sunny January morning, Steve joined Samet, Dave and I on our trip to the Home Office in central London. We stopped at the M4 services for a coffee and toast en route early in the morning and caught up with the many messages of support coming in on Twitter and Facebook. People from all over the UK were tweeting selfies with 'I stand with Samet' messages. An article that I had written on Samet's plight had even been published that morning by the *Huffington Post* and we knew the press would be awaiting our arrival with the petition signatures to hand over to the Home Office.

Navigating London traffic was the usual nightmare, but we did manage to find an underground car park close to the Parliament buildings, so carrying banners and bags was not as bad as feared. Rima and her CHANGE colleagues arrived with their boxes of signatories' names. The boxes were of course symbolic as holding up a data stick would have looked distinctly unimpressive for the cameras. Rima, being experienced in petition deliveries, had arranged a small PA system for Steve to perform his 'I'm a Soldier' track outside the Home Office HQ. Being a child of the 1960s it felt very much like an echo of that 'Beatles playing on the Apple Building roof' performance, insofar as we were not sure if either the Home Office or the police would allow an impromptu performance in such a high profile place. Generally, petition deliveries would be purely a photo-op, so adding in an unscheduled music performance presented all sorts of logistical problems.

A coffee shop was conveniently situated opposite the delivery location and gave us the chance for some last-minute planning. We had not sought permission for the performance nor announced it, as we had felt that literally 'busking it' was our best chance of success. Why complicate a good plan. The whole experience seemed somewhat surreal, even after the last few months of publicity and public support. I had only met Rima online up until that day, but it was enough to give me the confidence that she would set up the logistical support and she certainly did not disappoint. The whole CHANGE.org involvement had been an amazing experience since day one. Less than three months earlier, I could not have imagined how all of this would evolve into such a huge story nationally.

After some negotiations, the Home Office agreed to receive the petition at their reception. Steve, meanwhile, went ahead with his performance, which entertained all the supporters that had turned up, as well as the office folk in the area. One wonderful elderly lady turned up with a shopping basket on wheels emblazoned with a handmade 'I stand with Samet' sign, having trekked across London. Samet and I duly delivered the petition followed by a series of TV and media interviews. Every coffee break was spent looking at the 'selfies' of supporters on Social Media so a successful day all round with the petition having reached 265,000 signatures.

Within a few days, we had passed 300,000 and by the end of January 400,000 had been reached, but there was still no positive news from the Home Office. Samet's case though, had been brought to the attention of the Council of Europe thanks to Bristol MP Kerry McCarthy. Kerry had been our MP and was very supportive when we had lived in Bristol during Ali's immigration fight. Once again Kerry showed her support by highlighting Samet's situation whilst addressing the Council of Europe Parliament. Our campaign had snowballed throughout the Winter and really was beginning to feel unstoppable. Sadly, of course as the dark winter nights were drawing to a close from out of nowhere came the Covid Spring and the world changed overnight.

One of my favourite times of the year is seeing the first signs of Spring emerging and the daffodils this year seemed earlier than ever. Sadly, over the few short weeks of their flowering, the world was to change like never before in my lifetime and 2020 was destined to be the year when everything just stopped. The momentum of the campaign was lost for us and back then we just didn't know for how long. What we did know was that the new UK Government was not to be one that would face problems if there was a way to avoid or deflect them. All of a sudden, our story was understandably insignificant in the grand scheme of things. So much was quickly lost in those dark early days of Covid. Truth and Honesty had been among the first casualties in the UK and our Government was happy to take full advantage. All the wonderful humanity and love, that I in particular had witnessed over recent months, seemed now to be pushed aside.

I had always accepted that our campaign and the resulting almost celebrity-like status would be temporary, but the swiftness that the momentum disappeared was just so disappointing. Fortunately, I have never suffered from an enlarged ego, so my sudden relegation back to relative anonymity was quite manageable. My 'famous for five minutes' phase had actually outlived my expectations, but as the clock of progress suddenly halted the doubts and fears regarding Samet's prospects came to the fore again.

As the world changed and so many people's hopes and dreams faded and disappeared, another bombshell had hit Samet and all of us. Our latest court appeal had been refused and Samet was once again plunged into even more fear and negativity. It felt like our full tank of optimism, fuelled by the petition, was nearly empty. It wasn't the end of the road, but it felt like we were stuck on the M25 with all exits closed, fuel running out and the sat nav totally confused.

It reminded me of a time in France, when the sat-nav was directing me to a petrol station through ever-narrowing country lanes, with the fuel gauge on empty for the last 20 kilometres. We ended up at a dead end by the entrance to a field. The petrol station was just across the field, but on the motorway and about six kilometres away by road. A voice from the sat nav said "you can now walk to your destination." Yes, once again our destination was in sight and yet seemingly unreachable. The pandemic now just added to our despondency. Our Barrister assured us that we could make a further appeal, but with the world on pause, how long would that be and could a very broken Samet once again find the resolve or hope to carry on. The inclination to follow so many young people who had gone before him into the dark side of our society was growing stronger. I really wasn't sure how much longer I could hold him.

As we headed towards the lockdown Summer I looked back and reflected on how Samet's situation had gone so differently from Ali's. In less than five years since jumping off that lorry in Bristol, Ali's life had been transformed. I had been fairly quiet on Twitter for a while at that point so trying to keep my mind focused, I tweeted a brief bio of Ali's story on his birthday. Before I knew it the whole thing had gone viral which was cause for some friendly banter between Ali and Samet. For months nothing had happened and it felt good to tweet a good news story. Samet had 400,000 signatories to his petition and Ali 400,000 views to his story. It was almost like they were trying to outdo each other with their stories. Several executives at the United Nations Refugee Agency in New York, Switzerland and the Middle East shared Ali's story. It seemed almost ridiculous that a Foster Carer like myself could have two boys, both of whom had their stories shared around the world as a source of inspiration to others. Despite his own situation, Samet was pleased to see the spotlight had turned to Ali and, as ever, was pleased for his success without any sign of envy. I felt such pride when realising that my boys' stories had touched and inspired so many people around the world.

By this time Samet, with all his disappointments and setbacks, had grown wary of all the publicity. He had understandably never spoken in any press interviews himself and had always been uncomfortable being in the media glare. He had accepted my reasons, as to why I felt it was necessary, but had finally asked me if I could refrain from anymore as he feared it was making the Government hostile to his situation. Whilst I didn't think that was the case, my first duty was to Samet and to adhere to his wishes. I sensed that refraining from publicity going forwards would mean that he would become yesterday's news. Admittedly, this time it was Ali's story once again attracting media enquiries, but

I knew that it was inevitable that Samet's story would be back in the news if I spoke to the media about Ali. I fended off numerous media enquiries after agreeing with Samet that I wouldn't do any more press until his case was concluded, however long that might be. It was a promise made with all sincerity, but without knowing that the resolution to his case could be many years away.

Summer as for most people in 2020 (well the lucky ones anyway), was largely uneventful and fortunately, we all stayed healthy. There was a lot of legal stuff to go through preparing Ali's new visa application and preparation for the next stage of Samet's appeal. I was beginning to feel like I should have had a legal career with the amount of legal knowledge I had accumulated. This was not part of the usual Foster Carers remit. Several trips to Cardiff for legal appointments were almost welcome as a justifiable reason to get away from Bristol for a few hours, although Wales had its own lockdown. Trying to get a coffee from anywhere but a machine was an adventure in itself. In covid times even a little success like getting a coffee somewhere was most welcome.

September arrived and with it came a 19th Birthday for Samet. It was no great cause for celebration, as it was just a stark reminder of the lack of progress we had made towards securing his Leave to Stay in the UK. It had generally been a year littered with setbacks and dashed hopes and was set to continue through the first Covid winter and beyond. A month later came yet another setback when we were refused the opportunity to take Samet's case to the Court of Appeal. It was not entirely unexpected but again made us fear actually raising our hopes at all. In boxing terms, I could say that Samet having got up from numerous knockdowns was now pinned on the ropes getting battered and almost ready to throw in the towel and concede. Even my usual positivity and resilience was ebbing away.

Our Barrister Usha had fortunately prepared for the refusal possibility and had a Plan B ready to go. The problem that we had faced every step of the way since losing the initial appeal a year earlier ,was that we had not been allowed to introduce any fresh evidence to our original claim. The past 12 months had at least given us time to consider an alternative strategy if the appeals failed. Samet now had the right to submit a fresh claim as the other appeals procedure had been exhausted. With this fresh claim, new evidence could be added and over the year we had gathered and prepared a strong body of evidence just for that eventuality. I had so hoped this next stage would not be necessary, but as it was then we were at least much better prepared than for the original appeal. It was by then November 2020 and the continuing pandemic was just adding to the gloom. We submitted Samet's fresh claim and prepared for another anxious wait.

December 2020 brought the welcome news that Ali's visa had finally been renewed, something that at least brought some relief at the end of a difficult and largely unproductive year. Samet's case was still continuing. As we edged towards the Covid Christmas it was good to receive again some messages of support from some of the people who had signed Samet's petition. Unknowingly, they had in a small but not insignificant way become a new support network of sorts. Over the year as I think I have mentioned, my regular updates to the petition had introduced Dave, Ali and even Marcus to our supporters. We had eased off in the second half of the year due to Samet's nervousness about publicity, but a few had kept in touch via the petition, the fundraiser and by email. One of those was an amazing lady from Ecuador, Elizabeth. Although we had only spoken by way of a few emails, she had a calming and reassuring air about her, that reminded me of both our Barrister and another Elizabeth, my most treasured and missed friend Liz.

Liz, of course in a spiritual way, will always be there as an advisor, a point of reference and as a guide. I am not a religious person but I believe a spirit can guide you whether the spirit is actually there or not. It might not be anything more than the fond memory of someone close and recalling how they dealt with situations but just knowing what they might advise if they were there can in fact be reassuring enough. It is the purest form of communication where no words or actions are needed or necessary, just accessing one's own memory and mentally having a conversation with the person that has passed. We can I believe continue to learn from the love, support and memories of anyone that meant so much to any of us. Their vital existence was a piece in the jigsaw of one's life and their departure from it does not take away the imprint of that piece. Just because we can no longer see that piece of our life, does not mean that it is no longer there. Therein lies the key, because our eyes do not always see what is right in front of us and yet we can sometimes sense it is there. I am not, as I have said, in any way a religious person, but the spirits of those departed undoubtedly guide me because they exist in my mind, my memory and my heart so for me they are tangible and real.

"A beautiful part of living is what we're left by the dead," *Bruce Springsteen 2020*

As the year was ending it was Elizabeth, that wonderful lady from Ecuador, who was the source of new inspiration for me. Her emailed messages suggested a person of learning and vast experience and took me back to Google again, where I discovered something of the fascinating life that she has lived. An educator, a communicator, an author and so much more. A groundbreaking woman, who just like Liz Wilson, had inspired so many others. During what had been a year of Lockdowns and isolation and the, all too often boredom, it was so refreshing to hear from such an amazing person who had taken time out to support Samet and my family in our struggle. I had received thousands of wonderful messages over the past year, but this stood out as she seemed in many ways like a kindred spirit who appeared at the right time to lift my spirits after such a difficult year.

A kindred spirit maybe, but a very different life. A life most recently spent working with remote tribes in the Amazon jungle. With my bug phobias, the thought of being in the jungle fills me with dread. I can't even handle a normal house spider without breaking out in a cold sweat and then getting Dave to arrange it's immediate removal. When we lived in Spain, the clicking noise of a visiting gecko at night would also cause me to summon Dave. Their detachable tails however did add an extra complication. When I thought about this lady in Ecuador, I wondered how a woman of a similar age to me could cope with working in such an environment. I guess it's a bit like watching someone like David Attenborough. Full of wonderment and admiration, but would I want to actually be there, to put up with the discomforts? No way, not in a million years, I think.

In a strange way though, there was a similarity in how others have often viewed my work with young people and my life. Many people including some friends and family have, over the years, said that whilst they were full of admiration for me, they don't really get why I do what I do. When that first explosive foster child Wayne burst into my life, my dear Mum and Dad were certainly among them. Imagine a David Attenborough programme on people like Wayne. Never mind 'Life on Earth', 'Life in Care' has its own mysteries and wonderment and some amazing creatures. The creatures that I've studied have been somewhat closer to home, some quite dangerous and yet largely invisible to most of our society, except when they've done something wrong. David Attenborough helps us to understand a world around us that would otherwise be beyond our comprehension, so I like to think that the hidden talents and qualities of so many of the boys that I have looked after could offer some great insights to people who have never seen their value. Wayne, for instance, with his instinctive ability to solve technical and mechanical problems and react to crisis situations with lightning precision.

I recall a few years ago when his technical knowledge was in great demand. Those were the times of the 'Sky TV Boxes'. Everyone seemed to want them, but as is always the case with a successful product the costs kept rising and so became hard to justify for many people. When that happened, people would cancel their subscriptions and that's where the black market economy took over. Someone in their wisdom found that they could chip boxes that had been taken out of circulation. Media companies at the time rarely bothered to get departing customers to return their set-top boxes, so the opportunists stepped in. By 'chipping' the boxes they could be put back online without the suppliers knowing. People would happily buy a box off their mate at a fraction of the cost of a subscription. All completely illegal of course but the market for them grew rapidly, nevertheless.

Once Wayne had chipped a few boxes, the demand for his services grew rapidly. Meanwhile the various media companies were pushing their technicians to develop new online ways of disabling these chips. It became like a constant battle between the big media companies and these pirate computer hackers. They would bring out a new system and overnight the boxes would become obsolete before the hackers would find a workaround to get them back up and running. I remember one time that a company announced that after months of research by their experts a perfect storm scenario had been found to shut down all the chipped boxes. I was at Wayne's the next day and he had already figured out a new workaround and was getting congratulatory messages from people pleased that their boxes were back up and running in such a short space of time.

To Wayne the whole thing was more of a sideline, as it was for many others. Hackers began to get raided and arrested, reminding me of the pirate radio days. Pirate stations were closed down for a few days before opening up again in a new location. One bright spark at one of the media companies, a sub-contractor, decided to help himself to a piece of the growing pie. He managed a number of the company's delivery drivers and offered them incentives to pick up boxes from ex-customers and get them re-chipped. He then sold them back to the customers at a fraction of the subscription price. Each driver would get a bonus per box so there was a nice incentive for a bit of cash to be made on the side. They would take the boxes up to Wayne's and collect the 'newly chipped' boxes the next day.

I remember going to visit Wayne one day and seeing a whole batch of the Media delivery vans parked in his street and a house full of salesmen. Wayne even had his own uniform from the company and would get a nights free beer from various pubs that wanted to show big games or fights but didn't want to pay subscriptions. Nobody would question a man in full company engineers uniform lifting a street cover and 'fixing' a problem. Of course, as the saying goes "all good things come to an end". A few months later, on another visit to Wayne's, rather than the Media vans outside his house there were instead several police cars. The game was up !

The door was wide open and the uniforms going in and out were definitely not media company ones. although there was a Media Company enforcement officer along with various policemen and other officials. Once inside there was a stream of people going up and downstairs, carrying the shells of numerous set top boxes. One very smug looking female official was clearly enjoying her day's work. All sorts of bits and pieces were put onto a large pile of equipment on the kitchen floor. Wayne really seemed quite relaxed about it all and was his usual cocky self, laughing and joking with the intruders. Eventually they had collected everything they wanted and Wayne asked for a receipt for everything so that he could have it all returned once they had concluded their investigation. The smug woman smirked as if to say that she had enough evidence.

As soon as the last policeman had left and the last car driven away Wayne went over to his washing machine, opened it and pulled out what looked like a piece of one of the boxes.

"Don't worry," he said, "they've got nothing".

The essential piece of equipment that they apparently needed was the device that he used to chip the boxes.

"This is what they needed".

In his hand was the very piece that he had just taken out of the washing machine. They had placed it on top of the high pile of equipment on his kitchen floor. Then as they were busy collecting more items they were momentarily distracted and Wayne seized the moment and quickly put the piece inside his washing machine unnoticed. All the rest of the equipment was from dozens of boxes that had no value to them whatsoever. It was many months later that his equipment was returned with no charges laid. I suspect that even if they had found some minor offences committed that the media company had nothing to gain from a prosecution that would highlight the involvement of so many of their employees. It was a near miss for Wayne, but not the first time that he had walked away from what appeared to be a hopeless situation. It certainly didn't harm his reputation and just added to the legend as a good few others involved also walked away unscathed from the experience.

Many people just couldn't understand why I decided to sacrifice so many of life's more pleasant aspects. Missing out on simple things, like having a social life and being able to welcome visitors without either hesitation or trepidation. In a funny sort of way, maybe like Elizabeth in Ecuador I have spent my life working in a jungle of sorts, communicating with people outside of society's norms. From the rare tribes of Knowle West, to car thieves and autistic teenage rappers who are treated like aliens by so many in our so-called developed society. Yes, Elizabeth and I are both in our own ways communicators and translators with those who fall outside of society's accepted social norms.

Elizabeth and I might work in different worlds and in very different ways but whether it's an Amazonian tribe or an Aspergic rapper, what we do is help people communicate with each other and be understood. It's all about communication and understanding people outside of our own social group. People from different cultures and with different beliefs. It's also about learning to develop our skills and abilities and increasing our own knowledge by helping others.

The more we understand ourselves the better communicators we can be. Communicating with our inner soul and with those that have passed through our lives can be the most important conversations that we ever have. An elder can tell this to a person of any age, but maybe only an elder can fully understand it and can truly feel at one with the world. The most comfortable place for one person can be the most uncomfortable place for another. Our houses are where we live at any given time, but our homes are where we belong whether they be physical, emotional or spiritual.

A spirit can guide you just by being there, or by you feeling that they are there. It is the purest form of communication, where no words or actions are needed or necessary. When I have a big decision to make, I often stop and think what would Mum or Dad say to do or if it's anything Social Work then what would Liz have said. Their existence may now just be in my imagination, but it is no less valuable for that. Without imagination how could we live or strive for better things.

For some people, these spirit guides are a necessary piece in the jigsaw of life. When a piece of the jigsaw is missing and we can't find it then maybe it's already there but our eyes have just not been opened to it. Our eyes can be blinkered, but not our imagination. We can't necessarily achieve all our dreams, but that doesn't mean that we shouldn't chase them anyway. They are like signposts when we're lost. The destination may change, but sometimes we need justification for taking a certain path. Feeling that someone close that has passed would approve can be so reassuring and keeps you moving along the path wherever it eventually leads. Most likely it will just lead to another path, rather than any specific destination but the journey is often more important than the destination.

Younger people neither need nor desire spirit guides but they have incredible imagination because life has yet to dull their enthusiasm or creativity. Unfortunately, life experiences for young people in the care system can often lead them to focus their energies on negative emotions, antisocial behaviour and criminality. This is precisely where mentors and foster carers, like myself, can sometimes help to make a difference.

Chapter 17

David's impact over the years on the culture of my house, its well-being and its atmosphere has made it so much easier for so many young people to settle in and make it their home. David is a creature of habit, who despite a chaotic early part of life, has long since found his home with me. Over the years he endured many disruptive foster children but was always safe in the knowledge that I would preserve his routines and his safety. Initially as a child, I was for his own protection but in later years David created himself a role as my wingman and I grew to realise that I protected him, as much for my well-being as for his. He has become a rock in a life that has lost too many rocks in recent years. He has enabled me to develop routines and coping mechanisms, so that age has not lessened my abilities in looking after foster children. I am sure that my fostering career would have long since ended by now, had it not been for the ever supportive and dependable Dave.

He reflects the environment around him. At boarding school, the daily manic chaos would sometimes break his routines and he would just lose it and get sent home. Only on rare occasions in recent years have his life routines been upset and then he would rush to Wayne's. He knew that Wayne was always there for me, so if he felt like he was losing control he would head for Wayne's. If my customary protective shield had been penetrated, then in Daves eyes only Wayne was strong enough to sort it and fix whatever had been broken. He calls Wayne the Fixer because whatever gets broken in life Wayne can usually fix it. Cars, plumbing, domestic repairs, computers and any threats to our peaceful life and security.

David is a guy that thrives on order and routine and, as such, sets the tone for the whole house. Many years ago, I had created the environment where he could be safe and secure. Somewhere along the way he had quietly taken control of first his life and then of the home environment. He brought calmness and order to a household that had, on occasions, contained some very volatile young men. We both learned to survive, surrounded by young people who demonstrated extremely disruptive and sometimes dangerous behaviour.

Undoubtedly, over the years I had honed my skills to reduce risk and damaging situations, but only recently have I fully appreciated the impact David has had on making my job so much easier. He evolved from foster child to wingman over many years. He had already become an essential part of my natural family and was the most amazing support, to first my father and then my mother, in their final years. They had by their own example shown him how to care more than I ever could and they had on many occasions gave him respite when things became a bit rocky in my house. They were the rock for me and him and as each of them were to leave our lives he very slowly became my rock, as much as me being his. The process was so gradual through my two periods of grief, that I never truly appreciated it until recently. Writing this book has been a very therapeutic and enlightening experience. I feel like I am truly understanding myself and my life for the first time. I had never really stopped to think about it much before.

"Yes. Liz once again it's that Analysis and Reflection thing working a treat."

I don't think it's something that David has necessarily thought about but he soaked up all the love and caring that my parents had shown him and now spreads the same around to just about everyone in his life, especially me with the reducing number of Elders in our lives. He is part of my parents legacy as are many others in the family. Legacy is like a baton passed in a relay race. It's passed on to us to run our race and then when our race is run, we pass it on if there is someone to take it. Life is passed through blood, but a legacy of love can be passed to any willing recipients, whether blood or not and it is the most wonderful gift that any of us can pass on.

As a foster carer, one of the greatest things that I have learned is that we can pass on such wonderful gifts to very damaged children. They can see how we demonstrate love and caring by our actions more so than words. So often we remark how a child is like one parent or another and whilst that can be true, just ask yourself, how does it make those children feel who have not had loving supportive families. Many of the damaged young people that I have worked with had such low self-worth, due to their family experiences. Many thought that they were powerless in trying to end an inherited cycle of negativity.

David's positivity comes from being able to retain positive images from the past and even in bad situations being able to find some joy. So, he will remember something that made him laugh or how much he loved or cared for someone, even if they were not deserving of it on occasions. He constantly observes and studies people and unintentionally mirrors behaviours and responses. Surrounding him with positive people in his early years with me gave him a comfort zone that he lacked as a young child. He now faithfully recreates that comfort zone on a daily basis and can then maintain an equilibrium in his life. Take him out of that comfort zone with a hostile or threatening situation, or even just a drink or two over his limit and his world is rocked to the foundations, albeit temporarily. Having caring, positive people around him always ensures the disruption is short lived.

This is why I feel it is so important that when life is good, we still need to keep working at it. To get to where life is good can, for a damaged child, take a long investment of time and energy. Just because a young person may have reached a good place in life, we should never lose sight of the unseen fragility that can still exist. A transformed life is, even after many years, still only a heartbeat away from chaos and confusion. There are tiny little things I do on a daily basis that constantly reinforce a safe and secure environment in Dave's world and in mine. We have rituals, like our morning 'coffee shop' routine, meaning almost every day me and Dave have some time that is exclusively ours whatever else is happening in our world.

This for me is a big reason why so many children leave Foster Care and experience renewed feelings of fear and insecurity. They miss that daily positive contact and the routines that often seemed fairly insignificant. This can trigger negative memories and drastically increase a young person's anxiety. Suddenly being without that safety net of foster care can be so isolating and damaging. David stayed with me and has never had to experience that, but the occasional wobble shows how easily the negativity could return even after so many years. This is why support for young people leaving foster care needs to be massively improved, or we risk undoing so much of the healing that has taken place. Care leavers need substantial support packages, and not just for the first few months, but for several years.

To the outsider, Dave is still very dependent on me, but in fact the truth is that I now depend on him for so many things. He helps me continue as a foster carer by creating harmony in the house and doing so many of the physical day-to-day chores. Without him I would not still be fostering. He has compensated for my reduced energy levels as I have aged, taking responsibility for looking after the house and maintaining a calming influence with troubled children. Above everything though, it's his ability to maintain stability by welcoming and smiling through each and every day, with as much enthusiasm as he did the previous one. That is such a gift. I get up every morning knowing that he will not need his spirits lifting and he will in fact lift mine if they are flagging. That is a blessing indeed. People always want to talk to him because he makes them laugh, he makes them feel good and he radiates happiness.

Going out for a coffee with Dave every morning may seem a little extravagant, but it is something we both look forward to, every single day. It's routine, it gets us moving each day and is our time to talk and plan the day ahead or the next trip, or the next holiday. These days we vary the venue as there is a good selection and we have coffee buddies in each place. We both study people although in different ways. Dave likes a bit of drama, whereas I remember coffee days with Liz analysing different acquaintances and children or colleagues. Dave would always be there, just taking in our conversations with occasional interjections.

Recently when I was sitting in our local Costa with David a young man came and sat down on an adjoining table. Dave had seen him before and was looking a little concerned. Nothing untoward in this lads appearance, but a distinct rigidity in his movements, placing his coffee very precisely on the table and making several adjustments to his seat as he sat down. In the quiet early morning ambience, the wooden legs of the chair scraped very noisily in what seemed like an echo chamber. The young man squirmed and very quietly muttered to himself, 'don't do it, don't do it'. He then moved a chair from the next table closer to his thus repeating the noisy disruption.

Unsurprisingly a young woman on the table from where he moved the chair hurriedly finished her coffee, gathered her belongings and left, all the time avoiding any hint of eye contact. The young man clearly used to such reactions, grimaced and had what looked like a nervous tick or spasm followed by some quiet inaudible words of self-censure. He finished his coffee, meticulously tidied his table and approached us. He asked if we were done with the tray which was loaded with the remnants of our breakfast. It was perched on the chair between David and me. This was David's morning ritual after coffee. Clear the table, put every item on the tray and put the tray on the chair where it would remain until I was finished with my coffee about 10 minutes later. It is always the same with Dave, but suddenly his routine was under threat by this odd young man looking to remove the tray. OCD 1 meets OCD 2 I thought to myself ,with a nod to Liz. I politely accepted the young man's proposal and briefly made eye contact, so as to avoid looking nervous at his request. David, as I expected, whilst clearly rattled, yielded to my decision and the tray was taken by the young man and placed on the counter as he left.

Dave looked at me, then nodded in the direction of the departing young man and remarked. "Bit of Aspergers I reckon".

This was Dave's way of dealing with any autistic encounter since Marcus had visited. Dave certainly has undiagnosed autistic traits which he prefers to see post Marcus as Aspergers. Anytime he sees anyone get angry now then out comes his stock phrase,

"Got a bit of Asperger's I reckon".

It was one of those moments where I could hear the echo of Liz laughing. Whereas Liz would have quietly said with a nod "On the spectrum John". followed by a somewhat more clinical diagnosis.

Dave as always was the unintentional mimic, as he is inclined to be. He didn't even realise it was Liz he was mimicking, but the tone was exactly right, just different words.

With Dave words are always different. Whether he's singing Kenny Rogers, Ed Sheeran or any Bristol City chant, he rarely grasps too many of the actual words. It's more about the sound and tone which is probably down to the hearing problems that he generally covers up well. The hearing aids were long ago discarded and to be fair, he picks up most things in conversations. Walking past the automatic checkouts in Morrisons, he will loudly echo repetitive instructions in mimicked tones

"Please take your change".

"If you have a Morrison's Card, please use it now".

Dave would always giggle when my Mum used to say, 'I just need to spend a penny" and when in company loves to repeat the phrase even now. For me it's one of those odd things that feels like a tribute to Mum and to the wonderful influence she had on him. I shudder to think what phrases or mannerisms of mine he will mimic when I've taken my leave. He tells people that he already has plans for my funeral and he probably has. As for the young man in the coffee shop, well Dave was noticeably unimpressed. I imagine OCD clashes could often be like that.

After over two decades with me Dave can still be unsettled by the wrong person, even if that person is the right person for me to mentor. Marcus is a good example. He and David get on really well, but living in the same house together for more than a few days and the impatient and frustrated David of 22 years ago begins to emerge. Writing this book has continually reminded me that our relationships, however strong and long established need constant attention to maintain them. Many, many times in the past I have taken David's presence and support for granted, without really appreciating how hard he works to maintain that balance between us and his position at my side.

Summer 2025 and its almost five years on from Samet being refused permission to go to the Court of Appeal. We put in a Fresh Claim in early 2021 followed by another refusal in May of that year. We appealed this decision and went back to court early in 2022 only to lose the Appeal despite a great amount of supporting evidence. We were then advised that we could ask for permission to appeal this latest decision due to what we believe are clear legal errors, but permission was refused. It then took until November 2022 before permission to Appeal to a higher court was granted to us. We duly did that and it was only in 2025 that we have now been told by the higher court (the Upper Tribunal) that they accepted our argument and the matter would be put back to the lower court to be heard again.

That outcome basically means that we start all over again. In the meantime, Samet is now into his mid 20's and is still not allowed to work. His age meant that he had to leave my care a couple of years ago and live with a sibling who is legally in the UK. His life has been virtually on hold since the day he became an adult. 'Disgraceful' just doesn't cut it. It's inhumane and the way that the previous Government created a backlog, both in processing immigration claims and in the Immigration Court system, means that there is yet to be any light at the end of this very long tunnel.

His life since the Pandemic has been much like most of our lives were during the pandemic. It has been on hold, almost as if someone had put him in the freezer in that Covid Spring and he has remained there ever since. Over recent years I have through Samet been involved with an amazing charity Shpresa, based in London. Shpresa has spent over 20 years helping Albanians living in the UK including many young people in similar situations to Samet. They have developed and inspired many great initiatives. In particular two amazing projects BREAKING THE CHAINS* and LOHST**(Lives On Hold our

Stories Told). The first has addressed the problems young Asylum Seekers face when encountering the Asylum System and the latter, the first detailed study on the effects on COVID 19 on Asylum Seeking Children and young people in the UK. The effects and delays on frontline services and the Immigration system have continued to this day. Samet's case is testament to that.

I have met many of these young people and have been shocked to discover that many others' lives have been put on hold for far longer than Samet's. Other young Albanians have eventually, after many years, won the right to remain in the UK. Sadly, many then find that they too are in their mid to late 20s and it's incredibly difficult to just jump into employment with no previous work history. Others suffer ongoing mental health problems from years of struggle without any income and lack of sufficient support. Added to that we had a Government that vilified Albanians as 'invaders'. Even young Albanian Children born in the UK are now suffering abuse and discrimination because of this invidious and inciteful rhetoric. The anti-Albanian attitude has been underpinned by articles in leading national newspapers. It really is a bad time to be an Albanian living in the UK.

Remember that many of these young people like Samet, have been trafficked as children to the UK, and often forced to work in Cannabis farms and other illegal enterprises, before being released into our society. Having visited Albania several times in recent years I have heard how trafficking gangs now buy up the debts of poor families and then take their children to work for them in other countries to pay off the family's debts. In the UK when the gangs release these children, they get picked up by our Social Care system and end up getting placed with Foster Carers like me. As with Samet and Ali they often then thrive both at home and in education, something many were deprived of back in Albania. A couple of years later they reach 18 and get thrust into the Immigration system trying to get permission to remain. Life then just stops as it has with Samet.

I have met other young Asylum Seekers who, having lost their appeals and without any financial support, have run away rather than return to a miserable future in Albania from where many only get re-trafficked again. Often, they are then picked up again by the gangs that brought them here. They then live off the grid, in constant fear and become virtual slaves to the gangs. Almost inevitably, the gangs force many of them into criminal activities in order to survive, thereby giving fuel to the right-wing rhetoric of 'Albanian Criminals'. Any young person returning back to Albania is seen as a failure and is still targeted by gangs. Little to no help is forthcoming from the authorities there either, so most end up destitute.

Absolutely nothing that recent Governments have done has in any way discouraged the gangs who push these children onto small boats. In fact, the evidence suggests the reverse is true as it's usually the victims that are punished rather than the gangs. Successive Governments have in fact created a situation for the gangs whereby they can traffic increasing numbers of children and adults with an ever decreasing risk of detection or prosecution. Just as long as politicians and the media can use migrants as a distraction from other unsolved societal problems, then both politicians and Traffickers see it as a win-win situation. The lack of humanity on both sides is appalling and whether intentional or not it feels like successive Governments have been as complicit as the traffickers in this abuse of children. The traffickers profit from bringing them here, then happily release them into society for a couple of years before Immigration refusal virtually hands them back to the traffickers. The Government in turn then profit from the anti-migrant feeling that can win them votes amongst their core support and extreme right wing supporters.

In my opinion therefore, the UK Government has effectively all but closed any legal routes of immigration and in so doing has created the perfect environment for traffickers. As a Foster Carer for Asylum Seeking children, I find myself also feeling complicit in this evil trade. We foster carers seem to be given temporary custody of these poor children before they return to their abusers, anglicised and better educated and of even better value to them. In the 19th century our Government was complicit in encouraging the Slave Trade. I see a parallel in these times, with Asylum Seeking and Trafficked children being the new cargo of choice. Slavery hasn't gone; it's just been repackaged and redefined to suit a right wing and populist ideology.

My interest in Albania and its people has led me to making several trips to Albania in recent years. One of those was when I was invited to meet families involved in Albanian Blood Feuds, which are one of the reasons some children, especially boys, flee Albania. The Kanun are traditional laws that were used in Northern Albania and Kosovo between the 15th and 20th centuries and then revived at the fall of the communist regime in the 1990s. Under the Kanun it is allowable to take revenge on someone that has done you or your family wrong, even if it was generations before. For instance, if a man killed his neighbour, then that neighbours family could take retribution on his family. If your grandfather had been killed by someone, then you or your family could exact revenge by taking the blood (killing) of that person or his male descendants. In turn that family could then take revenge on you or your family and the feud could then continue for generations unless both parties agreed to an end of it.

The Kanun has led to young men in particular, being virtually imprisoned for their own safety in their homes, rather than being targeted for death. The Albanian Government, keen to join the EU, played down the existence of these feuds and when children flee here it is consequently rarely accepted as a reason for granting asylum. Even though the United Nations acknowledges them, it suits our Government's purpose to deny their existence whenever used in Asylum cases.

Two years ago, I visited several families whilst in Albania at the invitation of an amazing teacher Liljana Luani. With meagre resources Liljana visits families where children are confined to their houses so as to help educate the children. Liljana was the recipient of the Albania Teacher of the year award in 2018 and was selected as one of the 50 Best Teachers in the World by organisers of the Global Teachers Prize, whilst also winning a Universal Peace Ambassador award. Liljana raises money to help feed the families who are amongst the poorest in Albania. She is one of the few people allowed to move freely between the blood feud families as people can be killed by just being in the wrong place at the wrong time. Very few other people get to visit these families and Liljana had to get special permission for my visit, or else I could have been mistakenly targeted.

All the families have to live on the equivalent of about 40 euros per month for all their food, irrespective of the number of family members who live in the house. In the first house that I was taken to, all the male family members (father and four sons), had fled to various countries. In another house, a young girl greeted me with her mother and grandmother. In Albania, irrespective of their circumstances, guests are always honoured. In each house I was offered either figs or raki (made from figs) as a welcome. The young girl who had greeted me was one of two sisters. Several years ago, her elder sister, then about 16, was in the garden with her grandfather picking figs when they were both gunned down and killed because of a blood feud.

In another house, where there were four children, including several young boys, I asked at what age they were safe until. I had heard that it was about 16, but it was explained to me that boys in these houses grow up knowing that either they will become a target or will themselves be expected to exact a revenge killing. At what age? I asked and was told that when they are old enough to handle a gun will be the time. Part of Liljana's work is also trying to mediate between families to try and bring an end to feuds.

Visiting these families was a shocking and humbling experience and yet the welcome that I received in every house was quite wonderful and typical of the welcome I have received everywhere that I have gone in Northern Albania. To think that the way that any of these young victims' claims for Asylum due to Blood Feuds can be so easily dismissed in the UK is both heartbreaking and infuriating, as is our Government's attitude to Asylum Seekers in general. I have myself witnessed in Immigration courts here, Home Office Barristers giving information about expected outcomes for returned asylum seeking children. It is information that contradicts everything that I have been told by various experts in Albania. I get the impression that the Home Office get their information from Albanian Government PR handouts rather than completing any meticulous research.

From everything that I have experienced in dealings with the Home Office, I sense that we still have a long fight ahead to secure Samet's future. I am beginning to think along the lines that I hope I live long enough to see the day that he eventually wins. I like to think that I am a forgiving person, but I don't think that I could ever forgive what they have put Samet and so many other young people through, just to score a few political points.

Much nearer to home, I have had another long battle trying to help young Marcus deal with day-to-day life as a young person virtually abandoned by the Care System at 18. With his Asperger's and mental health issues, almost every day has been a constant battle for him these past few years. He's had very little support from Social Services since turning 18 and eight years on he really struggles dealing with paying bills and entering into any correspondence in relation to his benefits. Consequently, he lost his benefits for the first half of 2022 and only survived with my financial support. I had to make regular food trips, taking him essential supplies because his poor budgeting skills made sending money often impractical. I then had to help him restart his benefits claim, take him to counselling and doctor's appointments, none of which he could cope with alone.

On top of everything else, I was helping him create his music, which required almost daily support by phone. Meltdowns on the phone and on my regular visits were frequent, due to the pressures that he was under. The walls of his flat were almost completely covered with dents from his punches and the flat itself was a health risk, due to his inability to clear stale food and rubbish, except on my visits, which involved a 90-mile round trip. Even when planned well in advance, a trip to visit Marcus was always unpredictable and numerous ones had to be swiftly abandoned as his mental health issues were overwhelming.

Working with Marcus over the last twelve years and more has been fascinating, enlightening and sometimes inspiring as well as frustrating, annoying and often exasperating. Unfortunately, the increasing and consistent intensity of his mental health and care issues also became the most physically and emotionally draining experience that I have ever encountered. As a result, it considerably diminished my own energies and creative abilities in recent times. After frequent attempts over a couple of years to reduce my support, I decided two years ago, as my 70th Birthday approached, that the decision had been put off for way too long and I needed to put my energies into other people and other interests. I wanted to move away from music, which was impossible with Marcus around and I needed for once to put myself first and channel my energies more into writing. Two years on my decision has paid dividends and Marcus has found God, just as his previous carers hoped and he has become much more settled in his life than ever before. Those seeds that his previous foster carers, Alice and Andrew, planted have now flowered.

Chapter 18

Looking back on a life spent looking after damaged children and I am asking myself how much has really changed over the last four decades since I started. The answer is not nearly enough, as we foster carers still have so many of the same problems as we did back then. I've changed; I've evolved and. of course. learned better ways to deal with the frustrations of dealing with the Care System. The kids were never the problem for me, but the system was and still can be on occasions, although age has mellowed me. In those days I could empathise with kids who got angry, that they didn't feel listened to, because that's exactly how I felt as a Foster Carer. Being one of the first single men to foster made me naturally defensive, abrasive even. I never had a great tolerance of people who didn't seem to appreciate a Foster Carer who was occasionally somewhat outspoken. Those in authority had a kind of 'know your place' attitude that can still be evident to this day.

These days, we are often told that we are part of the team as fellow professionals, although actions don't always back up their words. This, I gather, is a view shared by many carers across the country, so, is not unique to just me, or single carers, or to just one local authority or fostering agency. When carers like me speak out then Social Services are rarely happy. One reason that I have had so much success with my campaigns for Ali and then Samet is that I have written all my own press releases, backed up by my tweets and social media. It was strongly suggested that I run everything past the Council's own PR people before releasing anything, which, with all due respect, would have ended up as watered down statements with little public interest or response. Everything would be too sanitised and would not grab the media's attention. It's one of the reasons, in my opinion, that recruitment campaigns by local authorities up and down the country rarely have a great impact. They are generally written by Social Workers and are just too bland. When writing a press release, if the emphasis is more on what you can't say rather than what you can say, then the media will rarely give it much coverage.

Councils tend to take the attitude that Foster Carers work for them, so they should therefore toe the party line. I have, on occasions, needed to remind various local authorities that as carers we are self-employed and not directly employed by them. If they should choose to employ us then that would be a different matter. The problem, of course, is that although self-employed we cannot simply move to another Authority or Agency without going through a process that takes many months and has no guarantee of success. That is something that tends to keep many carers in line rather than expressing themselves. As for me, well, I am too long in the tooth to spend time worrying if telling the truth might impact my career anymore. When we Elders have things to say then we tend to say them whilst we still can. Ruffling a few feathers is if anything, an added bonus at my age.

If there is one thing I do know, then it's that Fostering needs to change radically. The Cost of living crisis may have brought matters to a head, but for too long

Fostering has been the cheap option. In an era where so much of the spend of Local Authority budgets ends up with Hedge Funds and shareholders then underpaying Foster Carers should no longer be acceptable. I question what has actually changed substantially over my fostering career when looking at some of the main issues.

1. *RECRUITMENT*

    This has always been poor but is probably harder than ever now. Covid and the cost of living crisis have certainly added to the problems in recruiting and too often the marketing and advertising is ineffective. Campaigns tend to hit the same demographic that they did thirty years ago, failing to reach or attract many people who might consider fostering.

2. RETENTION OF FOSTER CARERS

    Likewise! Always poor and getting worse by all accounts. Lack of adequate support (logistical, financial and in the well-being of carers) is still a common reason given for carers leaving. The difficulties in recruiting enough foster carers would be less acute if retention of existing carers was better.

3. IFA's (Independent Fostering Agencies) and Private Children's Homes.

    These have always been a much more expensive option and have become increasingly dominant in the sector over the last two decades. What were once mostly Not-For-Profit companies are now overwhelmingly profit-making. Huge profits made from accommodating looked-after-children go to shareholders and hedge-funds. I am pleased to hear that the Welsh Government intends to stop using all profit making companies for looked-after-children, but I suspect it will be hard to implement, due to resistance from the companies that currently control the sector. I hope that I'm wrong with that suspicion and I certainly don't expect that we will see any similar moves in Westminster any time soon.

4. TRAINING

    The range of training and the delivery of it has improved immensely over the years. Vast amounts of training can now be accessed through online portals, although I have to admit, being an old-school carer, that I still much prefer in-person training courses. They have the added benefit of providing opportunities to meet up with other carers and Social Work staff where often we can share and gather extra information and knowledge, aside from the topic of the course itself.

5. FINANCIAL SUPPORT (Fees and Allowances)

    For most carers, these have failed to keep up with increasing costs, especially now with the cost of living crisis. We are constantly reminded that Foster Caring is not about the money whilst being told the budgets don't give much scope for improvement. It is actually about the money, in so far as there needs to be a fairer distribution of financial resources. Spend less on the private sector and invest more in local authority fostering services. Many of the increased expectations placed on the roles of Foster Carers in recent years have generally not come with any extra financial inducements. For Carers like myself, on the higher rates there tends to be an all-inclusive rate. The expectation of what exactly is included by way of duties has been open to continual change and interpretation. One of the big problems is that there are no consistent rates among local authorities, so carers in different parts of the country can be paid very different amounts and given different increases annually, or whenever they occur. After minimal rises in fees and allowances over many years, some Local Authorities, like Bristol, have finally now begun to acknowledge the financial difficulties we are facing and are planning significant increases. Foster Carers in other parts of the country may not be so fortunate.

To be still fostering at 72 was never in my plans or expectations. I'm not really sure if I had any actual expectations of what being in my 70s would be like. Everything about 70 plus smacks of old age and decline, so it's not an age that people tend to look forward to, or make plans for, other than funeral plans or one's inheritance. I never planned a career in fostering; it just evolved as life went along. Probably the only serious plan that I ever had was for my Respite Centre and look how that turned out. No career plan, no retirement plan, no pension, but most importantly, no regrets either about dedicating my life to fostering. I have been lucky enough to have found a passion in fostering that despite occasional problems has never left me and is as strong today at 72 as it ever was.

My inheritance, my legacy if you like, is in the children that I have looked after and also possibly within my words in this book. Becoming old can be scary and depressing and one doesn't know what to expect, but whatever it is won't be for too long, so there is no time to waste. Becoming an Elder may seem like the same thing as growing old, but for me it's totally different. The realisation over recent years of the opportunity that being an Elder brings has given me a new passion. It's a chance to share one's knowledge and experience and one's wisdom. Learned over a lifetime. It seems a shame that Social Services have failed to capitalise on my knowledge and experience, but maybe it's the realisation that I am not someone who appreciates being used as a free resource, just happy to give a day up for a bit of petrol money. Social Workers don't work for free, so why should we. Most of my life's work has been spent working in the shadows of society, in the Shadowlands. Mostly out of the public gaze, Foster Carers go largely unseen by society as a whole. Confidentiality and privacy is a big part of our work. People tend to only see the best bits, the palatable bits, but not the worst parts of a job that is 24/7 and seven days a week. It's often intense and unrelenting but rarely seen or recognised as a proper job. We all know Mr and Mrs Jones the Foster Carers down the street.

"He has a proper job, so she looks after the kids for a bit of extra cash."

The understanding and appreciation of what we do rarely extends beyond one's immediate family and fellow Child Care workers, but that's how it's always been, as far back as I can remember. The horror and cruelty we sometimes see are not generally for sharing. Neither generally are the worst of the stories, the traumatic lives or the tales of broken children. Foster Caring is like life's repair shop, where young people, so broken by abuse, mistreatment and neglect come to be fixed. Some we can fully repair, some we can only patch up and send on their way and some will never be salvaged, even with all the love in the world. With irreparable damage we are left hoping for miracles that rarely come and we see lives in terminal decline as a result. Just like patients on life support they do not have the abilities or resolve to recover or recharge themselves. Foster Carers are then just part of a revolving door of life-supporting carers that largely disappear with time and with the flickering hopes of a meaningful life. It all may sound overwhelmingly depressing but fostering teaches us to be realistic in our hopes and thankful for the many successes that we do have. We really are one of the emergency services where reality is always front and centre in our work and we have no time to dwell on the bad times, because another child's needs and problems will soon demand our attention more.

I am so appreciative that my life has had meaning and purpose. Recognition was never part of that, at least not until recent times in the media spotlight. We don't care for children in order to be recognised, but from my own experience, recognition is nevertheless very welcome, especially when it feels that the essential work we do throughout our fostering lives often goes unnoticed. In 2022, I was surprised and humbled to be one of the people nominated for the UK's Children's Champion of the year. Apart from an Immigration Court judge making a point of thanking me for my service to our nation's children, it was probably the only worthwhile recognition that I have ever received. A now framed certificate may seem scant reward for a lifetime's work, but for me it felt like that brief moment in the spotlight was in fact recognition, not just for me, but for the many thousands of Foster Carers who are just as deserving as me, if not more so. Foster Carers are people who rarely get acknowledged, apart from some condescending lip service. In a selfish way I feel that most especially in being a single man, a man who has fostered in a world that has become increasingly judgemental and suspicious of single men that work with children. Sometimes it has felt almost like the world is embarrassed to give us any type of recognition, simply because we have chosen to dedicate our lives to children and young people.

Recognition, validation and legacy are things that take on more relevance in one's Elder years. Legacy for Foster Carers, or rather the lack of legacy, has been a continuous fault of Child Care practice for my entire career. By legacy I mean what we leave behind and what succeeding generations can learn from our lives. Let's take Social Work as an example. Social Work develops, with new practices and systems continually being developed and ultimately someone somewhere will be credited with the development or initiative. As Foster Carers we are consulted as to the service but rarely credited for any usable ideas. There has always been a hierarchy in Social Services that rarely involves any representation of foster carers. They are happy to canvas ideas from numerous carers, so as not to credit any individual carers with their ideas or suggestions. If something goes on to be incorporated in the working practice then any credit will go to the person (i.e. Social

Work manager), who leads the research and then adds it to their CV. You can call me a cynic, but that doesn't mean it's not true.

I am not the only person to be still caring for children as they move through their 70s, but the vast majority have left Foster Care long before my age, for a multitude of reasons. Stress related burnout, personal health, the handling of complaints and the day-to-day frustrations of working in a system where the foster carer is still the most valuable resource and yet the least valued asset. The cost of living crisis has added another ingredient to the mix. So much of our invaluable experience and knowledge is lost when foster carers leave, because unlike other professions there is no place to store that knowledge, no successor to learn from it. Foster Carers are a disposable resource, where experienced carers leaving are replaced by new and inexperienced ones. Their knowledge, wisdom and experience goes with them.

When a placement leaves, then so does the income. Take someone like me, who always has two placements. One child moves on and almost immediately my income is halved, until I get another placement. If I get sick there is no sick pay, the children would probably be moved, well at least on a temporary basis anyway and all income would cease. Is it really any wonder that financial pressures cause so many carers to leave the service. With no job security and no financial security, fostering can be a constant source of insecurity for people who are themselves trying to give security to damaged young people. Without security, without basic working rights, without full employment status, it is hard to see how recruitment will ever attract enough new foster carers to truly meet the needs of children in the care system. In all my years of fostering, recruitment has always been difficult. Over recent years, retention has, I believe, steadily fallen, so we have a severe lack of foster carers now and increasing pressures on the service and carers which will only get worse and lead to more carers giving up.

This is another reason why foster carers, even retired ones, should be employed at the heart of the service, in its management, its planning and its oversight. As I have said already, there is no means of progression for foster carers. Social Workers can progress through the management structure but not foster carers. Just like frontline troops we fight the battles, often with insufficient support, until we quit or fall. We are the cannon fodder, so to speak. Carers deserve better but once again that shows no signs of changing.

I know that not all carers want to be fully employed and it's why I believe that the structure of foster caring needs to be changed. There needs to be room for the traditional carer who maybe sees the income as a secondary income, but more emphasis should be placed on creating employed roles that are not dependent on maintaining one hundred percent occupancy. Again, taking my situation as a single carer of two placements, if I were paid a salary then it removes the financial pressure caused when one placement leaves. As fostering is my only income, I need to maintain two placements in order to be able to pay my bills. Those gaps between placements, or even times where taking a second placement is prevented due to the difficulty of an existing placement, should not impact the Carer financially. A salaried position eliminates those unnecessary and unhelpful pressures.

There is pressure on carers to maintain their occupancy levels, so placements need to be filled. If the salary was not dependent on maintaining maximum occupancy, then there would be a much better chance of recruiting new carers. I believe many more people would come forward if the salary for looking after just one child was a liveable wage. New carers should initially only be expected to take on one child, so why would anyone want to do that if they cannot earn enough to survive. Provide a reasonable wage with employment rights and holiday and sick pay and recruitment could at last begin to meet the demands.

Much of the argument about not seeing Carers as professionals is that there are no qualification routes. Social Workers can get a degree, Youth Workers get their qualifications but Foster Carers just do on job training, so will never truly be recognised as professionals, unless for example they are also Social Workers, Teachers, Youth Workers or Nurses. Whilst all those people are getting their qualifications, what if there were actual career employment opportunities in Foster Care for them to consider? That is something that could happen if Local Authorities actually start employing foster carers as employees. I describe Fostering as my career. although it is not recognised as a career choice, but if it was, it would provide new routes into fostering where you don't just need a spare room to qualify. Maybe fostering could then be incorporated into Social Work courses in colleges and universities. When students qualify in Social Work then at least fostering could be a viable option for them if it was a career choice. With qualifications, some could move later into Social Work management and we might even get Social Workers with a true understanding of the foster carers role. It would then mean that the experience and knowledge that foster carers gain would not be lost as it is now when they quit.

Furthermore, why can't local authorities who maintain their own housing stock provide a package, with salary and housing for existing foster carers who want to increase their capacity or for potential foster carers who lack space. The increasing cost of rental accommodation will put many people off looking to upsize their housing for fostering. Packages could then provide new incentives for recruitment teams and create much needed extra room space for placements. There have been numerous times where I could have comfortably taken a third placement, if I had space and I am sure many other experienced Carers have been in the same position. It's all about developing new solutions for age old problems. Look outside the box and consider new roles and new initiatives as the old solutions have continued to fail.

The last couple of years have surprisingly seen my fostering profile raise beyond what I thought could be possible, having made multiple national and local media appearances and interviews. After so many years in the shadows they have been interesting and unusual times. As the cost of living crisis developed I suddenly was in great demand again from the media because so many Foster Carers were quitting because of financial pressures. Following an article that I wrote about the negative impact that the crisis was having on Foster Carers I unwittingly became something of a spokesperson for Foster Carers. There are all too few Foster Carers who have a voice that enables them to speak up on behalf of carers, so I have taken the opportunity to use my voice to promote foster caring, whilst also highlighting issues of concern for Foster Carers and Foster children.

It has felt strange to find myself suddenly thrust into the national spotlight again, but nonetheless it has been a great opportunity to shine that light on the wonderful work done by so many Foster Carers for children in the Care System. With having a platform there also comes a responsibility to contribute to discussions on ways to improve fostering because historically our voices have largely gone unheard or ignored. As with my mentoring, I may not have all the answers, but I can sometimes ask the right questions.

My appearance on the main ITN News highlighted how the cost of living crisis was affecting Carers like myself. It also featured Marcus, who I had been supporting with regular food visits. Just like countless other Foster Carers I have on occasions continued to offer variable levels of support to former foster children at my own expense. Now as adults they can struggle to survive, having been virtually abandoned by the system after leaving foster care. This for me is yet another reason why foster carers should be employed. Rather than expecting young people to depend on handouts and food banks. Part of a Foster Carers work could then be to help support care-experienced young people who are struggling to get by day-to-day. If carers are below capacity, then it makes good use of their extra available time. Foster Carers can make great support workers, so what better way than to utilise their skills for the benefit of young people. When I worked in Children's Homes, part of our work was to support former residents and help them transition to independence. Why not do the same with foster carers who often have excellent relationships with those that they have previously cared for? Why should it be that carers who worry for their ex foster children are left to offer support that really should be provided by Social Services.

For Wayne, my first ever foster lad, the last few years have been relatively quiet, as he has developed his own mobile mechanics business. His police involvement these days is very different as he now has customers who are policemen, even senior police officers. How times have changed. For Ali too, there has been another visa renewal so another £5,500 spent but at least it's sorted for another 30 months. Ali is a head chef, Restaurant owner and a married man now. He is less than a year away from his 10-year settlement status and then being able to apply for Indefinite Leave to Remain. It makes Samet's situation all the more frustrating knowing that he has not even got over the first hurdle yet after eight years. All we can do is to keep fighting for him and for others in his situation.

It seems so ironic now, that had Samet been allowed to work, then he could have taken a carpentry apprenticeship and would have been a qualified carpenter by now. Recently the Government has added carpentry and other building trades to the shortage occupations list. That list is a priority legal immigration route for people to come to work in the UK, in trades where there is an urgent need for labour. He is one of many that could have been benefiting our country in difficult times but has instead been cast aside and unable to get on with his life. He was able to go to college, but not to take on an apprenticeship. Why can't the Government make it possible for young asylum them a safe space for a while and some time away from the pressures that have blighted their lives.

All of us are all on a journey through life, but sometimes we all need to stop and take a break. After moving constantly, seemingly endlessly, we just need to rest, refuel and reset. Never underestimate the value to the human soul of being in a safe place for a while and not having to move for a while, most especially for young people who have bounced around the care system for years. For them, the next placement is just a meltdown away, so coming somewhere where they can have a meltdown and not be moved on is a major step forward. When Dave first came to me, Social Workers told me that he had been through many placements in his few years in the Care system. In fact, they only ever counted places where he had stayed more than a few weeks. Dave, on the other hand, counted all the numerous short stay and respite placements. Until he came to me, he had understandably never settled anywhere. He could look forward to the next meal, but that was about it.

I like to think that any youngster coming to me can pause and glance back on where they have journeyed from. They can see what they have come through and think about where they would like their life to go. I say glance back, because for the typical child arriving to me anything more than a glance back can bring back so many traumas and troubling memories. I was well into my 60s before I could truly analyse my life experiences both good and bad and yet I feel too often we push traumatised young people into deep reflection on their lives. Whether it's reflecting on the nightmares and traumas that they have suffered or recalling the few fond memories that are now lost and left behind forever.

These children do not yet have the skills nor the understanding to make sense of their situations, other than what can be dealt with in their 'survival mode' that they exist in from day-to-day. The balance between good memories and bad is rarely good for them. Memories equate to pain; the present can be just a numb feeling and only their hopes for the future may get them through this long dark tunnel that their lives seem permanently in. Every good and positive memory and experience that I can give them in their time with us will make them stronger and more resilient when they next move on. I don't even necessarily have to personally give them the memory or even to have been with them for that memory. I just have to give them the safety, the time and the space to discover and experience life for themselves. The best memories at any time may be away from me and away from my home but can happen because of being in a safe place and having a safe place to return to at the end of the day. For many that is a totally new and empowering experience.

I have learned that Fostering is not necessarily a solution for a troubled child, but it is a chance to press pause and decide, if necessary, on a different route to take. Sometimes it is enough to realise that the destination is still changeable. The ticket of life is open-ended with no predetermined destinations. Some of the best memories on my journey have been the people and places that I saw 'en route' rather than those gained at any over-hyped destination.

I hope that you enjoy your own journey and maybe if you are looking for something more from life than you have right now, then why not make a difference to a young person's life and become a Foster Carer. It can help to make your life really mean something and it can also help you create your own legacy. I have shared good and bad memories in *A Life in the Shadowlands* but the fact that I am still loving this job at my age is testament to how fostering can enrich your life as well as the children that you look after.

C'est ma vie! In the Shadowlands !

I have left the baton for any of you who would like to pick up. x

Acknowledgments

As a first time author this book has been a labour of love but would never have happened without some amazing support. It's the book of my life, a life that would have been very different but for some special people.

First and undoubtedly foremost my mum and dad, who gave me a lifetime of unconditional love and support and a childhood that I am eternally grateful for. My dad never once let me down when I needed him even, when my childhood was just a distant memory and even if he doubted the wisdom of my actions on occasions. There was never a problem that he could not get me past. Equally my mum, a survivor of the blitz, who was the most selfless person I have ever known but had a hidden steel that never weakened. Still wearing her beloved high heels into her 90s still standing on tables to clean her windows she would not be denied by age.

Both Mum and Dad struggled to understand why I wanted to work with so many antisocial teenagers. Yet they backed me without hesitation, every step of the way, thus creating a template that has served me so well throughout my fostering career. Both have now passed but their legacy guides me every day.

Three of my ex-foster boys, Wayne, Dave and Ali have become my greatest support now and as each of them once depended on me I now depend on them.

My great friend Steve Redman has been there for me through so many years and was the prime mover in encouraging me to write this book.

My greatly missed, dear friend Liz Wilson, who encouraged me and advised me on Social Work and fostering matters for many years. Liz was my confidant and guide on so many occasions but most of all brought fun and laughter every time she visited my house even in the darkest moments.

Finally, my dear friend and former business partner Patrick Hart who has done so much to help and inspire me and my kids over the years. Once more he has stepped up, this time to help turn my manuscript into a book.

www.ingramcontent.com/pod-product-compliance
Lightning Source LLC
Chambersburg PA
CBHW020830160426
43192CB00007B/598